House-Keeping

→IN THE←

SUNNY SOUTH

By Mrs. E. R. TENNENT.

THE UNIVERSITY OF GEORGIA PRESS
ATHENS, GEORGIA

Paperback reissue published in 2025
Foreword, Pantry Ingredient List, and Indices © 2025
by the University of Georgia Press
Athens, Georgia
www.ugapress.org
All rights reserved

Most University of Georgia Press titles are
available from popular e-book vendors.

Printed digitally

EU Authorized Representative
Easy Access System Europe—Mustamäe tee 50, 10621
Tallinn, Estonia, gpsr.requests@easproject.com

Library of Congress Control Number: 2025001869
ISBN: 9780820374062 (paperback)
ISBN: 9780820374079 (epub)
ISBN: 9780820374086 (PDF)

Originally published in 1885 by Jas. P. Harrison & Co.

To every fond and faithful lover of home this Book is dedicated
with the earnest hope that it may lessen the cares and
multiply the joys of every one seeking
instruction from its pages.

"Give us this day our daily bread."

CONTENTS.

Preface	vii
Foreword	ix
Pantry Ingredient List	xix
List of Contributors	xxiii
The Table	1
Bread Making	3
Coffee, Tea and Chocolate	20
Milk, Butter and Cheese	24
Soups	32
Oysters	40
Fish	44
Salads	47
Meat Sauces and Salad Dressings	51
Pickles	58
Catsups	70
Eggs	72
Omelettes	75
Vegetables	77
Meats	92
Cake Making	114
Icing	136
Pastry	138

Puddings and Pies	141
Sauces for Puddings	157
Fancy Desserts	161
Fruits	174
Jellies	176
Preserves	180
Canned Fruits and Vegetables	189
Ice Cream	194
Sherbet	198
Beverages	202
Confectionary	210
Diet for the Sick	213
Remedies	217
Household	224
Vestibule and Hall	231
Parlor and Library	234
The Family Room	238
The Kitchen	244
The Laundry	248
Poultry	253
Flowers	263
Advice to Young Wives	281
Index of Foods	285
Index of Proper Names	301

PREFACE.

IN August, 1883, the Phœnix Agricultural Club of Cobb County, Georgia, was organized. It has ever fostered the interests of the housekeeper as well as those of the farmer. Each month a special premium has been offered for some specimen of cookery. The premium exhibit has always been the best of its kind, with scarcely the possibility of improvement. It was these triumphs of Cobb County women that suggested the idea of a New Cook Book; but we are not indebted alone to Cobb County, or the South. Many noted housekeepers, all over the land, have contributed their tried and valued receipts.

Chiefest among the defects of all previous Cook Books stands the one glaring, unfortunate mistake that the receipts are, as a rule, costly. Necessity calls for such an adaptation as will meet the pressure of the times, and present to the public the highest attainment of the culinary artist in a form at once tasty and inexpensive.

The great majority of our receipts have been collected from private sources. We acknowledge our indebtedness, however, to the "Kentucky Home Cook Book," edited by the ladies of the Methodist Church, Maysville, Ky., "Housekeeping in the Blue Grass," by the Presbyterian ladies of Paris, Ky., "Housekeeping in old Virginia," by Marion Cabell Tyree, and "The Dixie Cook Book." Whenever a receipt has been copied, the name and the book from which it was taken have been given. "Housekeeping in the Sunny South," is now sent forth with the hope that the public may be benefited by the good it contains, and that its imperfections and omissions may be excused.

THE AUTHOR.

MARIETTA, GA., Feb. 1st, 1885.

FOREWORD.

A crow flying southwest from Marietta's town square along Georgia State Route 360 would look down on the modern hustle-bustle of apartments, car washes, and restaurants. Between a pharmacy and a trailer repair shop, a small patch of woods with some stone ruins makes for a peaceful stop. Our crow has landed on the remains of Nesbitt Union Chapel. Almost a century and a half earlier, the bird's three-mile flight would have been along a muddy wagon road and the chapel with its Gothic arch windows would have stood above the fields as a landmark. Back then the building was a rural gathering place for ecumenical worship as well as educational and social events such as meetings of the Phoenix Agricultural Club.[1] It was here that club members shared homesteading ideas and organized an annual fair with premiums (prizes) awarded for the best livestock, handiwork, and cooking. In fact, an old cookbook from 1885—the reprint that you now hold in your hands—has its roots in this club.[2] It offers almost eight hundred food recipes, over seventy formulas for household compounds or medicines, and eight essays on gardening, raising poultry, and managing various rooms of the house. The pages reveal intriguing details about home life in the Atlanta area and the South in the last quarter of the nineteenth century.[3]

We rarely stop to think of cookbooks as products of time and place, yet they are. When the preface of this Marietta cookbook states that the recipes are inexpensive to "meet the pressure of the times," it is hinting that the nation was still rebounding from an economic depression.[4] In addition, the Civil War was only two decades in the past and Reconstruction had ended only eight years before; the community, like much of the South, was in a process of recovery. At the same time, the cookbook also shows substantial cultural transitions and advances in technology. It is sprinkled with recipes from Georgia hotels and food businesses, suggesting that trade and commerce were growing. Although it is very much a community-centered cookbook, additional recipe contributors are spread across twenty-two states, showing that improvements in travel and communication were impacting social networks. Similarly, when the cookbook is compared with ones written a few decades earlier, there are more ingredients from other regions. Greater efficiency in the shipping of goods meant these items were now more affordable for middle-class kitchens. Through the cookbook we glimpse a world more "hands on" than our own with instructions for hog-killing time, a dairy section that includes advice for preventing your cow from kicking, and a recipe for barbecued turkey that instructs driving an anchor peg in the wall so the bird can be suspended over the fireplace by a cord.[5] But while the cookbook calls for many ingredients that would have been foraged or hunted locally, such as fox grapes, persimmons, squirrel, and venison, it also calls for over a dozen commercially-produced ingredients that reveal the rumble of the Industrial Revolution beneath the recipes. The cookbook offers instructions about the time-intensive process of capturing and nurturing wild yeast for baking bread—as well as recipes calling for ready yeast purchased at a store.[6] And by the time of this cookbook, technological changes in refrigeration had resulted in more affordable year-round kitchen ice for urban and suburban homes, which is seen in the increased number of recipes requiring chilling. In all these ways, the cookbook reflects Georgia's rapidly changing kitchens.

In the early 1990s, historian Alan Grubb noted that some researchers were slow to understand how useful cookbooks can be for understanding life in the past.[7] Decades later, foodways past and present is such a popular topic that there are countless television shows, books, cookbooks, blogs, podcasts, and video clips readily available that focus on food history. Many archives are actively collecting old cookbooks and making them available to researchers online. But even if they are now embraced as primary sources, are these old cookbooks still useful in the kitchen? Absolutely. Some ingredients that were popular in the 1880s may be difficult to find now, such as quince, guinea fowl, and salsify. (The internet, however, can often help with tracking down rare ingredients or determining substitutions.) Some of the recipes can be challenging, assuming well-practiced cooking skills on the part of the reader. But even if a little background reading or comparing with modern recipes is needed, cooking with older recipes can be just as compelling as gourmet or international recipes—and give us an intriguing sense of the past. In this cookbook you will find period recipes for classics such as Ginger Snaps, mac 'n' cheese, and Charlotte Russe.[8] If you like old-fashioned cakes, there are over eighty recipes ranging from coconut to dried apple to Marietta Cake studded with figs, raisins, and citron.[9] Some recipes are so old that they are new again to current generations—Celery Vinegar, Cucumber Catsup, To Preserve Green Peaches, and Potato Snow, to name a few.[10] Even some of the recipes that seem ordinary at first glance may have interesting twists. For example, the Banana Pie is spiced and has both top and bottom crust.[11] Egg Salad starts off like familiar deviled eggs but swaps mayonnaise for buttered breadcrumbs, creating a warm comfort food complete with a drizzle of warm gravy.[12] The recipes may also simply serve as inspiration; instead of following a recipe to the letter, we can try out its unfamiliar techniques or old-fashioned flavor combinations.

The 1885 recipes are fascinating and so are the people behind them. Mrs. E. R. Tennent was the compiler and contributed recipes of her own. She added cooking commentary for almost half of the recipe sections and, at the end of the volume, offered extensive guides for home organizing and decorating. This author, just shy of age thirty when the book came out, was born Ella Ruth Offutt in Scott County, Kentucky in 1855 to Benjamin Offutt and Ruth Downing Offutt.[13] While still a young child, Ella's mother died and thus she was raised in neighboring Bourbon County by an aunt and uncle.[14] In 1874, eighteen-year-old Ella married thirty-year-old Virgil M. Ogden from a family of merchants.[15] The following year, Ella gave birth to a son, but he lived only a few months.[16] After this difficult start, tragedy seemed to be behind the couple. They traveled for a time in Ohio where they welcomed a daughter.[17] By the 1880 census, the Ogdens had moved to Georgia and were farming in Marietta. The family's moves, however, may have been for medical reasons as Virgil suffered from consumption (likely tuberculosis).[18] By the 1880s, a pamphlet put out by the Western and Atlanta Railroad promoted Marietta for its clean water and "pure atmosphere" in a region claimed to be "the healthiest in America."[19] Regardless, in March of 1882, Ella became a widow at age twenty-six.[20] Spring turned to summer. Autumn arrived. And then a few days before Christmas Ella married town physician and lifelong bachelor Gilbert Tennent, Jr. (1833–1917).[21]

The life of Ella Tennent, like her cookbook, reveals a society in transition. One Georgia history book explained cultural norms for women before the Civil War this way: "No greater humiliation could befall a family than to have one of its girls go to work to earn money."[22] In contrast, Ella encouraged her readers: "Every woman in good health, no matter where she lives, can make money. . . . No honorable work is degrading."[23] Despite her gender, marriage, and motherhood, for the next twenty-seven years Georgia newspapers reported on the array of Ella's creative money-making pursuits. Ella used the Marietta newspaper to hawk homemade ink, chutney, and quilting lessons.[24] Beginning in the early 1890s, Ella was employed by the large advertising agency N. W. Ayer & Sons.[25] And Tennent's pen did not rest. In 1887, the Atlanta periodical *Southern Cultivator* hired her to "take charge" of their Household Department while later that same year Athens publisher T. L. Mitchell hired Tennent to edit a housekeeping journal called *Women's Work*.[26] The latter publication, a sixteen-page monthly periodical with a cost of fifty cents per year, was advertised as far away as Kansas.[27] Just a few months later, Ella began editing *Tennent's Home Magazine* with the annual subscription price of one dollar.[28] As late as 1903, Ella also wrote articles for Atlanta publications *The Old Homestead* and *The Sunny South*.[29] Then, unexpectedly, Ella died in 1909 after a brief illness.[30]

After perusing the cookbook, particularly the detailed room-by-room essays, the reader can imagine walking through the Victorian home that fifty-three-year-old Ella Tennent left behind when she died. The small-town community around that house is more difficult to picture yet comes into stronger focus through the recipes Tennent collected. Over one hundred and thirty Georgians contributed recipes to the cookbook. Tennent seemed to take a light hand with editing, allowing her contributor's voices to remain; some recipes are sparse and no-nonsense while others are descriptive and even a little poetic. The cumulative effect—remarkable in something as prosaic as a collection of recipes—is to perceive unique individuals behind the contributions. The citizens of Old Georgia begin to feel like real people.

The census and other surviving records show that the recipes came from the households of former governors and well-known politicians as well as locally prominent doctors, pastors, judges, and military leaders. State and county histories tell more about these people and their surnames can still be found in the names of buildings or streets. Yet the cookbook is more middle class than "upper crust," and Tennent's cookbook leans towards social diversity more than many other cookbooks of the time. Tennent included recipes from the wives of laborers and modest farmers. A Protestant minister is credited with one recipe while a few pages away there is one gleaned from the *Catholic Herald*.[31] There are contributor surnames that are traditionally Jewish. Unusual for the time, over a dozen contributors are male. Black cooks are also here, even if they are obscured by the prejudiced conventions of the day. Recipes from wealthy homes are credited to the woman of the house even though she may have spent little time in the kitchen, the foods praised at her table developed and perfected by a hired cook who, in the South, was usually a woman of color. Four recipes in the cookbook may be directly from Black cooks judging by the different handling of their credits—the title "aunt/auntie" is given to three of the four and their names appear in quotation marks.[32] Since the cookbook is reproduced just as it appeared to nineteenth-century readers, a race-related term for a hired worker in "Advice to Young Wives"— an ordinary word in Tennent's day—will make modern readers wince yet serves as a reminder that 1885 society had many necessary transitions and advances yet to come.[33]

Our imaginary crow flying from the center of town to its outskirts—whether in the nineteenth century or today—would have a valuable vantage point for understanding the lay of the land and the daily lives unfolding there. Much would be under the cover of the trees or otherwise hidden, so this wouldn't be a perfect way for understanding the whole, yet it would be helpful. The bird's eye view is a metaphor for the way this old cookbook offers a unique perspective on a historical community in a particular time and place, including changes unfolding within it. This viewpoint, like our hypothetical crow's, is imperfect and incomplete. Still, this home-focused primary source helps us ask new questions about domestic life in Georgia's past. It also helps us to touch, smell, and taste that past in our modern kitchens. You can beat dough until it is soft and bubbly to recreate Union Chapel landowner Rebecca Nesbitt's Premium Cracker Biscuit.[34] You can open your oven door to take a whiff of Phoenix Club Pound Cake.[35] If you're looking for a condiment with a "decidedly superior" taste for your next picnic, give the Baked Tomato Catsup from "Auntie Barnes" a try.[36] Or serve Lemon Biscuits, small cakes that the cookbook tells us were "so popular at the festivals in Marietta" much longer ago than first-person human memory can reach.[37] Through *Housekeeping in the Sunny-South*, we touch the past.

An Important Word of Caution

Food safety is crucial, so when using older preservation or pickling recipes please turn to modern guides for effective instructions. Up-to-date practices concerning safe handling of raw proteins, use of unpasteurized dairy products, and sanitary procedures should be similarly followed. If you are unfamiliar with an ingredient or method, research it well to be sure it is considered safe in this age of improved food science. Finally, the cookbook includes remedies and household formulas.[38] While a facial mask of honey and whiskey is likely benign as is dyeing lace with coffee, some advice and ingredients could be downright harmful.[39] It is unwise to use outdated or scientifically unproven treatments on people or animals, so these sections are reprinted strictly for historical interest.

NOTES.

1. The ruins of the chapel are located at 1305 Powder Springs Road SW across from the entrance to Chapel Drive and have a historic marker. The name of the Phoenix Agricultural Club was chosen to recall the ancient mythical symbol of rebirth as the chapel was built "over the ashes of an antebellum structure." *Southern Cultivator and Dixie Farmer* or *SCDF* (Atlanta), Volume 44, No. 10. October 1886, 413; The Cobb Land Trust Inc., www.cobblandtrust.org/html/NUhist.htm.

2. I discovered this cookbook while conducting keyword searches in Georgia Historic Newspapers, a database available through the Digital Library of Georgia. More information about the cookbook and its author can be found in my book published through UGA Press, *Georgia's Historical Recipes* (2025). This book explores what we can learn from old recipes and cookbooks, expanding on concepts touched upon in this foreword and placing Tennent's work in a larger historical context.

3. Sybil Williams, "Old Book Offers Helpful Recipes," *Marietta Daily Journal* 28 February 1962.

4. Tennent, *Housekeeping in the Sunny-South*, vii/Preface.

5. Ibid., 95, 25, and 108.

6. Ibid., 4.

7. Alan Grubb, "House and Home in the Victorian South: The Cookbook as Guide," pages 154–175) in *In Joy and in Sorrow: Women, Family, and Marriage in the Victorian South* edited by Carol Bleser. NY: Oxford University Press, 1991.

8. Tennent, *Housekeeping*, 134, 84 (Boiled Macaroni), 164, and 172.

9. Ibid., Cake Making section 114–135. Marietta Cake on 129.

10. Ibid., 53, 71, 182, and 77.

11. Ibid., 155.

12. Ibid., 50.

13. *Kentucky Birth Records*, 1852–1910 and *Kentucky Marriage Records*, 1852–1914 via Ancestry.com; 1860 Census.

14. Mrs. Ella Ruth Tennent, "Pathetic Southern Romance of James G. Blaine," *Sunny South*, 12 September 1903.

15. *Kentucky Marriage Records, 1852–1915* via Ancestry.com.

16. *Kentucky Death Records, 1852–1965* via Ancestry.com.

17. Online family trees and the 1900 census show that Ella may have had other children but no additional documentation was found. The 1880 census lists Ella's surviving child as a male, but later census and death records show that "Virgie" was

a daughter who later married Captain Dallas T. Ward of North Carolina. Her death certificate (17 June 1959, Richmond VA) viewed via Ancestry.com, corroborated by census records, indicates she was born in Cincinnati.

18. *Bourbon News* (Paris, KY), 17 March 1882.

19. Jos. M. Brown, "Marietta: 'The Gem City of Georgia,'" NY: Buffalo, Matthews, Northrup & Co., 1885.

20. *Bourbon News* (Paris, KY), 17 March 1882.

21. *Atlanta Weekly Intelligencer and Cherokee Weekly Advocate*, 13 July 1855. *Atlanta Georgian and News*, 7 April 1911; *Edgefield Advertiser* (SC), 7 March 1855; Sarah Blackwell Gober Temple, *The First Hundred Years: A Short History of Cobb County, in Georgia*. Atlanta: Walter W. Brown, 1935, 89; 1850 Census; Tombstone of Gilbert Tennent, Jr., Marietta City Cemetery; *Cobb County Probate Court, Marriage, Volume C 1882–1890* on microfilm; *Atlanta Constitution*, 24 December 1900.

22. Governor Treutlen Chapter, Daughters of the American Revolution, *History of Peach County*, Atlanta: Cherokee, 1972, 9.

23. Tennent, *Housekeeping*, 282.

24. *Marietta Journal* or *MJ*, 7 March 1889, 4 January 1906, and 29 November 1906.

25. *MJ*, 20 August 1891 and 24 September 1908.

26. *MJ*, 13 October 1887. *SCDF*, Volume 45, No. 4. April 1887, 178.

27. *Concordia Empire* (Kansas), 24 November 1887.

28. *MJ*, 13 October 1887.

29. *Tennessean* (Nashville), 3 January 1892; *Atlanta Constitution*, 11 September 1903.

30. *MJ*, 4 February 1909. Ella's son and first husband are buried in Paris City Cemetery, Kentucky, while her second husband is buried in Marietta City Cemetery. A grave has not been found for Ella Tennent. In terms of other locations, a descriptive real estate advertisement in the April 1887 issue of the *Southern Cultivator and Dixie Farmer* (Atlanta) indicates Ella (likely with her first husband) owned thirty acres "in the suburbs of Marietta." Not long after the cookbook came out, Dr. Tennent placed newspaper announcements for a medical office on the west side of main public square (*MJ*, 17 June 1886). According to another ad, his office was later on the south side in the "Masonic Building" and the Tennent residence was on Cemetery Street (*MJ*, 18 February 1892). The 1900 census shows the couple living on Powder Springs Street, but the next year they moved to Roswell Street (*MJ*, 7 February 1901).

31. Tennent, *Housekeeping*, 206–207 and 173. The likely minister was Daniel Pierce Young (1832–1878) of Scott County, Kentucky. 1860 and 1870 census. "Death of a Presbyterian Divine," *The Saint Paul Globe* (Minnesota), 1 July 1878.

32. "Aunt Polly," 15; "Auntie Barnes," 70; "Aunt America," 118; "Bossy," 119. Additionally, there is a recipe credited in its title to Aunt Sally on page 150. Unfortunately, these cooks do not appear in the list of contributors and census records from Cobb County did not help with further identification. As for the honorific term "aunt," Jessica B. Harris discusses the origins of this practice in *High on the Hog: A Culinary Journey from Africa to America* (NY: Bloomsbury, 2011), page 108.

33. Tennent, *Housekeeping*, 282.
34. Ibid., 9.
35. Ibid., 117.
36. Ibid., 70.
37. Ibid., 134–135.
38. Ibid., 217–230 as well as 249–252.
39. Ibid., 218 and 250–251.

PANTRY INGREDIENT LIST

Tennent's cookbook includes essays such as The Family Dining Room (240–243) and The Kitchen (244–247), the latter of which includes a list of Utensils Necessary in the Kitchen of a Small Family. These sections are a boon to modern readers wishing to picture southern kitchens of the 1880s. To aid with understanding the pantry, the list of ingredients below was culled from the book's recipes. These items may not have been "at the ready" in every kitchen, but it stands to reason that Tennent felt her readers could easily obtain them.

Acids – citric acid, cream of tartar, lemon acid, salicylic acid, tartaric acid

Beverages – ale, brandy, champagne, cider, cordial, milk, rum, tea, whisky, wine (including claret, port, sherry)

Colorings – annattoine/annatto, cochineal, Price's brand cake coloring, Prussian blue

Condiments – catsup, prepared/mixed/made mustard, Worcestershire sauce

Dairy Products – butter, buttermilk, cheese, clabber, cream, milk (including fresh, canned condensed, sweet), sour cream

Eggs

Fats – butter, lard, fat pork, olive oil, salad oil, suet, sweet oil

Flavorings and Additions, Savory – anchovies, bacon/fat pork, capers, garlic, horseradish, juniper berries, pickles, pine needles (for beer), sassafras root

Flavorings and Additions, Sweet – almonds (regular and bitter, usually blanched and beaten), citrus rind (lemon and orange, grated or candied), chocolate (bar form and cocoa powder), coconut (grated), coconut milk, dried fruit (apples, cherries, raisins), essence/extract (bitter almond, lemon, nutmeg), oil of lemon, peach kernels/pits, rose oil/water, preserves (jam, jelly, marmalade), vanilla

Fruit, Berries – blackberries, cranberries, currants, gooseberries, raspberries, strawberries

Fruits – apples, bananas, cherries, citron, crab apples, figs, grapes (sometimes fox grapes or scuppernongs), lemons, oranges, peaches, pears, persimmons, pineapple, plums (sometimes damson or blue), quince, raisins, watermelon

Grain Products – bran, cornmeal/Indian meal, corn starch, crackers, flour (regular wheat and graham/whole wheat), grits, hominy, malt, oatmeal

Grains – buckwheat, corn, oats, rice, rye, wheat

Herbs/Leaves – bay leaf, grape leaves, hops, marjoram, mint, parsley, peach leaves, sage, sassafras, summer savory, sweet basil, tarragon, thyme

Ice

Leavenings, Chemical – ammonia/ammonium carbonate, baking powder, soda/bicarbonate of soda, pearlash

Legumes – beans (butter, lima, white)

Macaroni

Meats, Fowl – chicken, duck, goose, guinea fowl, partridge, pigeon, quail, robin, snipe, turkey

Meats, Red – beef/veal, mutton, pork/ham/bacon/cracklins

Meats, Seafood – clams (fresh), fresh fish (bass, eels, rock, shad), salted fish (cod, herring, mackerel), canned fish (salmon), lobster (canned), oysters (fresh and canned)

Meats, Wild Game – squirrel, turtle, venison, woodchuck/groundhog

Mineral Products – alum, lime, salt/brine, saltpeter/saltpetre

Nuts – almond (regular and bitter), hickory, peanut, walnut

Rainwater

Spices (most used both whole and ground) – African cayenne, allspice, black pepper, cayenne pepper, celery seed, cinnamon, cloves, coriander seed, curry powder, ginger, Jamaica ginger, mace, mustard seed (black and white), nutmeg, red pepper, turmeric

Sweeteners – sugar in loaf/cone and granulated forms ("powdered" often meant pulverized loaf sugar), brown sugar, confectioner's sugar, honey, icing sugar, maple syrup, molasses (sometimes black or New Orleans), syrup (likely sugarcane)

Thickeners – arrow root, biscuit or bread crumbs, calf's foot jelly, cornstarch, cracker dust, gelatine, gum arabic, isinglass, lady fingers, rennet (for cheese production), tapioca

Vegetables – asparagus, beets, broccoli, cabbage, carrots, cauliflower, celery, collards, corn, cucumbers, eggplant, lettuce, mushrooms, okra, onions (sometimes eschalots), parsnips, peas, peppers (red and green), potatoes (white/Irish and sweet), pumpkin, salsify, spinach, squash (sometimes cashaw/cushaw), tomatoes, turnips

Vinegar (sometimes cider vinegar)

Yeast – liquid and cake form, homemade and store-bought

List of Contributors.

Anderson, Mrs. W. P. .... Marietta, Ga.
Anderson, Mrs. S. A. .... Marietta, Ga.
Anderson, Mrs. Dovie .... Richmond, Ky.
Atkinson, Col. S. J. .... Marietta, Ga.
Atkinson, Mrs. M. A. .... Marietta. Ga.
Atkinson, Mrs. T. J. .... Manetta, Ga.
Alston, Mrs. Dr. Wm. .... Marietta, Ga.
Alston, Miss Sabine .... Marietta, Ga.
Akin, Mrs. Warren .... Cartersville. Ga.
Acton, Miss Eliza .... New York City.
Agricola, Miss Kate .... Marietta. Ga.
Arnold, Mrs. J. M. .... Hannibal, Mo.
Adair, Mrs. Dr. .... Carlisle, Ky.
Alexander, Mrs. Kate .... Paris, Ky.
Ashurst, Mrs. Harvey .... Philadelphia, Pa.
Atlanta Constitution .... Atlanta, Ga.
Atlantic and Pacific Tea Co. .... Vesey Street, N. Y.
Brown, Mrs. Joseph E. .... Atlanta, Ga.
Brown, Miss Etta .... Kansas City, Mo.
Buttolph, Mrs. Dr. .... Marietta, Ga.
Buttolph, Mrs. James .... Marietta, Ga.
Bishop. Mrs. Wm. .... Marietta, Ga.
Buckner. Mrs. H. C. .... Paris, Ky.
Black, Mrs. Lemuel .... Marietta, Ga.
Beall, Mrs. Milton .... Rich Hill, Mo.
Blanton; Mr. Baker .... Farmville, Va.
Barlowe, Mrs. Sue .... Bayou Sara, La.
Berry, Mrs. Sarah .... Carlisle, Ky.
Bell, Mrs. Orville .... Liberty, W. Va.
Barnes, Miss .... Marietta, Ga.

Barnes, Mrs. Wm.	Marietta, Ga.
Barnes, Mrs. L. D.	Paris, Ky.
Bridges, Mrs. Amanda	Maysville, Ky.
Bledsoe, Mrs.	Maysville, Ky.
Brumby, Mrs. C. C.	Marietta, Ga.
Baker, Mrs. J. W.	Marietta, Ga.
Baker, Miss Cleff	Marietta, Ga.
Baker, Mrs. Hattie	White Plains, Ala.
Brooks, Mrs. Sam	Paris, Ky.
Bowie, Miss Kate	Smyrna, Ga.
Bellamy, Dr. W. C	Atlanta, Ga.
Bellamy, Mrs. F. L.	Atlanta, Ga.
Bashford, Mrs. Allen	Paris, Ky.
Brent, Mrs. Dr.	Cincinnati, O.
Brent, Mrs. Harry	Paris, Ky.
Boulden, Mrs. Sam	Grand Rapids, Mich.
Bean, Mr. A. L.	North Middletown, Ky.
Bean, Mrs. Dana	North Middletown, Ky.
Berrien, Mrs.	Savannah, Ga.
Breckenridge, Mrs. W. P. C.	Lexington, Ky.
Chamberlin, Mrs. E. P.	Atlanta, Ga.
Chamberlain, Mrs. J.	Marietta, Ga.
Campbell, Mrs. Belah	Marietta, Ga.
Campbell, Mrs. Dr.	Glendale, Cin., O.
Cumpstey, Mrs. Wm.	Marietta, Ga.
Curtis, Mr. D. M.	Fort Atkinson, Iowa.
Collier, Mrs.	Memphis, Tenn.
Clifton, Mrs. J. C.	Marietta, Ga.
Cheek, Mrs. T. H.	Marietta, Ga.
Cheek, Miss Mary	Marietta, Ga.
Cox, Mrs. L. S.	Marietta, Ga.
Coleman, Mrs. Dr.	Williamsburg, Va.
Carroll, Mrs. C.	Maysville, Ky.
Cunningham, Mrs. W.	Paris, Ky.
Cabell, Mrs. M. C.	Buckingham Co., Va.
Catholic Herald	New York City.

LIST OF CONTRIBUTORS.

Clay, Mrs. Brutus	Paris, Ky.
Carson, Mrs. T. M.	Lynchburg, Va.
Cortelyou, Mrs. Dr.	Marietta, Ga.
Chambers, Mrs. Kate	Paris, Ky.
Capital City Club Restaurant	Atlanta, Ga.
Duncan, Mrs. M. B.	Marietta, Ga.
Duncan, Mrs. Mary	Paris, Ky.
Dobbs, Mrs. Mattie	Marietta, Ga.
Dairyman's Journal	New York City.
Duffey, Mrs. J. A.	Atlanta, Ga.
Dorsey, Mrs.	Washington City.
Dimmitt, Mrs. L. C.	Maysville, Ky.
Dick, Mrs.	Marietta, Ga.
Dick, Miss Sallie	Marietta, Ga.
Downey, Mrs. Bettie	Owingville, Ky.
Downey, Miss Mollie	Owingville, Ky.
Demorest's Monthly	New York City.
Davis, Mrs. Arthur	Cartersville, Ga.
Davis, Miss Mary	Paris, Ky.
Diamond Cook Book.	
DeBard, Mrs. Allie	Natchez, Miss.
Dole and Merrell	New York City.
Dudley, Mrs.	Lexington, Ky.
Dabney, Miss Ann	Sharpsburg, Ky.
Earle, Mrs. Eliza	Marietta, Ga.
Edmonston, Mrs. A. S.	Marietta, Ga.
Edmonston, Mrs. Wm.	Marietta, Ga.
Ellis, Mrs.	Richmond, Ky.
Edwards, Mrs. Patsey	Paris, Ky.
Falks, Miss J. H.	Augusta, Ga.
Frey, Mrs. Wm.	Marietta, Ga.
Forest City Hotel.	Cleveland, O.
Ficklin, Col.	Virginia.
Fulton Street Market	New York City.
Fessenden, Mrs. G.	Hartford, Conn.
Ford, Dr.	Augusta, Ga.

LIST OF CONTRIBUTORS.

Foster, Miss Fannie. .... Cincinnati, O.
Gable, Mis. G. J. .... Marietta, Ga.
Garrett, Mrs. Alice .... Paris, Ky.
Gibert, Mrs. Dr. .... Bordeaux, S. C.
Gunn, Dr. ....
Galt House .... Louisville, Ky.
Goodman, Mrs. Robert .... Marietta, Ga.
Gnadinger, Mr. John .... Paris, Ky.
Greer, Mrs. Dr. .... Marietta, Ga.
Gordon, Mrs. John B. .... Atlanta, Ga.
Gilbert, Mrs. Albin .... Marietta, Ga.
Guerrant, Mrs. Ed .... Mt. Sterling, Ky.
Gilman, Mrs. V. C. .... St. Paul, Minn.
Hughes, Capt. J. M. .... Marietta, Ga.
Hughes, Mrs. J. M .... Marietta, Ga.
Hughes, Miss Dora.. Marietta, Ga.
Hendricks, Mrs. T. A. .... Indianapolis, Ind.
Harrison, Mrs. .... Purley, N. C.
Hibler, Mrs. Teresa .... Paris, Ky.
Hill, Mrs. K. Y. .... Georgia.
Heggie, Mrs. A. C. .... Marietta, Ga.
Hirsch, Mrs. R. .... Marietta, Ga.
Hamby, Mrs. T. K. .... Marietta, Ga.
Hamby, Mrs. Ben .... Marietta, Ga.
Hazard, Mrs. R. N. .... Kirkwood, Mo.
Hanley, Mrs. J. A. .... Paris, Ky.
Holton, Mrs. Dr. .... Maysville, Ky.
Hale, Mrs. S. J. .... New York City.
Harland, Marion .... Mobile, Ala.
Hunt's Hotel .... Cincinnati, O.
Home Guest .... New York City.
Hotel Emery .... Cincinnati, O.
Holstein, Mr. M. .... Middle Bass, Lake Erie.
Howell, Miss Kate .... Marietta, Ga.
Haynes, Mrs. .... Marietta, Ga.
Hollinshead. Mrs. John .... Cartersville, Ga.

LIST OF CONTRIBUTORS.

Hegman, Mr. C. E. F. .... Cincinnati, O.
Harper, Mrs. Charles .... Augusta, Ga.
Henry, Mrs. Fannie .... Atlanta. Ga.
Howard Lewis & Bro. .... Paris, Ky.
Hollingsworth, V. .... Toronto, Canada.
Hale, Miss Lizzie .... Smyrna, Ga.
Harding, Mrs. M. G. .... Staunton, Va.
Inman, Mrs. Hugh .... Atlanta, Ga.
Irwin, Mrs. Robert .... Marietta, Ga.
Irwin. Mrs. Tom .... Marietta, Ga.
Jenkins, Mrs. Gov. .... Georgia.
Jones, Mrs. Eva .... Baltimore, Md.
James, Miss Kate .... Maysville, Ky.
Jaynes, Miss Tillie .... Paris, Ky.
Johnston. Mrs. Stoddard .... Frankfort, Ky.
Jack, Mr. F. M. .... Atlanta, Ga.
Jack, Ward & Co. .... Atlanta, Ga.
Kolb, Mrs. P. V. .... Marietta, Ga.
Kirk, Mrs. .... Chattanooga, Tenn.
Keiningham, Mrs. L. .... Augusta, Ga.
Kirkpatrick, Miss Nettie .... Marietta, Ga.
Kennon, Mrs. .... Milledgeville, Ga.
Lofton, Miss C. B. .... Marietta, Ga.
Lofton, Miss Ruby .... Marietta, Ga.
Lester, Mrs. Judge .... Atlanta, Ga.
Lanehan, Miss Flora .... Meridian, Miss.
Lattimer, Mrs. .... Marietta, Ga.
Lemon, Mrs. H. C. .... Colorado Springs.
Lansing, Mrs. Tillie .... Little Rock, Ark.
Lagomarsino. Mrs. Mary .... Atlanta, Ga.
Massie, Mrs. W. W .... Paris, Ky.
Massey, Mrs. J. A. .... Marietta, Ga.
Massa, Mr. Fred .... Atlanta, Ga.
Magee, Miss .... Marietta, Ga.
Moore, Mrs. N. B. .... Augusta, Ga.
Mitchell, House .... Thomasville, Ga.

LIST OF CONTRIBUTORS.

Mitchell, Miss Ella .... Paris, Ky.
Moore, Mrs. Sue .... Atlanta, Ga.
Marlowe, Miss Idelle .... Marietta, Ga.
Meade. Mrs. R. H. .... Petersburg, Va.
Miller, Mrs. Sue .... Millersburg, Ky.
McLelland, Mrs. .... Marietta, Ga.
McGill, Miss Peachie .... Olympian Springs, Ky.
Moore, Miss Eva .... Marietta, Ga.
McIntosh, Mrs. B. L. .... Savannah, Ga.
McGavock, Mrs. .... Pulaski County, Va.
McCreary, Mrs. Gov. .... Richmond, Ky.
McCarney, Mrs. E. .... Paris, Ky.
Metcalfe, Mrs. James .... Lexington, Ky.
Manget, Miss Jennie .... Marietta, Ga.
Nesbett, Mrs. R. T. .... Marietta, Ga.
Nisbet, Mrs. T. C. .... Augusta, Ga.
Nippert, Mr. Phillip .... Paris, Ky.
New Haven Cook Book ....
Offutt, Mrs. Nancy .... North Middletown, Ky
Oakman, Mrs. Amanda .... Marietta, Ga.
Ogden, Mrs. E. J. .... Paris, Ky.
Osburn, Miss .... New Orleans, La.
Pinkerton. Mrs. S. J. .... Augusta, Ga.
Phillips, Mrs. Gen. Wm. .... Marietta, Ga.
Phillips, Mrs. Col. Charles .... Marietta, Ga.
Parloa, Miss .... New York City.
Parlor, Mrs. Mary .... Marietta, Ga.
Puckett, Mrs. Sylvester .... Portsmouth, Ohio.
Pitner, Mrs. James .... Marietta, Ga.
Pierce, Mrs. Dwight .... Bethlehem, Pa.
Parrott, Miss Sallie .... Cartersville, Ga.
Pollock, Mrs. G. .... Paris, Ky.
Payne, Mrs. M. V. .... Georgetown, Ky.
Preston, Mrs. Gen. Wm. .... Lexington, Ky.
Palace Hotel. .... San Francisco.
Park, Mrs. G. S. .... Parkville, Mo.

LIST OF CONTRIBUTORS.

Price, Miss Willie .... Fernandina, Fla.
Put-In-Bay House .... Lake Erie.
Powell, Mrs. Dr. .... Louisville, Ky.
Paris True Kentuckian ....
Roberts, Judge George .... Big Shanty, Ga.
Roberts, Mrs. Jno .... Big Shanty, Ga.
Robarts, Miss Lou .... Marietta, Ga.
Robarts, Miss Mary .... Marietta, Ga.
Riddell, Mrs. Beri .... Rugby, Tenn.
Reed, Mrs. Humphrey .... Marietta, Ga.
Reed, Mrs. Baxter .... Ball Ground, Ga.
Redmon, Mrs. Chas .... Paris, Ky.
Rusk, Mrs. Sallie .... Canton, Ga.
Rule, Mrs. David .... Denver, Col.
Rav, Mrs. John .... Paris, Ky.
Royal Pastry Cook .... New York City.
Robinson, Mrs. J. H. .... Marysville, Ky.
Rockwell, Mrs. Dr. .... Springfield, Ohio.
Rogers, Mrs. M. L. .... Paris, Ky.
Starnes, Mrs. H. N. .... Marietta, Ga.
Stewart, Dr. .... Marietta, Ga.
Stewart. Mrs. Dr. .... Marietta, Ga.
Shirley House .... Richmond, Ky.
Shellman, Mrs. Ples .... Dalton, Ga.
Scoville and Beerman .... Atlanta, Ga.
Slade, Mrs. Lela .... Drummondsyille, Can.
Simmes, Mrs. Wm. ....
Scott, Mrs. James .... North Middletown, Ky.
Scott, Miss Nannie .... North Middletown, Ky.
Scott, Miss Emma .... North Middletown, Ky.
Screven, Mrs. Nellie .... Savannah, Ga.
Smith, Mrs. W. K. .... Whitney Station, Ky.
Shipp, Mrs. Fannie .... Raleigh, N. C.
Singer, Miss Etta .... San Antonio, Mexico.
St. Nicholas Hotel .... Cincinnati, Ohio.
Strother, Mrs. W. A. .... Lynchburg, Va.

LIST OF CONTRIBUTORS.

Southern Cultivator .... Atlanta, Ga.
Setz, Mrs. Dr. .... Marietta, Ga.
Stevens, Mrs. F. M. .... Waterbury, Conn.
Smidt, Miss Anna .... Cincinnati, O.
Sibley, Mrs. Josiah .... Augusta, Ga.
Stevens, Mrs. W. P. .... Marietta, Ga.
Stevens, Mr. W. P. .... Marietta, Ga.
Tubman, Mrs. Emily .... Augusta, Ga.
Tabb, Mrs. C. E. .... Maysville, Ky.
Tyree, Mrs. M. C. .... Lynchburg, Va.
The Complete Home ....
Tarleton, Mrs. .... Cedar City, Mo.
Tolleson, Mrs. Ida .... Spartanburg, S. C.
Tennent, Dr. Gilbert .... Marietta, Ga.
Toombs, Mrs. Robert .... Washington, Ga.
The Shakers .... Mercer County, Ky.
Tucker, Mrs. Sophronia .... Gainesville, Ga.
Turney, Mrs. Matt .... Paris, Ky.
Tuttle, Mrs. .... Ansonia, Conn.
Taggart, Mrs. Dr. .... Loundsville, S. C.
Tyree, Mrs. Samuel. .... Lynchburg, Va.
Tennent, Mrs. Louis .... Indian Territory.
Upson, Mrs. C. R. .... Atlanta, Ga.
Vienna Bakery .... Philadelphia.
Washington, Mrs. Martha .... Virginia.
Woodrow, Mrs. James .... Columbia, S. C.
Wright, Mrs. Julia McNair .... New York City.
Whitney, Mrs. E. G. .... Whitney Station, Ky.
Winn, Mrs. Maj .... Marietta, Ga.
Winn; Mrs. W. J. .... Marietta, Ga.
Whitlock, Mrs. M. G. .... Marietta, Ga.
Walsh, Mrs. .... Augusta, Ga.
Wallace, Mrs. Bird .... Marietta, Ga.
White, Mrs. Ben .... Marietta, Ga.
White, Miss Hettie .... Marietta, Ga.
Williams, Mrs. Gates .... Lexington, Ky.

Wyatt, Mrs.	Marietta, Ga.
Wrenn, Mrs. B. W.	Atlanta, Ga.
Young, Rev. D. P.	Nicholasville, Ky.
Yorston, Mrs. Eliza	Atlanta, Ga.
Youman's Dictionary	

THE TABLE.

It is thoughtless and uncivilized, and worse—it is sinful, to partake of our meals and never return thanks to the Great Giver. You may be silent, and yet feel thankful, but speak it in words and let your children behold your reverence. A child of five years can be taught it, and if necessary should take the place of absent father and mother. A touching tale is told of a little girl who, in days of prosperity, was taught to say, "I thank Thee, Lord, for my good dinner." Reverses came, bad grew worse, and worse merged into utter destitution. One day she had a dry crust of corn bread and a glass of water, and with bowed head and clasped hands, and a deep reverential feeling she said: "I thank Thee, Lord, for my good dinner." The table linen should be faultlessly neat and free from stains. A pure white cloth is prettiest for dinner and supper, a colored one is not inappropriate for breakfast. It is a luxury to have a woolen or felt cover under the tablecloth. It deadens the noise made in moving dishes. Be sure that you have everything on the table that will be needed during the meal. It is annoying to every one present to be obliged to leave the table in search of some forgotten article.

Do not use small plates for dinner, or dinner plates for supper. In the first instance they will be crowded; in the next the supper which is generally a meal of less variety, will leave a very noticeable margin on the plate. The goblets should be highly polished and the napkins either put in them loosely or laid on the plate. Do not cross the knives and forks, but lay them side by side. Slice the butter evenly and always place a butter knife on the dish. If individual plates are used do not have the butter looking ragged but smooth it nicely with a knife dipped in hot water and leave the impress of some small and dainty design on top. Always have your cruets filled The pepper, salt, mustard, vinegar, and catsup will do but little good if not in easy reach. Nearly every one, and especially a guest, will do without rather than ask for them. Natural flowers add much to the appearance of a table, and often divert attention from a very short bill of fare. A pitcher of clear, cold water is indispensable; have your water in a glass pitcher. There is a popular prejudice against drinking water from a china cup, and it extends to the pitcher also. Bread should be sliced evenly, and all rough edges detached. Nothing looks worse than a slovenly bread plate. If the first course consists of soup, bring it to the table in a covered tureen with a large soup ladle. Do not fill the plates too full. When this is partaken of, remove the plates and tureen, and bring the coffee, vegetables, and meats as quickly as possible. Never, except for your own family, with whose tastes you are acquainted, trust yourself to add the sugar and cream to coffee. Every one can do it best for himself. Your coffee may be clear, strong and well flavored, and for the lack of *one more* spoonful of sugar or on account of *too much* cream, it is partaken of sparingly—just enough to save your feelings. When you are ready for dessert remove everything except the pitcher of water; brush off the crumbs, and if there is a fruit piece place it directly in the centre. The host generally slices the cake and the hostess serves the plates. Finger bowls should be provided, and they are made ornamental by placing a fragrant leaf on top of the water. Coffee, instead of being served at the beginning of a dinner, is often served at the last. Use "after dinner" coffee cups and beaten or cracker biscuit.

BREAD MAKING.

WE often hear excellent housekeepers remark that their failures were the cost of their triumphs. It is a mistaken economy to deny young girls access to the kitchen on account of the loss of material it incurs. It is not a high price to pay for the accumulated wisdom which renders its owner a blessing to the household ever afterwards No department is of more importance than that of bread-making. Fancy desserts, salads, etc., though extremely palatable, can be dispensed with, but bread is a necessity. There is no flowery path to success; no book which can alone teach the art. Experience is the school in which these lessons are taught, and you may expect to be "turned down" often before you can " go up head." Finally, with patience and determination, you will amass great storehouses of wisdom which will remain unshaken by the blasts of adversity. First of all, good flour is requisite. There are varieties and brands innumerable, and tastes differ widely. Competent judges all agree that the best flour is of a creamy tint and the particles round and distinct to the touch. Bread of every description is much improved by sunning the flour or subjecting it to a stove heat. Set the rising in a stone crock with a tightly fitting cover. When the bread is worked for the last time allow it to rise to its full capacity before baking. The failure to do this accounts for split, cracked and broken loaves. A gentle and steady heat is required. When taken from the stove grease the sides and top with butter, place them in such a position on a folded tablecloth that the air may circulate freely about them. Always break warm bread or cut it with a heated knife. That intended to be kept should be wrapped in a linen cloth and laid in a box or drawer.

The following instructions were given personally by the baker at F. M. Jack's celebrated establishment, Atlanta, Ga.:

RECEIPT FOR MAKING THE YEAST.

One ounce of hops, four ounces of flour, two quarts of water. Put the hops in the water and let them boil ten minutes. Strain through a sieve. Take a half pint of this hop water and make it into a stiff dough with the flour, then pour all the hop water on the dough. Let it remain till cool; then stir into the mixture a handful of malt. At the expiration of forty-eight hours the yeast will rise to the top as thin and clear as water and of a yellowish tinge. It is not fit for use until it is clear.

RECEIPT FOR MAKING THE BREAD.

Take two tablespoonsful of the yeast prepared as above and put it into a pint of milk-warm water; add flour enough to make a stiff dough and set it to rise; then work in more flour, a teaspoonful of salt and an even tablespoonful of lard. A thorough kneading is important. Mould into any desired shape, and when again risen bake in a moderate oven.

MRS. TENNENT'S PREMIUM BREAD.

Into one pint of milk-warm water dissolve a National yeast cake; stir in sufficient flour to make a stiff batter. Set it in a covered crock in a warm place to rise. Add a teaspoonful of salt, a tablespoonful of sugar, a piece of butter the size of a walnut and enough flour to knead. Work well, put on a large dish, grease on top and set in the sun or under the stove. When fully risen work again; grease the pan and the dough on top; let it rise the third time, then set it in a moderate oven to bake.

NATIONAL YEAST LIGHT ROLLS.

Follow the above directions, only after the last kneading roll out, cut with a biscuit cutter, grease on top and fold over. Lay in a greased pan, set in a warm place, and, when light, bake. If pressed for time the third rising may be omitted, making the dough into rolls after the first kneading.

MRS. J. I CHAMBERLAIN'S PREMIUM ROLLS.

Take a half pint of fresh milk and a half-pint of milk-warm water. Dissolve in it a yeast cake, and stir in enough flour to make a stiff batter. When risen add a teaspoonful of salt, a little butter and sugar. Knead well, make into rolls, and when they rise again set to bake.

Always set your rolls to rise over a large pan of hot (not boiling) water and cover with a large napkin. The heat from a stove or fireplace hardens the upper surface before they have a chance to rise.

Fleischman's yeast is deservedly popular, the only objection being its perishable character. City people can be supplied with it in a fresh state every day, but it is well for those in the country to use it in making dry yeast cakes.

BREAD MADE WITH FLEISCHMAN'S YEAST.

Dissolve half a cake of Fleischman's yeast in a quart of milk-warm water. Stir in enough flour to make a stiff dough. Set in a warm place and when risen work in more flour, a teaspoonful of salt and a tablespoonful of lard. Knead well, set to rise, then bake.—*Mrs. J. A. Duffey.*

FLEISCHMAN'S YEAST ROLLS.

Set the sponge as in preceeding receipt, and after you have kneaded the dough, make into rolls, set to rise, and bake.

YEAST CAKES.

Take a handful of hops and pour over them a quart of boiling water. Put them in a covered porcelain vessel and let them draw, but not boil. Strain over a quart of sifted flour; boil two large Irish potatoes, mash and mix with it, and when cool add three cakes of yeast dissolved. Let it rise, and add sifted corn meal enough to make it into cakes. Dry in the shade.—*Mrs. A. S. Edmonston.*

LIQUID YEAST.

Put five or six good sized potatoes with a handful of hops tied in a thin bag into a half gallon of boiling water. Boil all together until the potatoes are done; then remove the sack of hops, squeezing well. Pour the water off the potatoes and place it where it will keep hot. Mash very fine and smooth, add half a teaspoonful of salt and one teacupful of sugar; then gradually, the water in which the potatoes were boiled. Stir all together; pour into a gallon stone iar and put a saucer over the top. When milk-warm break in two cakes of yeast and leave it in a warm place to rise. Let it remain anywhere in the kitchen for two or three days, stirring from the bottom once or twice a day; then set away in the cellar or some cool place. This yeast does not sour. It improves with age. One teacupful is sufficient for two or three loaves of bread. Always reserve a cupful to start the next yeast as it is preferable to the cake yeast for this purpose.—*Mrs C. E. Tabb, in Kentucky Home Cook Book.*

GOOD YEAST.

Six or eight large potatoes boiled with the skins on; mash well and work half a pint of flour in. The water the potatoes are boiled in, put to this to thin. When cold, put in one pint of yeast and set to rise. Then add one teacupful of sugar and a tablespoonful of ginger.—*Mrs. M. V. Payne.*

BUTTERMILK YEAST.

Into one cupful of water, quite warm, dissolve one yeast cake. Add to this a pint of fresh buttermilk, a tablespoonful of salt, and a tablespoonful of sugar. Stir in sifted corn meal sufficient to make a thick batter. Set in a warm place and when light stir in corn-meal again until thick enough to make out into cakes. Set in the sun to dry. For the bread use in the same manner as other forms of dry yeast. If you would keep the bread moist for several days, when setting the bread sponge, add two Irish potatoes pressed through a sieve. This is a most excellent bread, entirely free from any yeasty taste.—*Mrs. Wm. Cumpstey.*

SALT RISING BREAD.

This is a most delicious and wholesome bread, but is not so well understood, and consequently less used than any other. It is a fortunate table that can boast of it baked to perfection.

MISS MAGEE'S PREMIUM SALT RISING BREAD.

Take a cupful of morning's milk and bring it to the boiling point; add to this a cupful of cold water. Stir in a teaspoonful of salt, three tablespoonsful of meal and sufficient flour to make a stiff batter. Put this mixture in a covered bucket, and set the bucket in a vessel of warm water. Never allow the temperature of the water to change, but add warm water from time to time. When risen add flour enough to knead, another teaspoonful of salt, three tablespoonsful of sugar and a tablespoonful of butter. Work well, put into a greased pan and grease the dough on top. Put in a warm place, and when fully risen set to bake in a moderate oven.

SALT RISING BREAD.

At night pour half a pint of boiling milk with a teaspoonful of salt added, over two tablespoonsful of sifted meal. Set in a warm place. Next morning, add a half pint of milk-warm water, and when light add flour, another teaspoonful of salt, and a teaspoonful of lard. Set again in a warm place, and when it rises bake.—*Mrs. Ben. Riddell.*

SALT RISING BREAD.

Take a pint of wheat bran, pour over it a quart of water and boil. Strain it, add a teaspoonful of salt and flour enough to make a thick batter. This is the rising. When it is light proceed as in other bread receipts. Some use corn meal instead of wheat bran.—*Mrs. Wm. Bishop.*

SALT RISING BREAD.

Take a pint of milk-warm water and add a fourth of a teacupful of fresh milk and a teaspoonful of salt. Stir in flour enough to make a stiff batter, cover and set to rise. When light add flour enough to knead, a teaspoonful of salt and a small piece of butter. Work well, mould and set in a warm place. When twice its original height it is ready for the oven.—*Mrs. Harrison.*

NICE LIGHT BREAD.

Make a soft buttermilk biscuit dough. Put in a greased pan near the fire, and when it rises bake in a moderate oven.—*Mrs. Geo. J. Gable.*

SODA BISCUIT.

One quart of flour, half pint of buttermilk, half a teaspoonful of soda, one teaspoonful of salt, lard the size of a hen's egg. Handle very little. If clabber and butter are used instead of buttermilk and lard the biscuit will be much better. It requires a little more butter than lard.—*Mrs. E. R. Tennent.*

BAKING POWDER BISCUIT.

Take one quart of sifted flour, a piece of lard size of a hen's egg, two teaspoonsful of Royal baking powder, a teaspoonful of salt. Mix into a soft dough with sweet milk or water.—*Mrs. Belah Campbell.*

BREAKFAST BISCUIT.

Take one quart of sweet milk, a half cupful of melted butter, a little salt, two tablespoonsful of Royal baking powder and flour enough to make a stiff batter. Do not knead into a dough but drop in buttered tins from a spoon. Bake in a hot oven; unless it is hot they will not be light and tender.

ENGLISH BISCUITS.

One and a half pints of flour, one cupful of corn starch, three tablespoonsful of sugar, large pinch of salt, two teaspoonfuls of baking powder, three tablespoonsful of lard, one egg, half a pint of milk, half a cup of currants, one tablespoonful of coriander seed. Sift together flour, corn-starch, sugar, salt and powder; rub in lard cold; add beaten eggs, milk, currants and coriander seeds; mix into a smooth dough, cut half an inch thick, lay in a greased pan and bake quickly.

CREAM BISCUIT.

Beat two eggs well; add a pint of cream and a large spoonful of yeast; stir in flour until the dough is stiff; make into biscuit and let them rise for five hours.—*Mrs. N. B. Moore.*

MRS. NESBITT'S PREMIUM CRACKER BISCUIT.

To each quart of floor use a heaping tablespoonful of lard, one even teaspoonful of Royal baking powder, and sufficient milk or water to make a stiff dough. Beat with an iron beater until the dough is soft and blisters. After rolling the dough half an inch in thickness cut the biscuits the desired size and prick with a fork. Bake in a quick oven. The dough should be beaten until it is perfectly smooth.

BEATEN BISCUIT.

Sift a teaspoonful of salt into a quart of flour; mix into a stiff dough with equal parts of sweet milk and water. Work in, a little at a time, two tablespoonsful of butter. Knead for an hour, wash over with milk, prick and bake.—*Mrs. Jas. M. Arnold.*

SWEET POTATO BISCUIT.

One pint of mashed potato, two tablespoonsful of sugar, two tablespoonsful of milk, a tablespoonful of lard, half teaspoonful of soda, flour sufficient to make a soft dough.—*Mrs. J. H. Falks.*

SOUR CREAM BISCUIT.

Sift one teaspoonful of salt and one of soda with a quart of flour; one pint of sour cream. Beat an egg and add to the cream; mix, roll, cut, and bake as quickly as possible.—*Mrs. Teresa Hibler.*

PATRICK BREAD.

One pint of sifted flour, two dessert spoonsful of sugar, two of butter, two of baking powder, two cupfuls of milk. Beat these well together and pour into your greased cake pan. Bake quickly and serve very hot; or, you may bake in pie plates, butter each one, stack up, and cut like jelly cake.—*Mrs. Eva Jones.*

RICE BREAD.

One cupful of sifted flour, one cupful of boiled rice, one pint of milk, two eggs, pinch of soda, salt to taste.—*Mrs. Peter Kolb.*

THOMAS BREAD.

One tumbler of sweet milk, two eggs well beaten, salt to taste, two teaspoonsful of melted butter, two teaspoonsful of sugar, a dessert spoonful of yeast powder, flour to make a stiff batter.—*Miss Mary Robarts.*

VICTORIA BREAD.

One pint of cornmeal moistened with buttermilk or clabber, one cup of sweet milk, one teaspoonful of soda, one of butter, one of sugar, one of syrup, one of salt, two eggs.—*Mrs. Harvey Ashurst.*

SWEET ROLLS.

Make a rich biscuit dough, spread with butter and sprinkle with sugar. Roll and cut an inch thick, and lay flat in the biscuit pan. Bake quickly. *Mrs. Hugh Inman.*

CLABBER BREAD.

Beat four eggs separately, two teacupful of clabber, one tablespoonful of butter, placed in a pan upon the stove long enough to soften; a teaspoonful of soda, the same of salt; mix with flour to a stiff batter; grease the pan in which the bread is to be baked; pour in the batter, let it stand an hour and bake.—*Mrs. E. Y. Hill.*

SALLY LUNN.

One quart of flour, three eggs, one tablespoonful of butter; add half a cupful of good yeast. Mix at ten o'clock A. M. for tea.

SALLY LUNN.

Melt two ounces of butter, stir it into three gills of tepid milk; mix in this one ounce of fresh yeast, a good pinch of salt, two ounces of sifted sugar and two eggs. Stir this into two pounds of sifted flour, and work all well together. Let the dough rise for half an hour; then knead and put into tins, allowing the cakes to rise well before baking.—*Mrs. H. N. Starnes.*

WAFFLES.

One pint of flour, two eggs, one dessert spoonful of lard, one and one-fourth pints of buttermilk, one half teaspoonful of soda.

WAFFLES.

One quart of sour cream or buttermilk in which has been dissolved a teaspoonful of soda and one of salt; two eggs well beaten; add them to the cream, stir in the flour, then a tablespoonful of melted lard or butter.—*Mrs. Baxter Reid.*

WAFFLES WITHOUT EGGS.

Take one quart of sifted flour and stir into it very thoroughly two teaspoonsful of baking powder; add a pinch of salt and make into a batter with sweet milk; add a tablespoonful of lard.

WAFFLES MADE WITH YEAST.

One quart of flour, one quart of sweet milk, with a tablespoonful of butter melted into it, and mixed with the flour gradually so as to be free from lumps; one teaspoonful of salt, three tablespoonsful of yeast. When well risen add two well beaten eggs.—*Miss. Ella Mitchell, in Blue Grass Cook Book.*

RICE WAFFLES.

To one cupful and a half of boiled rice add two cupfuls of flour; mix it with milk. It must be a little thicker than pancake batter; add a little salt and two well beaten eggs. Give it a good beating.—*Miss Emma Scott.*

CREAM MUFFINS.

Take one and a half pints of flour, whites only of two eggs, a little salt, just enough sweet cream to make the batter right consistency. Grease muffin irons; have hot and pour them half full. Bake quickly.—*Mrs. H. C. Buckner, in Blue Grass Cook Book.*

WHEAT MUFFINS.

Take one quart of flour, one quart of buttermilk, a teaspoonful of soda, a teaspoonful of salt, and a piece of lard size of a hen's egg. Add lastly two eggs well beaten.—*Mrs. Lemuel Black.*

WHEAT GEMS.

Take a quart of flour, sift in teaspoonful of salt; make into a batter with sweet milk· add a tablespoonful of melted butter and two eggs well beaten. Bake in muffin irons.
—*Mrs. Dr. Buttolph.*

WHEAT BATTERCAKES.

Take three eggs, froth the whites, and and the well-beaten yolks; pour on a quart of buttermilk in which has been dissolved a teaspoonful of soda; add a a little salt and one and a half quarts of sifted flour. The addition of cold boiled rice is an improvement. Grease the griddle with bacon rind. - *Mrs. T. H. Shockley.*

LAPLANDERS.

Three eggs well beaten, a pint of sweet milk, a pinch of salt, a tablespoonful of baking powder, half a cupful of lard or butter, flour enough to make the consistency of pound cake batter. Bake in greased pie pans and cut in eight pieces. You can use sour milk and a scant teaspoonful of soda. This batter is unsurpassed for waffles, muffins, or battercakes.—*Mrs. Dr. Stewart.*

FRENCH ROLLS.

Sift a pound of flour into a pan and rub into it two ounces of butter; mix in the whites of two eggs beaten to a stiff froth, and a tablespoonful of good strong yeast; add sufficient milk to make a stiff dough and a salt-spoon of salt. Cover and set before the fire to rise; after it has become light, put it to bake either in pans or plates, greased between the layers of dough.—*Mrs. A. C. Heggie.*

PASSOVER BREAD.

Mix with cold water enough flour to make a soft dough and add salt. Handle but little, roll out very thin, and bake.

VANITIES.

Take two eggs, beat without separating, as light as possible; add a teaspoonful of salt, and wet up as much flour as will roll; they should be quite stiff; take small bits of dough, not larger than a teaspoon bowl, roll them in the hand till quite round; then roll as thin as possible and fry in sweet lard.—*Mrs. R. T. Nesbitt.*

Rub the griddle on which you bake buckwheat battercakes with half a ripe turnip; it is said to be much better than lard or bacon rind.

BUCKWHEAT BATTER-CAKES.

To one pint of buckwheat add two tablespoonsful of corn meal, and one yeast cake. Mix into a thick batter with salt to taste. Add in the morning, just before baking, one tablespoonful of syrup. If acid add a pinch of soda. — *Mrs. R. T. Nesbitt.*

BUCKWHEAT BATTER-CAKES.

Take one cake of National, or half a cake of Fleischman's, yeast and dissolve in a pint of warm water; add enough buckwheat flour to make a stiff dough and a tablespoonful of lard. Set in a warm place over night. In the morning, add two well beaten eggs, a little salt, and sweet milk to thin the batter.— *Shirley House, Richmond, Ky.*

QUICK BUCKWHEAT CAKES.

To a pint of buchwheat flour add a teaspoonful of salt, a teaspoonful of baking powder, a tablespoonful of brown sugar and a tablespoonful of lard. Mix with sweet milk, or you can use buttermilk and soda.

SALT RISING BATTER-CAKES.

Make the sponge as for bread and when it is light add a little more flour, two well beaten eggs and a little lard.— *Mrs. T. K. Hamby.*

CORN BATTER-CAKES.

One pint of sifted corn meal and three-fourths of a pint of buttermilk or clabber, with a half teaspoonful of soda. Two eggs beaten separately, and add last a tablespoonful of flour.— *Mary Parlor.*

CORN MEAL MUFFINS.

Into one pint of buttermilk stir half a teaspoonful of soda. Beat the whites and yolks of two eggs separately, and then together, and stir it into the buttermilk. Add a tablespoonful of lard, a teaspoonful of salt and enough corn meal to make a thick batter. Pour into muffin irons hot and well greased. *Mrs. Ples. Shellman, National Hotel, Dalton, Ga.*

KENTUCKY CORN EGG BREAD.

Take one and one-half pints of meal, one pint of buttermilk, one egg, a small teaspoonful of soda, one of salt, one tablespoonful of lard.—*Mrs. Milton Beall*

OLD FASHIONED CORN DODGERS.

Into a quart of sifted meal stir two teaspoonsful of salt. Add a teaspoonful of soda to a pint of fresh buttermilk, and when it foams stir in the meal. Mould, lay in a greased pan and bake.—*Rachel Lowe.*

CORN HOE CAKE.

Mix into a stiff dough one pint of corn meal with cold water; add a teaspoonful of salt. Dust the gridiron with meal and lay on in thin cakes.—*"Aunt Polly."*

VIRGINIA ASH CAKE.

Add a teaspoonful of salt to a quart of sifted corn meal. Make up with water and knead well. Make into round, flat cakes. Sweep a clean place on the hottest part of the hearth. Put the cakes on and cover with hot wood ashes. Wash and wipe it dry before eating.—*Marion Cabell Tyree.*

CRACKLIN BREAD.

Take one quart of corn meal and nearly a pint of cracklins. Rub them into the meal thoroughly, one teaspoonful of salt and make up with warm water into a stiff dough. Make into pones and eat hot.—*Mrs. Wm. Frey.*

PUMPKIN BREAD.

To one quart of corn meal, add one pint of stewed pumpkin, a tablespoonful of lard, a teaspoonful of salt. Mix with warm water.

GRAHAM BREAD.

Take a half pint of warm water and a half pint of fresh milk. Break into it a cake of yeast and stir in enough meal to make a thick batter. Let it rise overnight. Next morning work in a cupful of black molasses, a teaspoonful of lard and a little salt. Add enough Graham flour to make a stiff dough. Set to rise, and when light bake.

DELICATE GRAHAM BREAD FOR INVALIDS.

One pint of Graham flour, one pint of flour, one teaspoonful of sugar, one of salt, one of baking powder. Sift all well together, rejecting coarse bran left in the sieve; add one and a half pints of milk; mix quickly into smooth soft dough. Bake in greased tins.

GRAHAM BISCUIT.

One quart of flour, one cupful of sugar, sour cream enough to make a soft dough, one teaspoonful of soda, one tablespoonful of butter; work sugar, butter and flour together till very fine; then add the cream; work but little; make into biscuit and bake —*Mrs. Joseph Jones, in Blue Grass Cook Book.*

GRAHAM GEMS.

Mix a cup of fresh milk and a cup of boiling water. Stir in a pinch of salt and Graham flour until a stiff batter is formed. Drop into well greased muffin irons and bake quickly.—*Miss Mattie Hurt.*

GRAHAM BATTER CAKES.

Take two eggs, one and one-half pints of milk, one and one-half pints of Graham flour, one teaspoonful of salt, and dessert-spoonful of baking powder, three level tablespoonsful of melted lard. Beat the eggs, add the milk, then the salt, mix baking powder through the flour and add to this, then beat in the lard; beat hard like cake; bake quickly.

OATMEAL BREAD.

One half pint of oatmeal, one and a half pints of flour, half a teaspoonful of salt, three of baking powder, three-fourths of a pint of milk; boil oatmeal in one and a half pints of salted water one hour; add milk; set aside until cold. Then place in bowl, sift together flour, salt and powder, and add. Bake in greased pan.

BOSTON BROWN BREAD.

Half a pint of flour, one pint of meal, half a pint of rye flour, two potatoes, one teaspoonful of salt, two teaspoonsful of baking powder, a tablespoonful of brown sugar and a half pint of water. Let the loaf steam one hour, then bake for thirty minutes.

MRS. JAMES HUGHES' RUSK.

Half a pound of sugar and three pounds of flour sifted well together; pour on half a pint of good yeast; beat six eggs, add half a pint of milk, mix all together and knead well; if not soft enough add more milk; it should be softer than bread; make it at night; in the morning work in six ounces of butter and make in small rolls. When well risen bake.

WAFERS.

One pint of sweet milk, one teaspoonful of salt, one teaspoonful of butter, flour enough to make a thin batter.

SWEET WAFERS.

Half a pound of sugar, a quarter of a pound of butter, six eggs, as much flour as required for a stiff batter. Bake in wafer irons.

THE FAMOUS KIMBALL HOUSE BAKING POWDER.

Take one pound of bicarbonate of soda, one pound of cream of tartar, and six ounces of tartaric acid. Mix thoroughly by passing several times through a fine sieve.—*Scoville & Beerman.*

CRACKNELLS.

To one pint of rich milk, put two ounces of butter, and spoonful of yeast. Make it warm and mix enough flour to make a light dough; roll thin and cut in long pieces two inches broad. Prick well and bake in slow oven.

CORN STARCH CRACKERS.

One and a half pints of flour, a half pint of corn starch, half a teaspoonful of salt, one tablespoonful of sugar, one tablespoonful of lard, a half pint of milk and a teaspoonful of baking powder.

HAM SANDWICHES.

Butter thin slices of bread and spread with the following preparation: one-half pound of grated ham, the yolks of four hard-boiled eggs, two teaspoonsful of made mustard, one tablespoonful of tomato catsup, pepper to taste, and vinegar enough to make paste.—*Mrs. S. Edmonston.*

SANDWICHES.

Make yeast bread by any receipt preferred. Bake in pans fourteen inches long and eight inches wide. Be careful to have a very light-brown crust. Take out of the pan and wrap in towels wrung as dry as possible out of hot water. Wrap a blanket around all and let it remain an hour or more; then, with a very sharp knife, slice through the middle, or in three pieces if possible, and cut up into any length desired. Spread each piece with soft butter, slices of ham, grated ham or tongue.—*Miss Lou Robarts.*

HAM TOAST.

Mix one tablespoonful of finely chopped ham with the beaten yolk of an egg and a little cream and pepper. Heat over the fire and then spread the mixture on hot buttered toast or slices of bread fried crisp in butter.

MILK TOAST.

It is ruinous to toast bread inside the stove. Have a long toasting-fork and hold the bread near a steady fire; a bed of live coals is the best. When all is well browned lay in a deep dish and pour boiling milk over, previously salted, and with a little melted butter added.

CORN MEAL MUSH.

Stir sifted corn meal into sweet milk, and then into boiling water salted. Mush is rarely cooked long enough. It may be made of water alone, dropping the meal from the hands very slowly into boiling water until it thickens.

FRIED MUSH.

Let the mush remain over night in pie-pans. In the morning slice and drop in boiling lard.

FRIED HOMINY OR GRITS.

Soak over night in salted water and cook some time.

LYE HOMINY.

Boil in several waters and in the last add salt. When done pour into a bowl one-fifth full of boiled milk with a tablespoonful of butter dissolved in it.

CRACKED WHEAT.

Moisten your wheat with cold water and add a little salt. Put in a bag, tie securely and allow room for the wheat to swell. Throw in a vessel of boiling water. Serve with sugar and cream or maple syrup.

OAT MEAL PORRIDGE.

Soak the oat meal over night in cold water. Next morning strain through a cloth, pressing hard. Boil half an hour, stirring constantly towards the last. Use salt or sugar as preferred.—*Mrs. E. P. Chamberlin.*

Coffee, Tea and Chocolate.

COFFEE.

If you want this delightful beverage in the highest perfection, you must be exceedingly neat and careful in every step of the process. First, select good coffee and parch it evenly. No art in the making can supply this deficiency. After each meal empty the grounds from the coffee pot, rinse with cold water, set in the sun with the top raised. Two or three times a week fill with strong soda water and let it boil ten minutes. Sometimes coffee is left over, and if it is poured off the grounds into the pitcher you can add it to the next coffee you make; but never let it remain in the coffee pot on the grounds.

VIENNA COFFEE.

Scald the dripper with boiling water, and then put the coffee in the upper division. Pour over boiling water, previously measured, and if not strong enough repeat. Whip rich cream to a stiff froth. Put a teaspoonful in the bottom of the cup, add the sugar, and pour on the coffee; then lay a teaspoonful lightly on top. A house which prepared coffee in this way on the Philadelphia Centennial grounds cleared four thousand dollars from the sale of coffee alone.

MRS. TENNENT'S RECEIPT FOR MAKING COFFEE.

Do not grind coffee too fine. If you do it will be muddy. Allow a tablespoonful to each person. Put into a pure, sweet coffee pot, and break into it an egg—white, yolk and shell. Beat thoroughly with a spoon and add cold water. Let it boil ten minutes, and then pour in a tablespoonful of cold water. This sends the grounds to the bottom, and the coffee will pour out clear as wine. The yolk of the egg gives it a flavor not attainable from any other source.

COFFEE.

Never buy ground coffee. When about to make coffee take the brown berries and heat them hot, then grind, while hot. Have your coffee pot clean, empty, dry; allow no cold coffee or old grounds. Put the dry coffee in the pot, and pour over it as much *boiling, hard* boiling water, as you want coffee. If you have a French pot, with a sieve in the middle, keep it securely fastened up. Stand it where it will be hot, but not boil for ten minutes, and your coffee will be all right. But suppose that you have no French pot, tie your ground coffee loosely in a bit of lace net or tarlatane, or very thin swiss mull; put it in the coffee pot, pour on the boiling water as before, put a tight cork in the spout, and see that the lid fits closely; put a cloth in it if it does not, and let it stand back for ten minutes as before. The idea is to keep all the aroma-charged steam in the coffee pot, and have the subtle oil of the berries in your coffee pot, and not pervading all the house, wandering out of doors, and regaling the neighbors, while you are dolefully drinking brown warm water.—*Mrs. Julia McNair Wright.*

COFFEE.

Allow a tablespoonful of coffee to each person. Pour on a pint of boiling water, and in ten minutes pour on the rest of the water. The shell of an egg is sufficient to clear it.—*Mrs. Amanda Oakman.*

It is said to be a great improvement to coffee to pour it from the boiler into a coffee pot, sweeten and boil a few minutes longer. In this way the sugar is thoroughly dissolved, but one objection is that all persons do not like the same amount of sugar.

In the absence of cream, beat the whites and yolks of three eggs separately and then together; sweeten and add the least bit of melted butter. Use as you would cream.

TO MAKE GOOD TEA.

First, procure a good article of tea. Be sure the water is boiling; heat the tea-pot by rinsing it out with boiling water; put the tea in the pot and pour on all the boiling water at one time; steep over boiling water or on a warm stove, but avoid boiling the infusion. All teas are impaired by boiling. The weight of a silver dime will make three cups of as strong tea as should be used; if made too strong the flavor will be obscured. Always use a china or a stone tea-pot. Tannin, always present in tea, readily combines with metals; hence metallic tea-pots neutralize the flavor of tea. Connoisseurs usually prefer black tea, and take it without milk, but mollified with loaf sugar; no other should be used in tea.—*The Great Atlantic and Pacific Tea Company.*

TEA.

Use a brown earthen tea-pot, and dare to bring it to the table. Put your *dry* tea into this *dry* pot, cover it and let stand on the back of the stove until pot and tea are *hot*; this releases the aromatic oil of the leaves. Now pour on the boiling water as much as you want tea; cover it closely. In Scotland they use a close wadded bag, called a cosey, to cover the pot, and it is a valuable invention. Never boil tea, black or green; heat the leaves; steep in boiling water, and keep the steam in the pot, and the tea will be excellent.—*Mrs. Julia McNair Wright.*

ICED TEA.

Make a strong tea and strain it in a pitcher; set in a refrigerator or in cold water. It is better to add the sugar to the tea when first made, but you can sweeten it when used. Put cracked ice and a slice of lemon in the glass, then pour on the tea.

CHOCOLATE.

Let a pint of new milk come to the boiling point; then add a heaping tablespoonful of chocolate grated. (Baker's is the best.) Sweeten to taste. Some like the addition of grated nutmeg. Persons with weak digestion will prefer equal parts of milk and water to the milk alone.

CHOCOLATE.

Bring a quart of new milk to boiling point; take six tablespoonsful of grated chocolate, put it into a cup and pour half full of hot water; rub to a paste, and stir into the boiling milk. Sweeten to taste.—*St. Nicholas Hotel, Cincinnati, Ohio.*

CHOCOLATE.

Take a tablespoonful of grated chocolate, pour on it a half cupful of water; add the least bit of butter. After it has simmered for several minutes, pour on to it a pint of milk, which had sugar and frothed whites of eggs added to it; stir well.

COCOA.

To one pint of milk and one pint of cold water add three tablespoonsful of cocoa. Boil twenty minutes and sweeten.

Milk, Butter and Cheese.

CARE OF COWS.

First of all, feed your cows well. You could not be expected to be healthy, good natured and attentive to your business if you were half fed, at irregular times, and on the poorest quality of food. Just so with our dumb beasts; they cannot contribute to our profit and pleasure if not well cared for. Cows should have a shelter in inclement weather, and should be curried twice a week. Keep their bodies free from burrs and trash. Treat them kindly. Never in a fit of anger throw a stone at them. Kindness and gentleness seem to influence them greatly, but force never. Who ever heard of a kicking cow who had a patient and gentle milker? This habit of kicking is brought on by ill-treatment. It is the only way they have of remonstrating against tyranny. Some persons give their cows dry salt twice or three times a week, but it is better to salt their food moderately each meal. Cotton seed is objected to by many as an article of diet on account of it making the butter white and sticky, but if the seed is boiled this will be obviated. Give your cow, twice a day, three quarts of bran wet with water, and boiled peas and cotton seed mixed in; stir thoroughly with a large paddle. Pea hulls, apple and peach parings, remnants of cabbage, squashes, etc., are heartily enjoyed. At noon give them an armful of fodder and two or three ears of corn. Provide them with plenty of clean, fresh water. If possible let them have grass, lucerne is especially desirable.

FEEDING COWS.

A small area of rich land should be devoted to some forage crop with which to supplement the pastures in case of severe drouth. Frequent sowings of drilled corn or several plantings of cattail millet will answer the purpose. It often happens, where no provision of this kind is made, that cows fall back in their milk and never recover after the grass becomes abundant. Fodder corn or millet fed at such times would prevent the loss. For a supply of green food during the winter and spring a quarter of an acre kept for each cow should be thickly sown in rye or barley, or both, mixed. This should not be pastured, but cut and fed to the cows twice a day, in connection with dry roughness of some kind, and a mixture of bran with some kind of meal or cotton seed meal. Turnips, parsnips, sweet potatoes, pumpkins, beets or collard leaves may be used in connection with the green small grain and dry food.—*Dep't of Agriculture.*

TO MAKE COWS GIVE MILK.

A writer who says that his cow gives all the milk that is wanted in a family of eight persons, and from which was made two hundred and sixty pounds of butter during the year, gives the following as his mode of treatment: If you desire to get a large yield of rich milk, give your cows, three times a day, water slightly warm, slightly salted, in which bran has been stirred at the rate of one quart to two gallons of water. You will find twenty-five per cent. increase in milk immediately under the effect of it, and she will become so attached to the diet as to refuse clear water unless very thirsty; but this mess she will drink almost any time and ask for more. The amount of this drink necessary is an ordinary water pail full morning, noon and night.

COW'S INFLAMED UDDER.

To relieve, it should be well bathed and fomented with warm water several times a day. If there is difficulty in drawing the milk a solution of carbonate of soda or saleratus should be injected with a common syringe into the teat and milked out again repeatedly. The alkaline solution dissolves any milk that may have clotted in the udder, and which stops the flow. This reduces the inflammation.—*Capt. Jas. M. Hughes.*

MILKING.

Knead the udder well and wash clean with fresh water. Use a quart cup for milking, and when filled pour into a large bucket. Strain and pour in round shallow pans so that the cream may easily be skimmed off. If you do not churn the cream alone, pour all into a fresh scalded stone jar. The next milk is to be poured in and mixed thoroughly with a long spoon with the first, and so on until the jar is filled. In summer it is difficult to keep the milk from turning to whey before there is a churning, if you get only a small quantity of milk at a time. This can be obviated to a great extent by setting the jar in a tub of cold water. Put it where the sun cannot reach it. In winter the milk will turn more easily if you add a pint of fresh buttermilk and set it near the fire.

CHURNING.

There are many patent churns on the market, but after being used a short while they are generally discarded and the old fashioned ones brought out again. There should be the utmost simplicity about a churn, and in this particular the "dasher" is ahead of all the intricate interior arrangements of modern churns. Some like the stone jar, while others prefer those made of cedar. Pour your clabber carefully into the churn. It is destruction to butter to add hot or boiling water. Sometimes it will cause the butter to appear in less time, but the flavor, the color, and the grain are gone. If the milk is well turned and moderately warm, you will not need hot water. Churn as rapidly as possible. When the butter rises to the top as large as grains of wheat the churning is generally completed. Pour in a quart of cold water, throwing it against the sides of the churn to wash down the butter that has lodged there. Turn the "dasher" around gently, and when it has collected the butter into a solid lump, lift out into a butter bowl half filled with cold water. Press out the buttermilk gently with a paddle and change the water until no milkiness appears. Then add refined salt to taste. Cover, and set away for twelve or twenty-four hours. At the end of this time you can press out a great deal more water. It is then ready for use. Scald your churn thoroughly, and if it is a wooden one, leave a bucket of water in it to prevent its contraction and the loosening of the hoops. Keep all your pans, strainers, paddles, spoons, and cloths scrupulously neat. Untidiness will tell in butter, and if you make it for sale, you will generally get twenty cents per pound extra for your pains.

The Wisconsin Dairyman's Association offered prizes in 1883 for the best essay on butter making, not to exceed two hundred and fifty words in length. The following, by D. M. Curtis, of Fort Atkinson, took the prize:

Cows.—Select cows rich in butter-making qualities.

Feed.—Pastures should be dry, free from slough holes, well seeded with different kinds of tame grasses, so that good feed is assured. If timothy or clover, cut early and cure properly. Feed corn stalks, pumpkins, ensilage, and plenty of vegetables in winter.

Grain.—Corn and oats, corn and bran, oil meal in small quantities.

Water.—Let cows drink only such water as you would yourself.

Care of Cows.—Gentleness and cleanliness.

Milking.—Brush the udder to free it from impurities. Milk in a clean barn, well ventilated, quickly, cheerfully, with clean hands and pail; seldom change milkers.

Care of Milk.—Strain while warm, submerged in water forty-eight degrees; open setting sixty degrees.

Skimming.—Skim at twelve hours; at twenty-four hours.

Care of Cream—Care must be taken to ripen cream by frequent stirrings, keeping it at sixty degrees until slightly sour.

Utensils.—Better have one cow less than be without a thermometer, churns without inside fixtures, lever butter worker. Keep sweet and clean.

Churning.—Stir the cream thoroughly; temper to sixty degrees; warm or cool with water; churn immediately, when properly soured, slowly at first, with regular motion in forty to sixty minutes. When butter is formed in granules the size of wheat kernels, draw off the buttermilk; wash with cold water and brine until no trace of buttermilk is left.

Working and Salting.—Let the water drain out; weigh the butter; salt one ounce to the pound; sift salt on the butter and work with lever worker; set away two to four hours; lightly rework and pack.

In winter when cream is set near the fire to "turn," it is much better to have it in a tin vessel than a stone jar, for the reason that tin is a non-conductor of heat, and the milk cannot be scalded.

BAKED MILK.

Place half a gallon of new milk in a jar, cover with paper, and set in a slow oven for eight hours. It will be thick and nourishing.—*Atlanta Constitution*.

To Prepare Milk for Infants.—Take the new milk and bring it to a boil; add one-third cold water; sweeten with powdered loaf sugar.

For a Fevered Patient.—Pour the new milk in a pitcher and set it in a refrigerator or cool place. Do not skim, but stir with a spoon. Put cracked ice as large as marbles in the bottom of a goblet and pour the milk over.

To Preserve Milk for a Journey.—Bring it to the boiling point; pour in bottles and cork tightly.

Annattoine Coloring for Butter.—Dissolve one pound of best potash and one half pound of sal-soda in ten quarts of water, stirring occasionally and allowing it to stand until well dissolved, and until the impurities have all settled to the bottom of the vessel. Pour off all the clear liquor possible, let it settle again and pour off more, and repeat until only the sediment remains. Dissolve one pound of annattoine in eight quarts of cold water. and let it stand in a cool place from one to two days, until perfectly dissolved stirring occasionally and thoroughly. This mixture will ferment if too warm. Mix the two liquids together and let the compound stand until the annattoine is perfectly united with the alkali and the liquid becomes clear, stirring occasionally. Store in earthen jars, or, if in glass, keep in a dark place. Immediately before churning, shake the bottle, and put into the cream a large tablespoonful of the liquid for each gallon of cream, and stir it at once. More or less may be used, according to the depth of color desired; more for butter to be sold fresh than for that which is to be salted down, as the tint will become stronger with time. It costs about ten cents per hundred pounds of butter.—*Capt. James M. Hughes.*

To Keep Butter Sweet.—Take one teaspoonful of loaf sugar, one of soda, and one of saltpetre. Dissolve in nearly a cupful of cold water. Dip nice old linen cloths in the mixture, wrap securely around the balls of butter and pack in a jar.—*Mrs. Martha Duncan.*

TO MAKE CHEESE.

Strain the night's milk into the tub, and in the morning stir in the cream. If you want rich cheese do not allow a spoonful to be taken off. Put a part of the milk over a clear fire in the brass kettle. Heat it enough to make the milk which is in the tub quite warm, but not hot; pour it back in the tub and stir in the morning's milk. Put in a spoonful or two of rennet; stir it well and let it stand half an hour undisturbed. If the curd does not form well by that time put in more rennet. To prepare rennet; this is the stomach of a calf, and it is often the case that a piece of curd, the last milk eaten by the calf, is found in it. See if there is anything inside which should be removed, and then return the curd to its place in the rennet; it is the best part of it. Soak the rennet in a quart of water and then hang it up to dry where the flies will not reach it; keep the water in a jar or bottle. There is a great difference in the strength of rennets; some will make a thousand weight of cheese, while others will scarcely make fifty. When the curd is well formed, cut in squares, making the knife go down to the bottom of the tub; let it stand fifteen minutes for the whey to separate, then break it up very gently, putting the hand down through all parts. It should be done gently, or some of the milk will be lost in the whey; this causes white whey. The greener the whey, the richer the cheese. Lay the strainer on top of the curd, and dip off the whey that presses up through, until you have dipped about a third of it. Put this immediately over the fire to heat. When hot, but not boiling, pour it back upon the curd and then break up the curd small and as quickly as possible with your hands; then lay the strainer into the cheese basket, and pour the curd into it to drain. When this is done, return it to the tub, salt it, put it again into the strainer, and then into the cheese hoop. Do not twist up the strainer but layer it over smoothly ; lay a follower upon it, put it into the press and press it tight. Let it remain two days and increase the pressure four or five times, turning the cheese over each time. After this turn the cheese out upon a shelf in a dark closet. Rub every day the side upon the shelf and turn it over. Rub it all over with butter often. These things must be done for six months. If cheese is rich, a strip of new cotton as wide as the cheese should be sewed tightly around it when taken from the press.

SOUPS.

Soups should be made with cold water, and the salt added toward the last. If put in at first the meat is toughened and the juices retained. Be careful to remove all scum. Cabbage and beans require some time to cook, and should be put in early; corn, potatoes, tomatoes and okra may be added afterwards. For thickening use flour rubbed smooth in water or milk. If you wish the soup dark in color use browned flour. The herbs used for seasoning are sage, thyme, sweet marjoram, tarragon, mint, sweet basil, parsley and bay leaves; cloves, mace, allspice and celery seed are used in some kinds of soup to great advantage.

STOCK FOR SOUPS.

Get a knuckle of beef or veal. Have the bone well cracked in small pieces. For a medium knuckle add five or six quarts of water; let it come to a boil before you add salt or pepper. Put the pot on the back part of the stove after it commences to boil and keep it gently simmering all day; then strain it from the bones and meat into a jar and set in the cellar to cool. The next morning carefully remove all grease that has risen to the top and hardened and you will have a clear rich stock ready to be used in soups.

SOUP FROM STOCK.

To make soup from any stock, put on as much stock as needed; add seasoning, water, and vegetables. The potatoes should be peeled, sliced and laid in water for half an hour, the cabbage parboiled and drained, and all others either sliced or cut fine before adding to the soup. Boil until thoroughly dissolved, strain through a colander and serve at once.

CLEAR BEEF SOUP.

Cut up in a pot the following ingredients: four pounds of lean beef, two carrots, a knuckle of veal, a tablespoonful of butter, three small strips of pork, sweet middling or cold ham, two onions; put the onions in whole and stick six cloves in each; one blade of mace. Pour a cupful of water on this and let it stew fifteen minutes; then fill the pot with cold water, let it come to a good boil, carefully skimming off all scum. Set on the back of the stove and let it boil gently six hours. One-half hour before serving drop in a bunch of parsley; strain through a cloth, salt to taste and brown with burnt brown sugar.—*Mrs. Wm. Preston in Blue Grass Cook Book.*

GUMBO SOUP.

Take a chicken and fry half done; then pour over it three quarts of water; add two dozen pods of okra, fried, two slices of broiled or fried middling, half a cabbage chopped, a half dozen tomatoes, a little minced onion, a pod of red pepper, a sprig of parsley and salt to taste. Thicken with browned flour.—*Mrs. Ellen G. Whitney.*

DELICIOUS SOUP.

Have ready one quart of peeled tomatoes, one-half teaspoonful of soda; let this stew until the tomatoes are thoroughly cooked. Have one-half gallon of boiling milk, new and unskimmed; pour in the tomatoes, stirring well. Let all boil together about fifteen minutes; season with red pepper, salt and one tablespoonful of butter. Just before pouring up thicken with pounded crackers.—*Mrs. Alice Garrett in Blue Grass Cook Book.*

FINE VEGETABLE SOUP.

Take a large soup bone and pour over it one gallon of water; skim well; then add one chopped cabbage and three or four sliced turnips. After they have been in two hours add several sliced potatoes, a quart of tomatoes, a pint of corn, a dozen pods of okra, two red peppers, and salt to taste. Thicken with a large tablespoonful of flour rubbed smooth in a little water.—*Mrs. Emily Tubman.*

BEAN SOUP.

Take dried white beans, wash and pick carefully; cover with cold water and boil until the beans are soft; add more water as it boils away. Mash the beans, add as much water as you want, a tablespoonful of butter, salt and pepper to taste. Mashed yolks of eggs are an improvement.

PEA SOUP.

One quart of peas, three quarts of water, a piece of bacon, about half a pound. Boil until thoroughly done, then mash through a colander. Return to the pot, and if too thick add hot water. Season with salt and pepper to taste. Have two or three slices of bread toasted, cut into small pieces and put into the tureen. Pour the soup over it. A few slices of lemon greatly improves the taste of the soup.—*Mrs. H. N. Starnes.*

PEA SOUP.

Pour three quarts of water over a boiled or fried chicken, cook slowly and skim well. Take a quart of pea hulls and put in when the water first becomes hot; strain and thicken with a tablespoonful of flour stirred in a cup of cream. Salt and pepper to taste.—*Mrs. Dr. Gibert.*

CAKES FOR SOUP.

One pint of flour, a dessertspoonful of lard, a little salt, and cold water enough to mix. Roll thin, cut in squares, add to the soup, and boil ten minutes.

NOODLES FOR SOUP.

Beat an egg until light; add a pinch of salt and as much flour as it will absorb. Flour the board well, roll it over and over lightly, and with a sharp knife shave down from the end. Shake them out and drop into the soup.—*Mrs. R. Hirsch.*

PARTRIDGE SOUP.

Take a partridge and chop it into small pieces; cover it with water and let it remain two hours, then let it boil one hour, add pepper and salt, a little butter, and a half cupful of rich milk. Thicken with corn starch. Add a sprig of parsley. This is a delicate and delicious soup, and will be relished by invalids.

TURTLE SOUP.

Boil a turtle very tender in five quarts of water; remove bones and cut meat into small pieces; season with a tablespoonful, each, of marjoram, sweet basil, thyme and parsley, salt and pepper to taste, one nutmeg, a dozen cloves, same of allspice. Tie these in muslin, remove before sending soup to table. Stir a large tablespoonful of browned flour into a quarter of a pound of fresh butter, add to the soup. Fifteen minutes before serving add the green fat, then add half a pint of wine, a sliced lemon, seeds removed; also force-meat balls. Simmer five minutes, take out lemon peel, and serve. This is for a small turtle. Add a slice of good ham if the turtle is not fat.

MOCK TURTLE SOUP.

Make as above, substituting a calf's head for the turtle. Remove the brains before boiling the head; let it boil until the meat will fall from the bones; chop the meat, tongue, and brains which have been boiled, and return them to the kettle; then add the seasoning.

DR. STEWART'S RECEIPT FOR CHICKEN SOUP.

With a hatchet or meat cleaver chop a chicken into small pieces, bone and all. Cover with cold water; let it stand an hour, then boil until the juice is extracted; add salt and pepper, a cupful of rich, unskimmed milk and a tablespoonful of butter; rice and noodles, if liked, and a sprig of parsley. Thicken with corn starch or flour.

VIRGINIA BRUNSWICK STEW.

For a large family three gallons of water, to which add two chickens which have been cut up, with one pound of fat bacon. The bacon must be cut up very fine before putting it into the water. As soon as the chickens are sufficiently cooked for the meat to leave the bones, take them out and separate the meat from the bones. Return the meat to the water, then add half a gallon of Irish potatoes, which have been boiled and mashed; one and a half pints of green corn cut off; one pint of green butter beans; one quart of tomatoes, which have been skinned, and a good sized loaf of light bread. Season with black and red pepper, salt and butter. The bread must not be put in until the stew is nearly done. As soon as it begins to thicken it must be constantly stirred until done. If it should be too thick, add more water. Squirrels are a good substitute for chickens.—*Baker Blanton, in Blue Grass Cook Book.*

POTATO SOUP.

Take a quart of milk, six large potatoes, one stalk of celery; pare potatoes and boil thirty minutes; turn off the water and mash fine and light; add the boiling milk and the butter; pepper and salt to taste; rub through a strainer and serve immediately; a cupful of whipped cream added when in the tureen is a great improvement. This soup must not be allowed to stand even if kept hot. Served as soon as ready it is excellent.—*Southern Cultivator.*

GREEN CORN SOUP.

To one pint of boiling water add one quart of milk, three ears of green corn grated, one ear cut from the cob, salt and pepper. Boil till it thickens, and add butter when ready for the table.

TURKEY BONE SOUP.

After a roasted turkey has been served, a portion of the meat still adheres to the bones, especially about the neck; "drumsticks" are left, or parts of the wings and pieces rarely called for at the table. If there is three-fourths of a cupful left, cut off carefully and reserve for force-meat balls. Break the bones apart, and with stuffing still adhering to them put into a soup kettle with two quarts of water, a tablespoonful of salt, a pod of red pepper broken in pieces, three potatoes and two onions all sliced. Let it boil slowly but constantly till a half hour before dinner; leave out bones, strain through colander and return to soup kettle. A pint of hot milk or cream may be added if liked. Prepare the force meat balls by chopping the scraps of turkey very fine; take half a teacupful of cracker crumbs smoothly rolled, a small salt-spoon of cayenne pepper, double the quantity of salt, half a teaspoonful of powdered summer savory or thyme; mix these together and add a beaten raw egg to bind them. Roll mixture into balls the size of a hickory nut and drop into the soup ten minutes before serving.—*Mrs. R. N. Hazard, in Dixie Cook Book.*

TOMATO AND MILK SOUP.

One quart can of tomatoes, three pints of milk, one tablespoonful of sugar, one of corn starch, one of butter, pepper and salt to taste. Strain tomatoes and put in half an hour before serving. Let milk come to a boil and thicken with corn starch.—*Mrs. Eva Moore.*

CLAM SOUP.

Open fifty medium sized clams, cut off the hard parts, and put the soft pieces where it is cool. Strain the liquor and put it with the hard bits over the fire. Add a quart of hot water, one teaspoonful each of minced onion, and parsley and two blades of mace. Simmer, *not boil*, three-fourths of an hour. Put two cups of milk into another dish to heat, then stir in a tablespoonful of flour rubbed smooth in two teaspoonsful of butter. Set the dish in hot water till the soup is ready. At the expiration of three-fourths of an hour, strain the clam broth leaving out the hard parts. Now put in the soft parts, let come to boiling point; season with pepper, turn into the tureen; add the hot milk and serve.—*Mrs. Geo. J. Gable.*

WHITE SOUP.

Boil a few large potatoes in salted water till soft; mash to a paste, add a good sized piece of butter and one egg; season with celery or salt. Boil one pint of new milk and while hot pour upon the potatoes, stir quickly; add enough hot water to make a thin soup and serve hot. It is delicious for children and invalids. Some consider the addition of a little minced onion an improvement.

JULIENNE SOUP.

Place a small shank or piece of fat beef, weighing a half pound or less, in a pot with one gallon of cold water. Let this boil hard for two hours, skimming it often. Boil in another smaller pot a half pint of potatoes chopped, one pint of tomatoes, and half a pint of corn, a tablespoonful of finely chopped carrot, a tablespoonful of finely chopped turnip; boil all hard for two hours; put them in same pot, boil hard all together for an hour; mince finely and add a dessert spoonful of parsley, and thicken with a small quantity of flour made into a thick paste and stir hard when added. If any be left it can be again boiled for dinner next day, when it is usually better, as it is improved by long boiling.—*Mrs. W. W. Massie.*

FRENCH SOUP.

Three quarts of water, four pounds of meat, two teaspoonsful of salt, three small carrots, three small onions, one of them stuck with cloves, one head celery, a little thyme, a little parsley, one bay leaf, two turnips, one burnt onion. Put meat in a pot with water, boil slowly, carefully removing all scum. When no more rises, put in vegetables previously prepared. Cut carrots in slices; stick onion with cloves; cut turnips in four pieces; let boil two hours. A few bones improve the soup. If water boils away too much add a little hot water in addition.

OYSTERS.

OYSTER SOUP.

To two quarts of new milk add the liquor from a can of oysters. When it boils, add the oysters and boil two minutes longer. Pour in a tureen, over powdered crackers, a tablespoonful of butter, salt and pepper to taste. Never add the salt and butter while cooking, it is apt to curdle.—*Mrs. Fannie Edmonston.*

OYSTER SOUP.

To a can of oysters and liquor add the can full of water, seasoned with red pepper and salt to taste; cook till nearly done. Add yolks of four eggs, beaten and mixed in a pint of milk. Put in the oysters and stir till it thickens.—*Mrs. Burnley.*

CREAM OYSTERS.

Drain well two quarts of large oysters; in a hot kettle melt a cup of butter; put the oysters in the butter and let them remain long enough to plump them; lift them out with a skimmer into a hot platter. A good deal of juice will come out into the butter, to this add salt and pepper to taste, also a cupful of cream or milk; thicken smoothly with two tablespoonsful of flour. When this boils, turn back the oysters and let them stay long enough to get hot. Have a hot dish in which are thin slices of toast, pour in the oysters and gravy, and serve immediately. If the liquor should get too thick add a little milk or cream.—*Mrs. V. C. Gilman, in Kentucky Home Cook Book.*

OYSTERS.

ROASTED OYSTERS.

Put the oysters in a coarse dish which will stand a fierce heat. Add a little of the liquor, salt, pepper, and butter to taste. Place in front of the grate. Do not cook too much. Serve with celery, pickles or tomato catsup. A most delightful way to cook oysters.—*Mrs. E. R. Tennent.*

BROILED OYSTERS.

Dip fine large oysters in melted butter, then put carefully on a hot broiler. Have a dish with melted butter and pepper. The salt in the butter is generally sufficient.

BROILED OYSTERS ON THE HALF-SHELL.

Select large shells, clean with a brush, open, saving juice; put oysters in boiling water for a few minutes, remove and place each oyster in a half-shell with juice; place on a gridiron over a brisk fire, and when they begin to boil season with butter, salt, and pepper. Serve on the half-shell.

OYSTERS WITH POTATOES.

Take six large Irish potatoes, boil, skin and mash well. Add a small cup of cream, a tablespoonful of butter, and salt to taste, with two well beaten eggs. Stir in about the same quantity of finely chopped oysters. Put in a baking-dish, protect with a paper until the oysters are cooked, then remove the paper and brown. New.—*Mrs. Leila Slade.*

HALF-FRIED OYSTERS.

Take the largest and freshest oysters, drain the liquor off, dip them in beaten egg, to which salt is added, and then in cracker-dust, and fry in butter.—*Fred Massa.*

FRIED OYSTERS.

Drain the oysters from the liquor and wipe them dry on a napkin. Beat two eggs, add a little salt, dip the oysters into the beaten eggs, then in sifted corn meal. Fry in lard.—*Mrs. Dorsey.*

POACHED EGGS AND OYSTERS.

Boil the oysters in their liquor, with a little salt added, until done. Have a kettle of boiling water salted. Drop in the eggs carefully, and when the whites are cooked lay an oyster on top of each. Lift out carefully on a hot dish, pour melted butter over, and add a little cayenne pepper.—*Mrs. Sue Barbour.*

BAKED OYSTER DUMPLING.

Make a rich puff paste, cut with a large biscuit-cutter. Put three oysters in each, that have been plumped in butter. Bake until dough is brown. For the sauce, take a pint of new milk, a tablespoonful of butter, salt and pepper to taste, thicken with corn starch. Pour sauce over ten minutes before serving.

SCALLOPED OYSTERS.

Grate cracker or stale bread in the bottom of your dish. Moisten with oyster liquor, to which salt and pepper has been added. Put in a layer of oysters, with bits of butter, and then a layer of crumbs till all is in. If it seems dry pour on more oyster liquor. For the top layer beat three eggs light. Crumble in bread until thick, then spread on. Bake slowly.—*Mrs. Collier.*

A FINE OYSTER PIE.

Make a rich puff paste; after having greased the baking dish, line with the paste. Then season one quart of oysters with pepper and salt, one-half pound of butter, and half a cupful of bread crumbs; put this in with the oysters without the liquor, and cover with paste in strips; if in baking the crust browns too fast, put a paper over it. If it looks dry, add more liquor. Serve hot.

OYSTER OMELET.

Take twenty-four large oysters, eight eggs, one small cup of cream, two tablespoonsful of butter, pepper, salt and chopped parsley; chop the oysters fine; beat the eggs separately and very light; mix all together, stirring in the whites last, very lightly. Fry in fresh lard or butter until the omelet is of a light brown.

DRESSING FOR COVE OYSTERS.

Take the yolks of four hard-boiled eggs, mash them fine and add a teaspoonful of butter; also a little parsley. Heat a teacupful of tomato catsup and add this. You can use also a little minced cucumber pickle.

RAW OYSTERS.

Get a large square block of ice and make a large hollow with a hot flat iron. Pour the oysters in, and around the edge of this ice-bowl place an elaborate border of curled parsley, with celery tops here and there. In very cold weather make balls of snow, very hard pressed. In an indenture at the top place five or six oysters. These balls arranged on a large dish, with sprigs of parsley thrown carelessly here and there, make a charming appearance. This style was originated by a young girl in Drummondsville, Canada.

FISH.

Fresh fish may be known by their firm flesh, red gills and full bright eyes. Clean them carefully so as not to have any blood on the backbone, but do not make so large a cut as to spoil the looks of the fish. The sound adheres to bone and must be left; so must the hard and soft roes. Great care must be taken not to break gall, for it would make fish bitter. Never fry fish in butter; fry them in good dripping or lard; oil is best, but it is very expensive. Let the fish remain salted for several hours before cooking.

TO FRY FISH.

Dry them in a towel, roll over and over in sifted corn meal and fry in hot lard.

TO BROIL FISH.

Clean, wash and wipe dry; split so that when laid flat the backbone will be in the middle. Sprinkle with salt and lay inside down upon a buttered gridiron over a clear fire until it is nicely colored, then turn. When done put upon a hot dish, butter plentifully and pepper. Put a hot cover over it and send to table.

BAKED SHAD.

Baked shad does not require to be cut down the back, only cleaned, the roes removed and the inside filled with a stuffing made of bread crumbs, salt pork, an onion, sage, parsley, pepper and salt; chop all together fine, fill and sew up the shad; place in a pan with a pint of water, pieces of fat pork on top, the roes at the side and bake one hour.—*Mrs. Will J. Winn.*

CREAM GRAVY FOR BAKED FISH.

Have ready in saucepan one pint of cream, diluted with a few spoonsful of hot water, stir in tablespoonful of melted butter and a little chopped parsley; heat this in vessel filled with hot water. Pour in gravy from dripping pan of fish. Boil thick.

SAUCE FOR FISH.

Take the yolks of two hard boiled eggs; pulverize them well; add mixed mustard, pepper, salt, three tablespoonsful of salad oil; three of vinegar; one tablespoonful of tomato catsup.

BOILED BASS OR OTHER FISH.

Put sufficient water in pot to enable the fish, if alive, to swim easily. Add half a cup of vinegar, one teaspoonful of salt, one onion, one dozen whole black peppers, one blade of mace. Sew up fish in a piece of net or muslin fitted to shape. Heat slowly for first half an hour, then boil eight minutes to the pound quite fast. Unwrap and pour over it a cup of drawn butter based upon the liquid in which fish was boiled, with the juice of half a lemon stirred into it.

SALT MACKEREL.

Put to soak in water with the skin side uppermost. In six hours broil or fry as preferred.

TO PICKLE ROCK.

Cook a rock fish, cut in pieces in water enough to cover. Put in a handful of salt, a little white pepper, one tablespoonful of allspice, a few cloves and mace. When the fish is nearly done add a quart of vinegar. In putting away cover with liquor.

TO FRY EELS.

Skin them, wash well, season with pepper and salt, roll each piece in fine Indian meal, and fry in hot lard; or egg them and roll in cracker crumbs and fry. For sauce use melted butter sharpened with lemon juice.

BAKED HERRING.

Soak salt herring over night; roll in flour and butter, and place in a pan with a very little water over them. Season with pepper.

CODFISH BALLS.

Take codfish and soak one day and night; then boil it all to pieces and pick into shreds; pick out all the bones and let it drain. To one pound of fish allow one dozen Irish potatoes, boiled and mashed very fine. Season with pepper, salt, and a teacupful of sweet milk, break in one egg, then mix all well together. Make into cakes and bake a light brown.

FISH CAKE.

Put bones of fish with head and fins into a stewpan with about a pint of water; add pepper and salt to taste, a good sized onion, handful of sweet herbs, if you like; stew all slowly about two hours. Then mince fine clear meat of fish, mixing well with bread crumbs, cold mashed potatoes and a small quantity of finely chopped parsley; season with salt and pepper to taste; make whole into cake with an egg well beaten. Brush it over lightly with white of egg; strew with bread crumbs and fry rich amber brown. Strain gravy made from bones and pour it over. Serve hot with garnish of lemon slices and parsley.

SALADS.

MRS. GEN. PHILLIPS' CHICKEN SALAD.

To one large hen boiled and chopped fine, add half a dozen hard-boiled eggs; one-fourth of a pound of butter; season with mustard, vinegar, pepper and salt to taste. Melt the butter and cream it with the yolks of the eggs; add the seasoning and the whites of the eggs chopped fine. Mix thoroughly with the chicken.

CHICKEN SALAD.

One pound of chicken minced; one-third of a pound of lettuce or cabbage. Boil six eggs hard; separate yolks from white; mash yolks in half a tumbler full of sweet olive oil or melted butter, half a tumbler of vinegar, two tablespoonsful of dry mustard, a tablespoonful of loaf sugar dissolved in vinegar, a teaspoonful each of pepper and salt. Mix well and pour over minced chicken and lettuce or cabbage. Garnish with sprigs of parsley and the whites of eggs cut in rings.—*Mrs. Joe Clifton.*

TURKEY SALAD.

Take scraps of cold turkey and mince very fine. Take a pint of good apple vinegar, add to it the beaten yolks of four eggs, half a cupful of butter, a teaspoonful of loaf sugar, a teaspoonful of salt, a pinch of cayenne pepper, and a tablespoonful of mustard. Boil till thick, and when cold add a large tablespoonful of horse-radish. If it is added while cooking it is apt to curdle. Pour over the minced turkey and garnish with celery tops, whites of eggs cut in rings, and curled parsley.—*Palace Hotel, San Francisco.*

SALADS.

JELLIED CHICKEN.

Take a chicken and boil in salted water till it falls from the bones, then take it out and mince finely. Dissolve half a box of gelatine in the water in which the chicken was boiled, and add just enough vinegar to take off the gelatine taste. Pour over the chicken and turn into a mould.—*Mrs. Sue Moore.*

BEET SALAD.

Boil one large beet; when cold cut in small slices. Boil six Irish potatoes; when cold slice. Cut up one large head of lettuce or an equal amount of cabbage sliced on a potato slice. For a dressing take the yolks of three eggs, one teacupful of vinegar, one teaspoonful of ground mustard; heat them, stirring all the while until thick; add a tablespoonful of salad oil and a dessert-spoonful of sugar; pour over the salad. Cut up one or two hard boiled eggs and lay on the dish.—*Mrs. W. W. Massie.*

SALMON SALAD.

Turn out a can of salmon into a dish, and pour over it a dressing made as follows: Yolks of two hard boiled eggs, rubbed very fine and smooth; one teaspoonful of English mustard, one of salt, the yolks of two raw eggs beaten into the other, a dessert-spoonful of sugar, one tablespoonful of celery seed; add a lump of butter melted, and enough vinegar to thin. Pour over the salmon and stir well. Some persons like the addition of brown sugar, cayenne pepper and cloves.

LOBSTER SALAD.

Chop up one can of lobsters, cut in small pieces as much celery; then cream with one teacupful of butter, one tablespoonful of mustard, one of sugar, one teaspoonful of salt, and the yolks of four hard boiled eggs, rubbed smooth; stir in five tablespoonsful of pepper vinegar, and pour the mixture over the lobster and celery.—*Mrs. Geo. J. Gable.*

SALADS.

OYSTER SALAD.

Half a gallon each of fresh oysters and celery cut into slices, yolks of four hard boiled eggs, a raw egg whipped, two large spoonsful of melted butter, two teaspoonsful, each, of salt, black pepper, and made mustard, one teacupful of vinegar, two pickled cucumbers cut fine. Drain liquor from oysters, throw in hot vinegar on the fire, let them stay till plump, not cooked. Put at once into cold water, drain off, and set in cool place; prepare dressing; rub salt, pepper, and mustard with the yolks finely mashed, add butter, a few drops at a time. When smooth add beaten egg, then vinegar by the spoonful; set aside. Mix oysters, celery, and pickle, tossing up well with a silver fork; salt to taste. Pour dressing over all.—*Mrs. G. S. Park, in Dixie Cook Book.*

HAM SALAD.

Run the small bits of ham through your sausage mill and season with butter and pepper. Set a pint of sour cream on the fire, add a pinch of soda, a cupful of vinegar, a large tablespoonful of mustard, a tablespoonful of brown sugar, and the yolks of three eggs. Boil hard, and when cold pour over the minced ham —*Mrs. Rachel Downey.*

BOTTLED SALAD DRESSING.

Beat yolks of eight eggs, add to them a cup of sugar, one tablespoonful each of salt, mustard and black pepper, a little cayenne, and half a cup of cream; mix thoroughly; bring to a boil a pint and a half of vinegar, add one cup of butter; let it come to a boil; pour upon the mixture, stir well, and when cold put into bottles and set in a cool place. It will keep for weeks in the hottest weather, and is the equal, if not the superior, of Durkee's celebrated salad dressing.

COLD SLAW.

Cut fine a solid tender head of cabbage; sprinkle over with salt and pepper. Beat three eggs, six tablespoonsful of vinegar, four tablespoonsful of sugar, a teaspoonful of made mustard, a tablespoonful of melted butter or oil. Set this on the fire, stir till it becomes smooth. Set aside to cool and mix with the cabbage.—*Miss Idelle Marlowe.*

EGG SALAD.

Boil hard one dozen eggs, cut them in half, and lay the whites carefully on a dish. Mash the yolks and add a cupful of bread crumbs, a lump of butter, a little cayenne pepper, a teaspoonful of salt, and a cucumber pickle minced fine. Make into balls, put back into the egg and pour drawn butter or chicken gravy over.—*Mrs. T. H. Cheek.*

POTATO SALAD.

Take a teacupful of apple vinegar, dissolve in it a teaspoonful of loaf sugar, a teaspoonful of mustard, salt and pepper. Rub into it the yolks of three hard boiled eggs. Take a quart of mealy potatoes that have been pressed through a sieve, add this mixture to it, and set aside to get cold. Garnish with parsley and the whites of eggs cut in rings.—*Mrs. Saxon Anderson.*

Meat Sauces and Salad Dressings.

SAUCE REMOULADE.

Given to Mrs. W. W. Massie, at Hotel Belle Vue, Munich.

Put the yolks of four eggs in a bowl with half a teaspoonful each of salt and pepper, beat in olive oil until it thickens, then pour in tarragon vinegar and oil alternately, until half a liter (half a pint) has been used; chop fine five eschalots, one tablespoonful of capers, five small cucumber pickles, a little tarragon and spinach; beat them together with a tablespoonful of mustard into the prepared sauce. Add the juice of half a lemon and a little cayenne pepper. Excellent for cold chicken or meats.

PEPPER SAUCE.

Take one hundred ripe fresh red peppers, and to one gallon of vinegar put two tablespoonsful of mustard, two of salt, one of black pepper. Boil until the skin can be slipped from the pulp of the pepper, then strain and bottle. It is better to boil the pepper in water till soft, then strain, put in the other ingredients and boil.—*Whitlock House.*

CUCUMBER SAUCE.

Grate the cucumbers and season with salt to suit your taste. Let them stand four hours, then squeeze out every particle of water with the hands. To one cup of cucumber put four cupsful of best vinegar, four tablespoonsful of black pepper. Stir up, and if not salt enough add a little more.—*Mrs. James Pitner.*

ONION SAUCE.

Boil onions enough to fill a sauce tureen until they are soft; mash them into a pulp and add a tablespoonful of vinegar, a wine glass of wine, a tablespoonful of butter; salt and pepper to your taste.—*Mrs. H. N. Starnes.*

FISH SAUCE.

Put six teaspoonsful of water and four of vinegar in the saucepan; warm and thicken it with the yolks of two eggs. Make it quite hot, but do not boil it; strain in the juice of a lemon and strain through a sieve.—*Mrs. Geo. J. Gable.*

LONDON CLUB SAUCE.

One gallon of vinegar, one pound of black pepper, half a pound of cayenne pepper, half pound of mustard, four ounces of cloves, four ounces of salt, six ounces of burnt sugar. Put all in a stone jar and let steep for two weeks.—*Miss M. J. Redmon.*

DRAWN BUTTER.

Rub two teaspoonsful of flour into a quarter of a pound of butter; add five teaspoonsful of cold water; set it in boiling water till it melts, and when it begins to simmer it is done. Be careful always to work the flour in the butter so thoroughly as not to be lumpy. If the drawn butter is used with fish, add eggs hard boiled and chopped very fine. If used with boiled fowl, put in oysters while it is simmering, and let them become thoroughly heated.—*Miss Ella Mitchell, in Blue Grass Cook Book.*

VENISON SAUCE.

One pound of brown sugar, one tumbler of currant jelly, one pint of claret wine or tomato catsup, two tablespoonsful of ground mace and cinnamon, one pound of butter. Boil all well together.—*Mrs. Wm. Simmes.*

PEPPER VINEGAR.

One dozen pods of red pepper, fully ripe. Take out stems and cut them in two; add three pints of vinegar; boil down to one quart, strain through a sieve and bottle for use.

AROMATIC MUSTARD.

Four tablespoonsful of ground mustard, one tablespoonful of flour, one tablespoonful of sugar, one teaspoonful of salt, one teaspoonful of black pepper, one teaspoonful of cloves, one teaspoonful of cinnamon. Mix smoothly with boiling vinegar; add a little salad oil, and let it stand several hours before using. It will keep any length of time.
—*Mrs. R. K. Meade, in Virginia Cook Book.*

MORGAN'S TARTAN SAUCE.

Put into a bowl one spoonful of dry mustard, two spoonsful of salt, a little cayenne pepper, yolk of one raw egg; mix these together. Then add drop by drop one teacupful of sweet oil; stir into a thick mass. Add a little vinegar. Chop very fine two small cucumber pickles, two teaspoonsful of capers, two sprigs of parsley, one leek or small onion, and a little celery; stir all into the dressing. This is delicious with fish, cold meats, chicken or turkey.

CELERY VINEGAR.

Pound half a pint of celery seed and put in a quart bottle of vinegar. Let it stand two weeks, then strain and bottle.

APPLE SAUCE.

Pare and cut up tart apples; cover with water and boil to a pulp. Sweeten to taste and add a piece of butter. Nice accompaniment for fresh pork or roast turkey. Evaporated apples make very nice sauce.

CRANBERRY SAUCE.

Cover the berries with water and boil to a pulp. It will require two hours. Sweeten to taste.

HORSE RADISH SAUCE.

Three tablespoonsful of grated horse-radish, two tablespoonsful of sugar, five tablespoonsful of vinegar. Put all in a tumbler and fill to the top with cream.—*Mrs. Robinson.*

SAUCE FOR LETTUCE.

For one quart of lettuce boil three eggs hard; separate them from whites, mash a small Irish potato with a tablespoonful of thick rich cream; mix with the egg a tablespoonful of mustard, one of loaf sugar, a teaspoonful of salt, wineglassful of good vinegar, essence of ham poured on lettuce.—*Mrs. Will J. Winn.*

SALAD DRESSING.
(Excellent.)

Four eggs boiled very hard. Let them get entirely cold; remove the whites and rub the yolks to a paste; add one teaspoonful of sugar, one teaspoonful of French mustard, one salt spoon of salt. Rub all together slowly adding olive oil till the mixture is the consistency of thick cream; add two tablespoonsful of vinegar and the whites of the eggs chopped, not too fine.—*Mrs. Mattie Dobbs.*

FRENCH SALAD DRESSING.

Beat the yolks of six eggs very light, add a teaspoonful of sugar, a teaspoonful of black and cayenne pepper mixed, half a cup of butter, and half a cup of vinegar. Boil till thick, and when perfectly cold add minced cucumber pickle and chopped celery. Pour on the prepared chicken.—*Forest City Hotel, Cleveland, Ohio.*

GREEN TOMATO SAUCE.

One gallon of green but full tomatoes, one pint of onions chopped very fine, one pint of sugar, two tablespoonsful of salt, one of ground black pepper, one of ground cloves, one of cinnamon, one and a half of ground mustard, one teaspoonful of cayenne pepper, two pints of vinegar. Boil all together in a porcelain-lined kettle until quite tender. Put in air tight jars.—*Mrs. George Lester.*

WORCESTERSHIRE SAUCE.

All the English sauces in popular use are founded upon walnut catsup. To make a catsup of walnuts, the green shells are taken in these proportions; two gallons of walnut juice, five pounds of salt, mixed and bruised and allowed to lie a week; the liquor is then pressed out, and to every gallon is added four ounces of allspice, three ounces of ginger, and of pepper and cloves two ounces each, all bruised. The whole is then simmered for thirty minutes and is then set aside to clear. This is the catsup. To make a sauce of this similar to Worcestershire, take one gallon of port wine, three-fourths of a gallon of catsup, two pounds of anchovies with their liquor, eight lemons, forty-eight eschallots, or small onions, one and three-fourth pounds of scraped horse-radish; mace one ounce, cayenne two ounces, mustard eight ounces. Boil the whole gently, then strain and bottle.—*Youman's Dictionary.*

CHUTNEY SAUCE.

Pare and core sour apples; tomatoes, brown sugar, best raisins, and apples each eight ounces; salt four ounces; red pepper and powdered ginger two ounces each; garlic and small onions one ounce each. Pound the whole well, and add three quarts of best cider or wine vinegar, and one quart of lemon juice. Let it stand in the vessel a month, but give it a good shake daily. Then pour off the clear liquid and bottle it.

MIXED SAUCE.

Three apples chopped fine, two onions, one seeded cucumber, two green peppers, three tomatoes; chop well, mix with salt, pepper, mustard, vinegar and a little sugar.

SOYER SAUCE.

One spoonful of mustard, one spoonful of olive oil, one-half cupful catsup.

DRIED BEEF GRAVY.

Shave very thinly one-half teacupful of beef, put over it one quart of cold water, set on top of stove; let it simmer one or two hours, thicken with one and a half tablespoonsful of flour mixed with cold water, and butter size of a walnut; salt to taste.—*The Complete Home.*

FRENCH MUSTARD.

Slice an onion in a bowl; cover with good vinegar; after two days pour off the vinegar; add to it a teaspoonful of cayenne pepper, a teaspoonful of salt, a tablespoonful of sugar and mustard enough to thicken; mix. Set on the stove and stir till it boils. When cold it is fit for use.

RICH DUTCH SAUCE.

Put two ounces of butter with two tablespoonsful of flour into quarter of pint of water or gravy; simmer and stir, adding half a teacupful of cream, beaten with the yolks of four eggs, and three tablespoonsful of horse-radish vinegar, warm but do not boil together, add salt and the juice of half a lemon, and strain through a sieve.

COMMON EGG SAUCE.

Boil a couple of eggs hard, and when they are quite cold cut the whites and yolks separately; mix them well, put them in a very hot tureen and pour boiling to them a quarter of a pint of melted butter; stir, and serve the sauce immediately.

MUSTARD SAUCE.

Stir made mustard into melted butter in the proportion of two tablespoonsful of the former to a quarter of a pint of

MEAT SAUCES AND SALAD DRESSINGS.

the latter. This is a useful sauce for boiled tripe, herrings and hot lobsters.

MINT SAUCE.

Two tablespoonsful of mint, chopped fine, one tablespoonful of powdered sugar, a salt-spoonful of salt, half a teacupful of vinegar. Mix vinegar, sugar and salt together, then add the mint. Set in a cool place for fifteen minutes before serving. It is best to lay the mint in ice-water an hour before using, as this makes it fresh and tender.—*Mrs. L. C. Dimmitt, in The Home Cook Book.*

PICKLES.

THERE is no department of cooking more dependent on good materials than pickles. Be sure you have fresh, firm vegetables, pure, strong spices and peppers, and the best of apple vinegar. Always make your pickles in a porcelain kettle. It is extremely hazardous to health, and even to life itself, to use brass kettles. In the past they have been depended upon to give the pickles a bright color, but it can be done much more safely with cabbage leaves by lining the bottom and sides of the kettle with them and placing a layer over the top of the pickles. A small lump of alum will make them crisp and tender. When they are put away in jars place a saucer over the top of the pickles to keep them well under. Bits of horse-radish dropped in will preserve the vinegar. If white specks appear skim them off, add a handful of brown sugar to the vinegar, boil and skim and pour over the pickles hot. They are unfit for use if frozen. No care can restore them. In very cold weather remove them to a room where a fire is kept. Pickles are much better and can be kept indefinitely by putting up in glass bottles and sealing.

SPICED VINEGAR.

Two and one-half gallons of apple vinegar, two and one-half pounds of brown sugar, three-fourths of a pound of white mustard seed, one box of French mustard, a half pound of pepper, three ounces of cloves, three ounces of celery seed, one ounce of allspice, two grated nutmegs. Boil all together a half hour ; then add a pint of scraped horse-radish, a half dozen sliced lemons, a dozen sliced onions, and a little sweet basil.—*Mrs. Joseph E. Brown.*

CUCUMBER PICKLES.

Boil one and a half gallons of good cider vinegar with one tablespoonful of pulverized alum, one dozen onions, four pods of red pepper. Pour over the pickles and let stand several days. Take the same vinegar, to which add two ounces of turmeric, ten cents' worth of celery seed, ten cents' worth of cinnamon, a few pieces of white ginger, white and black mustard, handful of garlic, three pounds of brown sugar.—*Mrs. M. V. Payne.*

GOOD CUCUMBER PICKLE.

One gallon of strong cider vinegar, one pint of brown sugar, half a pint of white mustard seed, one large onion quartered, half a dozen garlic cloves, two tablespoonsful of celery seed, ten cents' worth of stick cinnamon, broken, three or four pieces of root ginger. Boil all hard and pour over pickles, which should be previously greened, and tie tight. These are ready for use in three days. —*Mrs. W. W. Massie.*

FRENCH PICKLE.

One large cabbage, two quarts of green tomatoes, two large onions, half a dozen peppers. Chop all together, put in a jar and sprinkle with salt. Let it remain over night. In the morning put in a colander and pour over cold water to extract salt; then take one teaspoonful of cloves, two teaspoonsful of cinnamon, two teaspoonsful of mace, a half pound of brown sugar, one-fourth of a pound of white mustard seed, with enough vinegar to cover pickles. Pour the spiced vinegar over pickles and cook ten minutes.—*Mrs. Maj. Winn.*

MIXED PICKLES.

Take a large head of cabbage, a half gallon of green tomatoes and two dozen cucumbers. Chop all very fine, mix thoroughly, and sprinkle with salt. Let it remain over night, and next day squeeze out the salty water. Cover with best vinegar, add a tablespoonful of white mustard seed, a tablespoonful of celery seed, a tablespoonful of cinnamon, nutmeg, cloves, and allspice ground, a teaspoonful of black pepper, a pinch of cayenne pepper, two small onions sliced, a cupful of brown sugar, and more salt if needed. Boil a long time, adding more vinegar as it boils away.—*Miss Sallie Dick.*

CABBAGE PICKLE.

For a two gallon jar take cabbage enough to fill it; then pour on hot brine; let the brine remain on them four days; squeeze them out of the brine and pour weak vinegar over them, letting it remain several days. Then take strong vinegar, put into it two ounces of cinnamon bark, essence of cloves to suit the taste, two ounces of turmeric. Put this over the cabbage and tie closely.—*Mrs. Patsey Edwards.*

This has taken the premium at Bourbon Fair several times.

PICKLED ONIONS.

Take small onions no larger than marbles; skin them carefully, throwing them in very strong brine. Let them remain eight days, changing the brine two or three times. Dry them between cloths, place them in bottles, add spices, and fill up with strong vinegar. A teaspoonful of olive oil poured on the top will prevent the onions turning yellow. The spices used are allspice, cloves, black pepper, and mustard seed.—*Mrs. James Woodrow.*

ONION PICKLE.

Peel the onions and boil in sweet milk fifteen minutes; take them out, place in bottles, and pour scalding spiced vinegar over them; seal.

PEACH PICKLES.

Pick the peaches carefully from the tree before they are entirely ripe; put them in jars and cover them with salt and water, strong enough to bear up an egg. Let them remain three days, take out and wipe carefully with a soft cloth to prevent bruising. To each gallon of white wine vinegar add one pint of mustard, two or three heads of garlic, one-fourth of a pound of ginger sliced, half an ounce each of cloves, mace, and nutmeg, two ounces of allspice. As the peaches are put in the jar sprinkle the spices among them. Have about a dozen small onions stuck with cloves. Add a good deal of horse-radish. Pour the cold vinegar and mustard on the peaches, and tie up tightly. In two months they are fit for use. If you choose you can take out the stones and fill the peaches with a mixture of the ingredients.—*Mrs. L. J. Pinkerton.*

SLICED PEACH PICKLE.

Slice the peaches but do not pare them. Boil in spiced vinegar till tender and seal. They look very pretty with three cloves stuck in the centre of each.

DELICIOUS CUCUMBER PICKLE.

Take cucumber pickles that have already been made, slice them, some lengthwise, some crosswise also; slice some onions rather thick. Lay the onions in salt water. In a kettle put one quart of best cider-vinegar made quite sweet with brown sugar and colored strongly with turmeric; season highly with cinnamon, cloves, allspice, mace, white and black mustard seed, celery seed, and curry powder, and let all boil well. Then put in cucumbers and onions. Boil until the pickles are a rich citron color; let them cool and tie or seal in jars.—*Mrs. John A. Hanley, in Blue Grass Cook Book.*

MUSTARD PICKLE.

Soak the salt from your cucumbers; have your kettle ready, and put in a layer of cucumbers and a layer of grape leaves. Sprinkle in a little pulverized alum, a little allspice, cinnamon, black and red pepper, a few slices of onion, two tablespoonsful of sugar, and so on until your kettle is full; then cover with good vinegar, and let it simmer over a slow fire until the cucumbers are green. Take five boxes of mustard, and allow one and a half cups of sugar to each box; rub them together with vinegar until smooth; to each box put one tablespoonful of cinnamon, one of cloves, one of mace, one of allspice, four dessert-spoonsful of salad oil, one of turmeric, one of celery seed, one pound of white mustard seed. Mix these well, and pour the mixture over the pickles when cold.—*Mrs. H. N. Starnes.*

RIPE TOMATO PICKLE.

Take one peck of ripe tomatoes, stick with a fork three or four times; sprinkle them down, with salt and tomatoes alternately, and let them remain forty-eight hours; then take out and lay them in fresh water three or four hours; drain off, and lay them in a jar, alternately, a layer of tomatoes and a compound of sliced onion, allspice and black pepper, (whole grains) with a tablespoonful of mustard. The four ingredients are to be considered a layer until all the tomatoes are used, letting the top layer be of onions. Then pour scalding vinegar over the whole. Tie up tightly, and in eight or ten days they will be fit for use.—*Mrs. H. N. Starnes.*

GREEN TOMATO PICKLE.

One peck of tomatoes, twelve onions; slice them and sprinkle with a little salt and let them stand twenty-four hours; then drain the water from them and add two or three green peppers, one-fourth of a pound of mustard seed, half an ounce of cloves, one ounce of mace, one ounce of celery seed, one ounce of allspice, and two pounds of sugar. Cover with vinegar and boil until clear; when cold add one box of mustard.—*Miss Mollie Downey.*

WALNUT PICKLE.

As you peel the walnuts throw them into cold water. After they are all peeled put them into a vessel of cold water and let them remain twenty-four hours, then put them in strong salt water and let them remain eight or ten days. Scald them in vinegar and drop them in a jar of cold vinegar; add pepper, ginger, cloves, cinnamon, allspice, mustard seed, horse-radish and garlic, according to the quantity of pickles. Previous to adding the garlic and horse-radish, cut them in thin slices, cover with salt and let them stand twenty-four hours. Shake off the salt and put them in the sun to dry. If the spices are beaten, tie them in a cloth.—*Mrs. Judge Atkinson.*

HEYDEN SALAD.

Take equal quantities of cabbage and green tomatoes; season them with green pepper and onions to your taste. Chop the vegetables fine, put them in a jar and cover them with a handful of salt. Let them remain for a few hours, squeeze and put them in vinegar. Let them remain twenty-four hours, squeeze them out of the vinegar and put them in a jar with ground and seed mustard, cloves and horse-radish to your taste, and fill the jar with vinegar.—*Mrs. L. L. Cox.*

FOR GREENING PICKLES.

For two gallons of pickles take one teaspoonful of soda, put the pickles in a preserving kettle, sprinkling a little of the soda over each layer.—*Mrs. Jos. Black in Ky. Home Cook Book.*

SUPERIOR MIXED PICKLE.

Take any kind of fruit in season, chop fine, add corn scraped from the cob, finely chopped cabbage, tomatoes, cucumbers, beans and onions. Sprinkle salt over, and let them remain twenty-four hours; drain and add all kinds of spices, an ounce of each. To two gallons of pickles allow four pounds of sugar, one ounce of turmeric, and the yolks of one dozen hard-boiled eggs, mashed or creamed with the spices. Boil with strong cider vinegar.—*Mrs. Tarleton.*

PREMIUM SPANISH PICKLE.

Take three dozen cucumbers, two large heads of cabbage, one dozen onions. chopped fine or sliced, and four pods of green pepper. Peel and slice the cucumbers lengthwise and cut them in pieces one inch long; chop the cabbage and pepper, salt each separately, and let them stand over night; at morning squeeze out the salt water and add the following ingredients: one ounce of celery seed, one-half pound of white mustard seed, one ounce of turmeric, one tablespoonful of ground cloves, one tablespoonful of allspice, one half pint of grated horse-radish and one pound of brown sugar. Mix all well. Put into a kettle and cover well with vinegar, and scald. When cold, add a half-pound box of Lexington mustard. Put in jars and cover with cold vinegar, adding a little syrup of honey to prevent moulding. Seal up.—*Mrs. Dr. J. H. Holton in Ky. Home Cook Book.*

CUCUMBER MANGOES.

Take two dozen large, green cucumbers; cut a piece out of the side and fasten it to the cucumber with a needle and strong thread; scrape out the seeds and all the pulp, and lay them in weak salt water five hours. Make a dressing of two large heads of cabbage, four green peppers chopped fine, two ounces of celery seed, two ounces of white mustard seed, one ounce of ground black pepper, one ounce of salt and one teacupful of sugar. In filling the cucumbers, squeeze the water from the dressing, put two onion setts and two small beans in each cucumber; put back the piece, and tie a strip of cotton an inch wide around the cucumber, to hold it in place; then put in a porcelain kettle with a layer of grape or cabbage leaves and a tablespoonful of alum alternately. Cover with vinegar and scald three-quarters of an hour; then lift them out into jars, adding spices to taste. To a gallon of the best cider vinegar put one and one-half pounds of sugar, boil fifteen minutes and pour over the mangoes. Tie up closely or seal. Splendid.

PICKLED BEETS.

Wash them, but do not cut off any of the rootlets; boil them tender, peel them, or rub off the outside with a coarse cloth, cut them in slices, put them in a jar, cover with cold vinegar, black pepper and ginger.—*Mrs. Sarah Josepha Hale.*

MRS. GABLE'S LILY PICKLE.

One quart each of finely chopped cabbage and green tomatoes, one pint of sliced cucumbers. Sprinkle salt over and let them remain twelve hours, then press as dry as possible and put in a preserving kettle; cover with best vinegar, add a pod of red pepper, a teacupful of brown sugar, a large tablespoonful of mustard, a grated nutmeg, a dozen whole cloves, a stick of cinnamon, several pieces of root ginger, and a small teacupful of grated horse-radish. Add more vinegar as it boils away, and cook until perfectly tender. A little turmeric gives it a brilliant yellow appearance.

TO MAKE VINEGAR.

Five gallons of rain water, two quarts of whisky, two quarts of molasses, half a pint of good fresh yeast. Lay a sheet of foolscap paper in the bottom of a keg; place it in the sun. After pouring in the mixture put in the bung loosely; do not put it in tight till fermentation ceases. Good in six weeks.—*Mrs. R. T. Nesbitt.*

PYFER PICKLES.

Salt pickles down dry for ten days, soak in fresh water one day; pour off water, place in a porcelain kettle, cover with water and vinegar and add a teaspoonful of pulverized alum to each gallon; set over night on a stove which had fire in it during the day; wash and put in a jar with cloves, allspice, pepper, horse-radish, and onions or garlic; boil fresh vinegar and pour over all. In two weeks they will be ready for use. These pickles are always fresh and crisp.

CHOW-CHOW.

Take one peck of green tomatoes, one dozen large cucumbers, one dozen onions, six red peppers, one head of cabbage. Chop all separately, then mix together and sprinkle with salt. After remaining six hours press out all salty water and add a handful each of white and black mustard seed, one tablespoonful of celery seed, three of ground black pepper, a pinch of cayenne and a teacupful of grated horse-radish. Cover with good cider vinegar.—*Mrs. Sarah Berry.*

CHOW-CHOW.

One-fourth of a peck of green tomatoes, one large head of cabbage, six large onions, one dozen cucumbers, half a pint of grated horse-radish, half a pound of white mustard seed, half an ounce of celery seed, a few small onions, one-fourth of a teacupful of ground pepper, turmeric, ground cinnamon, and a little brown sugar. Cut the cabbage, onions and cucumbers into small pieces and pack them down in salt one night, then put in vinegar poured over hot. Do this three mornings. The third morning mix one box of ground mustard with one-quarter of a pint of salad oil. To be mixed in while warm.—*Mrs. Orville Bell.*

KENTUCKY PICKLE.

Take green tomatoes, cabbage and onions about equal quantities; grind them in a sausage machine. Salt, and put the mixture in a bag and let it hang all night, or until the juice has run from it; then season with red and black pepper, mustard, celery seed, cloves and sugar. Pack in jars and cover with strong cold vinegar.

TABLE OF WEIGHTS AND MEASURES FOR SPICES.

Two tablespoonsful, (well heaped) of ground spices weigh one ounce.

Two and one-half tablespoonsful of whole spices weigh one ounce.

Two tablespoonsful, (well heaped) of mustard seed weigh one ounce.

Two and a half tablespoonsful of turmeric weigh one ounce.

Three tablespoonsful of celery seed weigh one ounce.

SWEET PICKLES—SPICED PEACHES.

Seven pounds of peeled peaches not quite ripe, three pounds of sugar and one quart of good vinegar, one teaspoonful each of ground cloves and cinnamon. Let the vinegar, sugar and spices become thoroughly heated; put the peaches in and let them remain till quite soft. Put up in air tight jars.—*Mrs. Kilgour.*

A DELICIOUS WATERMELON PICKLE.

Peel, cut and weigh ten pounds of rind; cover well with clear water and let it boil until tender; fold a large towel and lay in the bottom of a dish or waiter; lay the rind on it to drain. It will take nearly all day. Take two pounds and a half of sugar and a quart of vinegar; boil together; pour over rind. Second morning boil again. Third morning add one ounce of ground cinnamon, half an ounce of ground cloves, half an ounce of ground allspice. Tie the spices in a cloth, drop in three minutes; take out spices and pour the vinegar over the rind; tie up closely. Do not use for ten days.—*Mrs. Dovie Anderson.*

CUCUMBER SWEET PICKLE.

Take the cucumbers out of brine, soak them one day in clear water; then slice them a quarter of an inch thick, and same lengthwise. You can cut them in fanciful designs. Boil them in enough water to cover, with a small piece of alum, for half an hour; then drain off the water and for every quart of cucumbers take a quart of good vinegar and three pints of brown sugar. When the sugar and vinegar have boiled ten minutes add the cucumbers, and an ounce each of all kinds of whole spices, one grated nutmeg, half an ounce each of celery seed and white mustard, and a little turmeric. Seal while hot.—*Mrs. E. R. Tennant.*

MRS. KIRK'S PREMIUM PICKLE.

Take seven pounds of large white Heath peaches; after they are peeled put them in stone cans. Make a syrup of one quart of best cider vinegar, three pounds of sugar, one ounce of cinnamon bark and one ounce of cloves; pour it over the fruit boiling hot for eight mornings. The ninth morning put all into a preserving kettle, and let it come to boiling. Seal hot.

SPICED CHERRIES.

Place cherries with stems on in a stone jar. Take enough vinegar to cover, and to each quart add three pints of brown sugar and whole spices. Pour hot over the cherries six mornings. *Mrs. James Scott.*

PICKLED RAISINS.

Leave two pounds of raisins on stem, add one pint of vinegar and half pound of sugar. Simmer over a slow fire half an hour.—*Mrs. Tolleson.*

SPICED TOMATOES.

Twenty pounds of ripe tomatoes scalded and peeled, two quarts of vinegar, eight pounds of sugar, four tablespoonsful each of cinnamon, cloves and allspice. Boil till thick, stirring often.

SPICED GRAPES.

Seven pounds of grapes, three pounds of sugar, one pint of vinegar, one tablespoonful of cloves, one tablespoonful of cinnamon.

SPICED CURRANTS.

Five pounds of currants, four pounds of brown sugar, two tablespoonsful of cloves, the same of cinnamon, one pint of vinegar. Boil till quite thick.

SWEET PICKLED BEETS.

Boil them in a porcelain kettle till they can be pierced with a silver fork; cut in slices and boil in equal parts of vinegar and sugar, with half tablespoonful of cloves tied in a cloth to each gallon. Pour boiling hot over the beets.

CATSUPS.

To one half bushel of skinned tomatoes, add one quart of good vinegar, one pound of salt, one-fourth of a pound of black pepper, one ounce of African cayenne, one-fourth of a pound of allspice, one ounce of cloves, three boxes of mustard, twenty cloves of garlic, six onions, two pounds of brown sugar, and one handful of peach leaves. Boil this mass constantly stirring for three hours to prevent burning. When cool, strain through a sieve and bottle. It will improve by age and create and give zest to appetite almost under the ribs of death.—*Dr. Gunn.*

BAKED TOMATO CATSUP.

Bake the tomatoes by putting them in a stove pan with enough water to keep from burning; then press them through a sieve. To every six quarts of juice add the same quantity of vinegar. Put on a slow fire and let it boil until it thickens; then add a half ounce each of cloves, allspice, and pepper, one-fourth ounce of cinnamon, two grated nutmegs. When almost as thick as mush, add a large tablespoonful of salt. Cool and bottle. The flavor of this catsup, though unlike all others, is decidedly superior. Baking the tomatoes renders a thin and watery catsup impossible.—*"Auntie Barnes."*

TOMATO SOY.

Half a peck of tomatoes, one large pepper cut fine, one large onion cut in slices, one tablespoonful each of ground allspice, black pepper, and celery seed, one-fourth of a cup of salt, half a pint of vinegar. Boil all together slowly, one hour. Cool and bottle. This is, by many, preferred to tomato catsup.

WALNUT CATSUP.

Put one hundred walnuts, beaten to pieces, in one gallon of vinegar and let it boil one hour; strain and return to the fire, with two tablespoonsful of black pepper, two of salt, three of eschalots chopped fine, both roots and tops, one tablespoonful of mace, one of cloves, five or six pieces of ginger, and a few sticks of cinnamon. Boil until it can be washed through a sieve and bottle it.—*Mrs. H. N. Starnes.*

CUCUMBER CATSUP.

Pare and grate the cucumbers. To one quart of cucumbers add three large onions grated, one teaspoonful of salt, one teaspoonful of black pepper, drain through a sieve. Measure the juice and add the same quantity of vinegar.

EGGS.

Eggs form a very nourishing diet, especially for the sick, but they should always be fresh. If the whites and yolks seem mixed and cannot be separated, do not use them for any purpose.

OLD FASHIONED SCRAMBLED EGGS.

Break into a bowl one dozen eggs, but do not beat them. Sprinkle over a teaspoonful of salt and one of pepper. Have a half cupful of melted butter or lard in a skillet. When it is boiling hot drop in the eggs, but do not stir until the whites are set. Then scrape briskly from the bottom, stir well and serve hot.

SCRAMBLED EGGS.

(Very delicate.)

Take one dozen eggs, beat the whites and yolks separately, and then together, add a teacupful of milk in which half a cupful of corn starch has been dissolved. Pour in a skillet containing hot melted butter and stir until done.

BOILED EGGS.

Drop in boiling water; two minutes cooks it very soft; three minutes harder; five minutes will give you a hard-boiled egg. If you wish them for traveling, lunch or picnic dinners better let them stay in seven minutes.

ROASTED EGGS.

Wet brown paper with water and wrap around the eggs. Place them in hot ashes. When they pop they are done. Serve with butter, pepper and salt.

A NICE WAY TO SERVE EGGS.

Take hard-boiled eggs and cut in half. Lay on a cloth and pour chicken or turkey gravy over.—*Mrs. T. H. Cheek.*

POACHED EGGS.

Have your skillet full of boiling water salted. Drop in the eggs gently from the shell. When the whites are set remove with a perforated skimmer to a flat dish: pepper them and pour melted butter over.

FRIED EGGS.

After frying your ham remove it and into the gravy drop the eggs; turn them over once, and on each slice of ham put an egg. They may also be fried in lard or butter. Always pepper them.

SCALLOPED EGGS.

Moisten a pint of bread with milk. Put a layer in a pudding dish, then a layer of hard boiled eggs, sliced, and bits of butter here and there; then a layer of minced ham, chicken, or turkey. End with a thick layer of dry bread crumbs.

PICKLED EGGS.

Pint of strong vinegar, half a pint of cold water, teaspoonful each of cinnamon, allspice and mace. Put the spices tied in a bag into the water to boil. Add the vinegar, and pour over the eggs; or, place them, after shelling, in a jar of beet pickles and the white will become red.

STUFFED EGGS.

Boil one dozen eggs hard. Cut them in two, take out the yolks, mix with a cupful of bread crumbs, a minced cucumber pickle, a tablespoonful of melted butter, a teaspoonful of mustard. Make into round balls and put back into the eggs. Dip them in melted butter, and then roll in cracker dust and set in the oven to brown.—*Galt House, Louisville, Ky.*

TO PRESERVE EGGS.

Take one gallon of water, one and one-half pints of common salt, and two pints of limestone lime. Dissolve the lime and salt in the water. Place perfectly fresh eggs in a stone jar and cover with this solution. Keep them in a dry cool place but do not let them freeze. Eggs put up in this way can be kept perfectly fresh for a year. This is really splendid.—*Mrs. Amanda Bridges, in Ky. Home Cook Book.*

To preserve eggs for winter, take the vessel you wish to pack them in and cover the bottom with a layer of oats; then place your eggs, the large end down, remember the large end, so they will not touch each other. Then cover well with oats.—*Atlanta Constitution.*

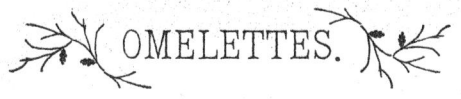

OMELETTES.

OMELETTE VERY FINE.

Six eggs beaten separately, one tumbler full of sweet milk, reserve about one-fourth, into which stir one tablespoonful of flour. When the milk boils stir in the paste, add salt and about one tablespoonful of butter; put aside to cool. Mince a little ham; chop fine some parsley and thyme, a spoonful of each and two of ham, stir in the yellows, ham, and herbs into thickened milk, adding the well beaten six whites. Grease the skillet. Bake in the stove. You can leave out ham and herbs if you choose.—*Mrs. Mary L. Rogers, in Blue Grass Cook Book.*

OMELETTE.

Soak a cupful of bread crumbs in a cupful of sweet milk overnight; three eggs, beat yolks and whites separately; mix yolks with the bread and milk, stir in the whites, add a teaspoonful of salt and fry brown. Sufficient for six persons.—*Mrs. Warren Akin.*

CHEESE OMELETTE.

Three eggs beaten to a stiff froth, half a teacupful of grated cracker, three tablespoonsful of grated cheese. Cook in a frying pan with butter. Some add chopped thyme and parsley.

TOMATO OMELETTE.

Skin two or three tomatoes, cut in slices; fry in butter; beat up some eggs to make omelette; season with salt and pepper. Warm some butter in a pan, put in eggs, stirring well to keep from adhering, mix in tomatoes, turn out omelette on a plate, doubling it in two. Another nice way is to roll up tomatoes in omelette and serve with sauce.

CREAM OMELETTE.

Break six eggs into a sauce pan; take four tablespoonsful of thick sweet cream, beat these well together; have some nice butter melted in a stew-pan, pour the eggs on it, and take care that it does not bake too much.—*Mrs. R. T. Nesbitt.*

BREAKFAST DISH.

If you have a few bits of meat or cold fowl and two or three cold potatoes left, put some dripping in a sauce-pan, slice the potatoes thin, cut up the meat fine and add salt and pepper to taste. Then beat up two or three eggs. Stir to them a cup of cream or milk and pour over the meat and potatoes. If eggs are not plentiful, use fewer eggs and more milk. If milk is scarce, add a dessert-spoonful of butter. Keep it over the fire, stirring constantly till the eggs are cooked. Do not leave it an instant till the eggs are done or they will burn and ruin the whole.—*Miss Jennie Manget.*

VEGETABLES.

CREAMED POTATOES.

PEEL the potatoes, throw them in boiling water, and when done mash thoroughly with a spoon; add salt to taste, rich cream and butter. Set on the stove and stir for two minutes.

ROASTED POTATOES.

Place inside the stove, and when done mash gently with the hands, to make them mealy. You can also roast them in wood ashes in open fire-place.

BOILED POTATOES.

Boil the potatoes, skin them and place in a deep dish. Take a pint of milk, add a tablespoonful of butter, and when it comes to a boil thicken with a little flour and pour over potatoes.

FRIED POTATO BALLS.

Boil the potatoes, salt to taste, make into cakes, roll over in flour, and fry in hot lard.

POTATO SNOW.

Peel and boil in a sauce-pan six large mealy white potatoes; add a little salt to the water, take them out one by one; rub through a sieve into a deep dish, letting it fall in a mound. Do not touch with a spoon or the hands. Have a sauce-boat of melted butter to serve with it at table.—*Marion Cabell Tyree.*

POTATO HASH.

Cut cold boiled potatoes in slices. Put in a pan with boiling water, adding pepper, salt and butter. Stir till thick and serve.

TO BOIL NEW POTATOES.

If very young rub the skin off with a coarse towel; lay them in cold water for an hour; cover with cold water salted; boil an hour. Drain, salt, and dry and send to table plain.

POTATO PUFF.

Take two cupsful of cold mashed potatoes and stir into it two tablespoonsful of melted butter, beating to a white cream before adding anything else. Then put with this two eggs whipped very light, and a teaspoonful of cream or milk, salting to taste. Beat all well, pour into a pan and bake in a quick oven until it is nicely browned.—*Marion Harland.*

SARATOGA CHIPS.

Slice the potatoes very thin with a sharp knife or a potato slicer; let them lie in cold salted water for an hour; Then drop them in boiling lard. Do not have a shallow vessel but a large deep one, such as is used for boiling vegetables. When nicely browned remove with a perforated skimmer, and lay on a folded tablecloth. When the linen has absorbed the grease, remove to a dish and serve.—*Hunt's Hotel, Cincinnati, Ohio.*

ROAST SWEET POTATOES.

Place inside the stove, and let them remain until you can pierce easily with a fork.

FRIED SWEET POTATOES.

Parboil, skim and slice and throw into boiling lard; or, you can wash, mix with an equal quantity of Irish potato, add a tablespoonful of butter, and stir until hot and slightly brown.

CANDIED SWEET POTATOES.

Parboil the potatoes, skin, slice and put a layer in the bottom of a baking dish; pour melted butter over, and sprinkle heavily with sugar; then another layer of potatoes, and so on, finishing with the sprinkling of sugar. When ready to bring to table lay five or six lumps of loaf sugar on top.

TO PRESERVE SWEET POTATOES FOR WINTER.

Boil or steam until thoroughly done; slice them and keep around the fire or in the sun until dry, then put away in paper sacks.

BOILED CABBAGE.

Pick off the outer leaves, quarter and lay in strong salt water. This will bring out the insects if there be any. Cover with cold water, add about one pound of middling and a pod of red pepper. When it has boiled an hour throw in a pinch of soda. Never add salt till the last half hour of cooking. Serve with pepper sauce, catsup or pickles.—*Mrs. W. W. Massie.*

BOILED CABBAGE.

Boil the cabbage fifteen minutes in hot water, then pour off and add fresh hot water, salted. When tender remove to a dish and add butter and pepper.

COLLARDS OR CABBAGE SPROUTS.

Pick over carefully, lay in cold water slightly salted half an hour; shake and put into boiling water; season with pork and red pepper.

STUFFED CABBAGE.
(Celebrated.)

Remove the centre from a firm, white cabbage, leaving sufficient of the outside to hold together. Chop the part taken out fine with one pound of sausage meat and a few strips of fat bacon; season highly with red pepper, black pepper and salt. Place in the cavity, bind tightly with a cord, put in a cloth and boil two hours.—*Augusta Cook Book.*

SCALLOPED CABBAGE.

Trim a medium sized cabbage, cut in half and put it to cook in cold water; let it boil fifteen minutes; then pour off the water and refill with boiling water; boil twenty minutes longer; then take the cabbage from the water, draining to dry, chop fine, seasoning it with salt, butter and pepper to taste. Beat together two fresh eggs and four spoonsful of sweet cream; add them to the seasoned cabbage and stir all together. Butter a pudding dish, put the cabbage in and bake.—*The Complete Home.*

LADIES' CABBAGE.

Boil a firm, white cabbage fifteen minutes, changing the water then for more from the tea-kettle. When tender, drain and set aside until perfectly cold. Chop fine and add two beaten eggs, a tablespoonful of butter, pepper and salt and three tablespoonsful of rich milk or cream. Stir all well together and bake in a buttered pudding dish until brown. Eat very hot. I can conscientiously recommend this dish even to those who are not fond of any of the ordinary preparations of cabbage. It is digestible and palatable, more nearly resembling cauliflower in taste than its coarser and commoner cousin-*german.*—*Marion Harland.*

ASPARAGUS.

Cut your asparagus, rejecting the hard lower portions. Cook till tender in water salted to taste. Take up in a dish, add butter and pepper. You may toast bread, dip it in the asparagus water, lay it in the dish and place the asparagus on top.—*Mrs. A. S. Edmonston.*

RAW TOMATOES.

Dip the tomatoes for a moment in hot water, then into cold water. This causes the skin to peel off easily. Slice, cutting out the hard parts. Sprinkle each layer with salt and a little sugar and pepper. Pour best cider vinegar over and place bits of ice on top. Keep in a cool place till needed. Some persons like French mustard with raw tomatoes.

STEWED TOMATOES.

Pare the tomatoes and cut in small pieces; put in a stew pan and when soft add pepper and salt, a tablespoonful of brown sugar and a lump of butter. You can vary this dish by adding as much green corn as you have tomatoes; okra may also be added.

BAKED TOMATOES.

Stew the tomatoes until done; add salt and pepper to taste. Put a layer in a baking dish, then a layer of bread crumbs with bits of butter here and there, then another layer of tomatoes, and so on, finishing off with bread crumbs. Bake until nicely browned.

BAKED TOMATOES.

Peel as many tomatoes as will cover the bottom of a pan, and after making an excavation in the center of each fill with crumbs of bread seasoned highly with pepper, a little salt, butter and sugar. Add a little water to prevent burning and bake two hours.

BROILED TOMATOES.

Place on a griddle smooth, flat tomatoes, the stem side

down; when brown turn and cook thoroughly. Serve with butter, pepper and salt.

FRIED TOMATOES.

Take smooth round tomatoes; cut in thin slices and roll in flour, sprinkle with salt and pepper and fry in equal parts of boiling lard and butter.

FRIED GREEN TOMATOES.

Slice the tomatoes and lay in salt water a half hour before cooking; drain them, roll in corn meal and fry in hot lard. Salt and pepper to taste.—*Mrs. Florence Hanley.*

FRIED PEACHES.

Take firm large freestone peaches, halve them and place them cup down in a skillet of boiling lard or butter. When the edges are nicely browned turn them up and fill the cups with white sugar and cook till thoroughly done.—*Mrs. Florence Hanley.*

TO BOIL GREEN PEAS.

Shell them, and cover with cold water for an hour; then put them in hot, but not boiling water, slightly salted; when done remove to a hot dish with a little of the water, add a tablespoonful of butter, pepper and more salt, if needed.

TO STEW YOUNG ONIONS.

Let them lie in cold salt water for an hour; then put in boiling water, and when tender add butter, pepper and salt.

TO COOK SQUASHES.

Pare the squashes, cut up in small bits and cover with cold water; when cooked to a jelly add salt, butter, pepper and milk. Stir thoroughly and cook a little longer.

HOW TO MAKE SAUER KRAUT.

Barrels having held wine or vinegar are used to prepare the sauer kraut in. It is better however, to have a special barrel for the purpose. Strasburg as well as Alsace has a well-acquired fame for preparing the cabbages. They slice very thin and firm cabbages into fine shreds with a machine made for the purpose. At the bottom of a small barrel they place a layer of coarse salt, and alternately layers of cabbage and salt, being careful to have a layer of salt on top. As each layer of cabbage is added it must be pressed down by a large and heavy pestle, and fresh layers are added as soon as the juice floats on the surface. The cabbage must be seasoned with a few grains of coriander and juniper berries. When the barrel is full it must be put in a dry cellar, covered with a cloth under a plank, and on this heavy weights are placed. At the end of a few days it will begin to ferment, when the pickle must be drawn off and replaced by fresh, until the liquor becomes clear. This should be done every day. Rinse the cloth and wash the cover, put the weights back, and let it stand for a month. By that time it will be ready for use. Care must be taken to let the least air possible enter the sauer kraut, and to have the cover perfectly clean. Each time the barrel is opened it must be properly closed again.

FRIED SQUASH.

Pare the squashes and slice thin; let them lie in salt water two hours, ice water is best; then dry in a towel, roll in flour and fry in boiling lard. Pepper them when laid on a flat dish.—*Mrs. Dr. Tennent, Sr.*

BAKED SQUASH.

Stew the squashes quite low, season with butter. salt and pepper; then put a layer in a baking dish, then a layer of bread crumbs and crumbled yolks of eggs; next comes a layer of squash, and so on till dish is full. Brown.

FRIED EGG PLANT.

Peel a nice large egg plant, cut in thin slices, lay in salt water two or three hours; then steam until tender. Make a batter of two or three eggs, first beaten separately and then together; a teacupful of sour cream, a teaspoonful of salt, half a teaspoonful of soda, and flour to thicken; dip the slices of egg plant in the butter and fry in boiling lard till light brown; serve hot. An excellent breakfast dish. *Mrs. Florence Hanley.*

RAW CUCUMBERS.

Peel carefully, leaving no green streaks, lay them in cold, salt water for an hour, then slice and pour spiced vinegar over with crushed ice mixed in.

FRIED CUCUMBERS.

Slice the cucumbers lengthwise, lay in salt water awhile, drain, and roll in corn meal and fry in hot lard; salt and pepper to taste.

BOILED MACARONI.

Boil the macaroni in salt water till tender; drain and lay in a hot dish; take a pint of milk and when it comes to a boil add grated cheese, a tablespoonful of butter, two beaten eggs, and a little corn starch rubbed smooth in milk. Pour over the macaroni.

SCALLOPED MACARONI.

Boil the macaroni till tender in salt water. Put a layer in a baking dish then a layer of bread crumbs, crumbled yolks of eggs, and bits of butter. Arrange alternately, finishing with breadcrumbs and egg. Pour over half a pint or less of cream or milk, and bake till a nice brown.—*Mrs. T. H. Cheek.*

TO BOIL CORN.

Put on in a kettle of warm water salted, and boil rapidly till tender. You can leave it on the cob or cut off with a sharp knife and add butter and pepper.

ROASTED GREEN CORN.

Turn back the husks upon the stalk, pick off the silk, recover with the husks as closely as possible and roast in the hot ashes of a wood fire. Eat with butter, salt, and pepper.

STEWED GREEN CORN.

Cut from the cob and stew fifteen minutes in boiling water. Turn off most of this, cover with cold milk and stew until very tender, adding before you take it up a large lump of butter cut into bits and rolled in flour. Season with salt and pepper to taste. Boil five minutes and serve.

CORN PUDDING.

One pint of milk, three eggs, whites and yolks beaten separately, three tablespoonsful of melted butter, one dessert spoonful of white sugar, one heaping teaspoonful of corn starch or flour, one teaspoonful of salt, six ears of corn. With a sharp knife slit each row of corn in the centre, then shave. Add the corn to the yolks of the eggs, next the butter, corn starch, sugar, and salt; then the milk, gradually, and lastly the whites. Bake in a hot oven.—*Mrs. Sallie Rusk.*

CORN PUDDING.

Scrape the corn from the cob, add enough morning's milk to make it tolerably thin, add butter and salt according to judgment. Do not use pepper till served for the table.—*Mrs. H. C. Buckner.*

GREEN CORN FRITTERS.

Twelve ears of tender corn grated or scraped, as for the above pudding, one teaspoonful of salt, one of pepper, one egg beaten into two large tablespoonsful of flour. Mix thoroughly, make in small cakes, fry in hot lard or butter.
—*Mrs. Buckner in Blue Grass Cook Book.*

CORN PUDDING.

One pint of green corn grated, one large teacupful of cream, one heaped tablespoonful of flour, one of butter, four eggs beaten light, salt to the taste. Bake half an hour.

CORN OYSTERS.

Two cupsful of grated corn, half a cup of milk, two tablespoonsful of flour, salt and pepper to taste, half a teaspoonful of baking powder. Drop from a spoon into boiling lard.—*Mrs. Sylvester Puckett.*

CHICKEN CORN PIE.

A pint of rice boiled very soft and well buttered while hot, two chickens parboiled, six or eight large ears of corn boiled and the grains cut off. Put a small portion of the rice at the bottom of a baking dish, then the chicken cut up with a little of the liquor they were boiled in, with stewed tomatoes at discretion; then the corn with butter, pepper and salt. Cover with the rice, glaze with an egg, and bake a delicate brown.—*Mrs. Spalding.*

TO FRY OKRA.

Boil a quart of okra, strain it well from the water, mash it smooth and season with salt and pepper. Beat in one or two eggs, add flour enough to make a stiff batter, fry as fritters. Serve on a flat dish in a napkin.—*Mrs. Walsh.*

OKRA STEW.

Cut the okra in round slices, put in a stew-pan, and to a quart add one wineglassful of hot water, a tablespoonful of butter, into which has been rubbed an even teaspoonful of flour; salt and pepper to taste. Cover the pan and shake occasionally. When well done serve in a hot dish. A few tomatoes and a little onion is an improvement.—*Mrs. Walsh.*

TO COOK SALSIFY.

Wash and scrape well until perfectly white; throw in cold water to prevent discoloration. Cut up in pieces one inch long and cover with water salted; when done pour off the water, add a pint of milk, thickened with flour, a little butter, salt and pepper.

FRIED APPLES.

Wash carefully but do not pare, slice thin, throw in hot lard, and add a cupful of sugar. When they have cooked ten minutes, add a cupful of water.—*Mrs. T. H. Cheek.*

FRIED APPLES.

Make a thick syrup, and when it begins to boil drop in your thinly sliced apples. Get some variety that will not fall to pieces. Add a teaspoonful of butter and a little ground cinnamon. When they have boiled twenty minutes remove to a vessel with hot melted butter, and fry till lightly browned. Sift grated loaf sugar over.—*Mrs. Thomas A. Hendricks.*

CARROTS.

Slice the carrots into half-inch slices, put in a pot of boiling water with a piece of corned beef. When done serve as a garnish around the beef. They should be cooked for an hour and a half.

STEWED PARSNIPS.

Wash, scrape, and cut in slices; cover with cold water to cover; add a little salt and simmer slowly till nearly dry. Season with pepper and butter.

PARSNIP FRITTERS.

Scrape and wash three or four parsnips, cut them in slices, put them in salted hot water and cook for three quarters of an hour. Skim them out, dip them in batter made of two eggs, four tablespoonsful of flour, and milk to make right consistency. Dip the parsnips in the batter and fry in hot lard.—*Mrs. Lovelace.*

TURNIPS.

Select turnips of a good variety, peel and cut in slices about a quarter of an inch thick; throw them into well salted boiling water. Boil one hour, or until tender, then drain off the water and mash fine with a potato masher, adding to four or five turnips of medium size one tablespoonful of butter, half a teaspoonful of black pepper, and one teaspoonful of salt.

TO STEW TURNIPS WITH MEAT.

Prepare some fresh beef or pork, and stew in a small quantity of water until about half done, carefully removing the scum as it rises. Pour the water over cold and heat gradually; add a little salt, peel some turnips, slice tolerably thin, rinse well, then put them in with the meat and stew till soft. Remove the meat, add more salt to the turnips, if needed, pepper and a cupful of sweet cream; mash fine, stir them until they are nearly dry and perfectly smooth. Put into a covered dish and serve at once.

BOSTON BAKED BEANS.

Put one quart of beans on the back of the stove to simmer (not boil) until they are tender; then take them out of the pot and pour off the water; have a brown earthen pot, in the bottom of which place a very small onion, then the beans, one tablespoonful of molasses, one teaspoonful of salt, one half teaspoonful of black pepper, one quarter of a pound of salt pork on top. Pour three pints of cold water on them, and put into the oven for about eight hours. The beans should be a nice brown when done. Serve hot, or eat cold with mayonnaise sauce. Neither the molasses nor the onion affects the taste of the beans, and are a great improvement.—*Kentucky Home Cook Book.*

TO COOK SPINACH.

Wash in several waters, as it is apt to be gritty. Cover with hot salted water and boil till tender; then drain the water; pour a tablespoonful of melted butter over and pepper to taste. Lay poached eggs on top.

JOWL AND GREENS.

Put one and a half pounds of meat, or half a good-sized jowl in three quarts of water. When it begins to boil skim carefully; in two hours add the greens, a pinch of soda, and a tablespoonful of salt. When done skin the jowl, remove to a dish, pile the greens around it, and garnish with slices of hard boiled eggs.

TO COOK CASHAW.

Cut and peel off the rind, steam or boil till tender and thoroughly dry. Mash well and free entirely from lumps; season plentifully with butter; add sugar to the taste. Place all in deep dish; sprinkle a little sugar over the top, and lay bits of butter in places over the cashaw.

TO BOIL BEETS.

Wash them; do not break or cut the roots. Leave an inch of the tops so that the color and juice cannot escape. Boil hard for two hours. When tender slice them, sprinkling over them sugar, then butter and salt to the taste.—*Marion Cabell Tyree.*

TO BAKE ONIONS.

Boil six onions in water, or milk and water, with a seasoning of salt and pepper. When done enough to mash, take them off, mash them with butter, grate bread crumbs over them, and set them to bake; or, place them whole in the baking dish with butter and bread crumbs.—*Home Guest.*

TO FRY ONIONS.

Wash and slice them; chop fine, put in a frying pan and cover with water; simmer till the water is dried up, then fry brown with a large slice of fat pork.—*Mrs. Samuel Tyree.*

CAULIFLOWER.

Remove the outside leaves; cut in four parts, tie them together; put in boiling water and let them simmer till the stalk is thoroughly tender, keeping it covered with water and removing the scum. Boil two hours, drain well and serve with melted butter. You may cook broccoli by the same receipt, except that you cut it in two pieces instead of four.

CANNED FRENCH PEAS.

Take off the top of can, place it with the peas remaining in it in boiling water. Add butter, salt and pepper.

SUCCOTASH.

One pint of shelled Lima beans; one quart of green corn, cut from the cob; one quart of tomatoes, peeled and chopped. Boil the corn and beans together till done; then drain off the water and put in a cupful of milk, a tablespoonful of butter, and salt to the taste. Let it boil up and then pour in the tomatoes. Let all simmer an hour.—*Mrs. Geo. J. Gable.*

RADISHES.

Arrange in a fancy dish first a white one, then a red one, and so on. Ornament with curled parsley.

CELERY.

Wash well and put in cold water until dinner. Remove all the green, as nothing is so ornamental as the pure white leaves of bleached celery. If the ends of the stalks have been broken, split and curl them.—*Virginia Cook Book*.

MEATS.

VIRGINIA HAMS.

SELECT well fatted pork that has hung up to cool well one night. Round the hams short or lengthy, according to size, and wished for weight in hams; trim smooth, avoiding gashes in the flesh, take off the feet at the bottom joint below the knee with the heel of a knife, and the bone too from each ham that connected them and salt quite lightly one or two days to draw out what blood it may have. To each one hundred pounds of ham use eight or ten pounds of salt, two ounces of salt-petre, two pounds of brown sugar, one ounce of red pepper dissolved, and mixed in tubs with four or five gallons of water, and poured over the hams packed in a tight barrel or hogshead, intending just to cover the hams, and chines, and shoulders. To be sure if the brine is strong enough, see if it will float a fresh egg. After four to six weeks in brine hang by the skin at the end of the leg, and smoke gently several weeks with green hickory wood till dry and brown; and before any balmy days in March that the flies may start, wrap each ham in a newspaper and have a bag for each, made from any coarse bags, and deep and narrow enough to put each in, hock end downward and erect, resting mainly on the ends. With twine fifteen inches and with the ends tied to form a double, hang a loop over a nail to wait till August or September to become bacon. Greater age is no improvement. Hams cured in this way will be sought for by epicures and judges of good bacon.—*Col. Ficklin.*

MEATS.

CURING HAMS.

To every bushel of salt a peck of ashes, not strong, one-fourth of a pound of salt-petre; break up red pepper pods in the mixture. Rub the hams well and pack them in the compound. Let them remain about six weeks, then hang them and smoke them well. After they have been thoroughly smoked, select a clear, bright day, have a pot of boiling water, plunge each ham in, letting it remain three or four minutes; then have some weak, sifted ashes ready, and roll the hams in until they stick well. Then wrap each ham in hay and tie up tightly in a bag fitting closely. Hang up till needed.—*Judge Geo. Roberts.*

TO BOIL A HAM.

Wash your ham after scraping well in strong soap suds; then rinse off in clear water; wash again in soda water, then again in clear water. Cover with water three inches above the ham. Have it cold. If at any time you need more water add it boiling. Do not boil too fast, and turn the ham over several times. When done remove skin, and turn and lay on a dish.

MRS. BLEDSOE'S PREMIUM HAM.

Take a ham that weighs sixteen pounds, wash very carefully and lay it in a boiler skin side down. Cover with hot water, adding two pounds of brown sugar, the kind used in making molasses. Boil rather slowly for five hours; take out, skin, turn and dress, and bake to a light brown.—*Kentucky Home Cook Book.*

TO BOIL A HAM IN CIDER.

Cover the ham with water and cider, equal quantities of both. When done dress and bake.

BAKED HAM.

Boil a ham, remove the skin and spread over the top a mixture made as follows: One tablespoonful of salt, two of sugar, one of mustard, one-half of pepper. Lay the ham in a pan and pour around it a cup of wine and one of water. Bake an hour, basting frequently.—*Mrs. S. J. Pinkerton.*

Baked ham is a noted Pennsylvania dish. It is roasted the same as beef, but requires a longer time in the oven. It is turned, cut in thin slices with a brown gravy made of beef stock and brown flour.

STUFFED HAM.

Take a pound of grated crackers, or crumbled corn muffins, half a pound of butter, a little minced onion and celery, a teaspoonful of pepper, three of sugar, one of nutmeg, one of ginger, one of mace, one of mustard, four eggs. Mix well; cut the ham to the bone in slices and press the dressing down.—*Mrs. Yorston.*

FRIED HAM.

Slice the ham and throw in boiling water for a few minutes. Put a very little lard in a hot skillet, lay the slices in and let cook till a delicate brown. Take up and thicken the gravy with a little flour stirred in milk or water.

BROILED HAM.

Soak the slices in cold water, lay them on a broiler over hot coals. When done remove to a dish in which you have put melted butter and pepper.

TO GLAZE A COLD HAM.

Cover the ham with the beaten yolk of an egg. Then sift on cracker dust. Cover with sweet cream and bake.—*Mrs. Dr. Alston.*

SAUSAGE MEAT.

To thirty pounds of meat add eight ounces of fine salt, three ounces of pepper, two teacupsful of sage, one teacup-

MEATS. 95

ful of summer savory. Excellent.—*Miss Jaynes, in Blue Grass Cook Book.*

W. P. STEVENS' SAUSAGE.

To twelve and a half pounds of meat put three large tablespoonsful of salt, two of black pepper, a half teaspoonful of red pepper, two of thyme powdered and sifted, two of sage, and a teaspoonful of salt-petre.

SMOKED SAUSAGE.

Make strong cotton bags and wring out of hot water. Put the sausage in, stuffing tightly, and smoke.—*Mrs. Judge Atkinson.*

ROAST PIG.

When roasted whole a pig should not be under four or over six weeks old. As soon as the pig is killed, throw it in a tub of cold water to make it tender. As soon as cold take it by the hind leg and plunge into scalding, not boiling water, and shake it about until the hair can be removed by the handful. When all that is possible has been taken off in this way, rub from the tail up to the end of the nose with a coarse cloth. Take off the hoofs, scrape and wash the ears and nose till perfectly clean. Hang it by the hind legs, open and take out the entrails; wash well with water with a little soda dissolved in it; rinse again and again, and leave hanging an hour. Wrap in a coarse cloth wrung out of cold water and lay on ice, or in a cool cellar, until next morning, when, if the weather is warm, it must be cooked. It should never be used the same day that it is killed. First, prepare the stuffing of the liver, heart and haslets of the pig stewed, seasoned and chopped. Mix with these an equal quantity of boiled potatoes mashed; add a large spoonful of butter with some hard boiled eggs, parsley and thyme chopped fine, pepper and salt. Scald the pig on the inside, dry it and rub with pepper and salt, fill and sew up. Bend the fore legs under the body the hind legs forward under the pig, and skewer to keep in position. Place in a large baking pan, pour over one quart of boiling water. Have a lump of fresh butter tied up in a clean rag, rub it all over the pig, then sprinkle over pepper and salt; put some in the pan with a bunch of herbs; invert over it a pan while it simmers and steam till perfectly done. Remove the pan, rub over with the butter and baste often. When of a fine brown cover the edges of a large dish with a deep fringe of curled parsley; first sift over the pig powdered cracker and place it kneeling in the green bed. Place in its mouth an orange or a red apple, and if eaten hot serve with the gravy in a tureen or sauce boat. It is much nicer cold. Serve with little mounds of grated horse-radish amongst the parsley.—*Marion Cabell Tyree.*

ROAST PORK.

Gash the roast crosswise with a knife; salt and pepper it well and lay in a pan with water and a little butter dissolved in it. Baste frequently. Thicken the gravy with flour, serve with tomato catsup, walnut catsup, or apple sauce.

PORK STEAKS OR CHOPS.

Beat them as you would beefsteak, salt and pepper them, dip in well beaten yolk of eggs, then in crumbled bread, and fry.

SPARE RIB.

Put into a pan with a half pint of water, a little butter, salt and pepper to taste. Baste frequently.

Common middling may be made extremely palatable by slicing, soaking three hours in cold water, broiling over hot embers and removing to a dish in which there is butter and pepper.

BREAKFAST BACON.

Slice very thin, dust with sifted corn meal, put on the broiler and when done butter, and pepper.–*Mrs. Bird Wallace.*

MEAT.

BACKBONE OR CHINE.

Put into a pot of salted water with a pod of red pepper in it. Boil an hour. Serve with potato balls.

BACKBONE PIE.

Cut the bone in pieces about three inches long. Stew till done, in salted water enough to cover, with a pod of red pepper. Line a baking dish or pan with paste. Lay in the bones, pour the water in which it was boiled over it, lay in bits of butter, cover with paste and bake.

PIG'S FEET SOUSE.

Cut off the horny parts of feet and toes; scrape, clean, and wash thoroughly; singe off the stray hairs, place in a kettle with plenty of water, boil, skim, pour off water and add fresh and boil until the bones will pull out easily; do not bone but pack in a stone jar with pepper and salt sprinkled between each layer; cover with good cider vinegar. When wanted for the table take out a sufficient quantity, put in a hot skillet, add more vinegar, salt and pepper, if needed, boil until thoroughly heated, stir in a smooth thickening of flour and water, and boil until flour is cooked; serve hot as a breakfast dish. Or, when the feet have boiled until perfectly tender, remove the bones and pack in stone jars as above. Slice down cold when wanted for use.

PIG'S FEET.

Parboil in salted water, dip in butter, and fry in hot lard.

HOG BRAINS.

Wash well and let them remain several hours in salt water. Beat the whites and yolks of three eggs separately and then together, adding a little flour. Stir the brains in and fry in hot lard. Serve with horse-radish sauce.—*Mrs. Dr. Taggart.*

STEWED BRAINS.

Put them on in enough water to cover, adding a little salt and cayenne pepper. Boil till done, pour off the water, add a little fresh milk, a beaten egg, and a tablespoonful of butter. Boil for five minutes and serve.

SWEET BREADS.

Parboil, wipe dry, split in half, rub with butter, pepper and salt, and cook inside the stove; or you can throw them in a little hot lard and fry.

TO STEW PIG'S HEAD AND JOWL.

Clean the head and feet; take out the bone above the nose, cut off the ears, clean them nicely, separate the jowl from the head; take care of the brains to add to the stew.

ROAST BEEF.

Rub the roast well with salt and pepper, put in a pan and pour in a pint of water. Cook slowly and baste frequently. Stick a fork in, if the juice that oozes from it is slightly red it is rare; an hour more will cook it well done.

BEEF A LA MODE.

Wash and wipe a round of beef; cut out the bone and fill the place with a rich stuffing made of bread crumbs highly seasoned with pepper, salt and onions. Have ready one teaspoonful of salt, one of pepper, cloves, mace and nutmeg; make incisions in the beef with a knife and put in them strips of fat pork rolled in the spices; sprinkle the remainder of the spices over the top of the beef, then cover the whole with fat pork to prevent burning. Tie the beef all around with tape and skewer it well to keep it in place; place in an oven with at least three quarts of water and let it bake five or six hours. Baste frequently with butter and lard mixed with a small quantity of flour. When nearly

MEAT. 99

done skim off the fat and thicken the gravy. Season with walnut catsup and wine.—*Mrs. Brutus J. Clay in Blue Grass Cook Book.*

BRINE FOR PICKLING BEEF,

One peck of common salt, two pails of clear water; stir with clean oak stick until the salt is dissolved. One ounce of saltpetre dissolved in one pint of luke-warm water. Stir all together and let settle for five minutes. Skim off the froth with a clean brush broom, pour over the beef until covered. This quantity of brine will do for about one hundred pounds of beef.—*Fulton Street Market, N. Y.*

CORNED BEEF,

Should be in the store-room of every farmer's wife during the winter and spring. The following, sent by a Virginia lady to the Georgia Department of Agriculture, is said to be a most excellent way of preparing it: Salt the beef as usual, adding a pinch of salt-petre to each piece. Let it remain in salt three days, draw off the bloody brine formed by the salt and wipe each piece with a clean towel and repack it in the tub—a syrup or molasses cask will answer. For the brine, take as much water as will cover the beef and add salt until it will no longer dissolve it, a teacupful of ground salt-petre and a quart of molasses, or its equivalent in brown sugar. Boil this and skim well. When entirely cold pour over the beef and keep it well pressed under the brine. These proportions will answer for two hundred pounds of beef. Pieces of beef which would be inferior if cooked while fresh make delicious meat when corned by this receipt. The round of beef, or a piece cut from the thigh where the best round steak is taken, cutting entirely through with a thickness of six or eight inches, makes, when corned by the above receipt, a delicious dish, either boiled and eaten cold or broiled with butter and pepper.

TO COOK CORNED BEEF.

If you would have it juicy after it is cold, when you put it on to cook let the water be cold, and when cooked do not take it out of the pot until cold.—*Mrs. J. M. Hughes.*

PICKLE FOR BEEF TONGUE OR CHIPPED BEEF.

Five pints of salt, half a pound of salt-petre, one quart of molasses, two gallons of water. Rub the beef well with salt and lay it away for twenty four hours to let the blood drain from it; rub it well in the pickle and pack it close down in a tight vessel. Pour the pickle over it and cover it. If a white scum should rise at any time boil, skim, and when cold pour over the beef again.—*Col. S. J. Atkinson.*

JERKED BEEF.

Take as much salt as will be sufficient to salt your beef, add salt-petre in the proportion of half a pound to a peck of salt. Rub molasses with it till it is perfectly wet, cut the beef into pieces weighing from three to four pounds; rub it well in the mixture. Pack it close in a vessel that will not leak; let it stand three or four hours; then put it on a scaffold four or five feet high in the sun. Make a good fire under it. The fire must be hot enough to dry it in a few days. Chipped beef is salted in the same way, only the pieces are cut much larger, and lie in salt a week.—*Mrs. R. T. Nesbitt.*

BEEF TONGUE.

Soak in cold water all night; then wash and boil four or five hours. When done take off the skin and cut in thin slices; or, it can be left whole. Garnish with parsley.

HUNTER'S ROUND OR SPICED BEEF.

To a round of beef that weighs twenty-five pounds take the following: Three ounces of salt-petre, one ounce of cloves, one ounce of nutmeg, one ounce of allspice, one pint of salt. Let the round of beef hang in a cool dry place twenty-four hours. Take out the bone and fill the space with suet and spices mixed. Rub the ingredients all over the round; put in a wooden box or tub; turn it over occasionally and rub a small amount of salt on it. Let it remain three weeks. Then make a stiff paste of flour and water; cover the round with it and set in the oven. Bake three hours slowly. Remove the paste when cold and turn neatly the rough outside, and slice horizontally. Serve only when cold.—*Mrs. Wm. A. Strother.*

The head and hoof of beeves are thrown away by some, while by others they are highly esteemed. Several choice dishes may be made from the beef's head. If boiled thoroughly and cut fine it may be made into pies or stews and placed in a dish with bread crumbs on top and thoroughly browned. These dishes are seasoned with pepper and salt and a little onion to suit the taste, and are both good and economical. Another dish is made from it by chopping it fine and mixing it with some cold ham, fat and lean, bread crumbs and an egg or two. Knead them well together; form into round or oval balls, roll in a little flour and fry a light brown. The head of a large beef will not cost at most more than twenty five cents, and will supply an ordinary family several days with choice dishes. The feet nicely dressed and thoroughly boiled, besides making nice neats-foot oil, if cut up fine, rolled in flour and egg and fried makes a choice dish. For making soup no part of the beef is equal to the tail.

POMPEY'S HEAD.

Two pounds of tender beef ground, one pound of bread crumbs, one-quarter of a pound of lard or butter, three onions minced well. Season highly with parsley, red and black pepper and sage. Mix the seasoning well; form into a loaf, put into a pan with half a tumbler of water and bake.—*Mrs. Mattie Dobbs.*

SCRAFFLE.

Boil a fresh killed hog's head tender; take it up and remove all the bones; chop the meat very fine and season it with salt, pepper and sage, as sausage meat; strain the liquor; wipe out the pot nicely; return the broth to the pot; there should be about a quart of this. Put the meat back and stir into the broth fine corn meal until the mass is the consistency of soft mush; let this simmer half an hour, stirring frequently; pour the mixture into pans three or four inches deep. When cold slice in thin slices, roll in corn meal or flour and fry in boiling lard a light brown. The neck of beef may be used instead of the hog's head, and prepared in this way is called white pudding.

BROILED STEAK.

When beef is butchered in cool weather, say in December, so much of it as is intended for steak may be hung in a cool place without salt, and steak cut from it as needed, rubbing a little dry meal over the freshly cut part to prevent drying and crusting. The longer the meat hangs without salt the more tender the steak will be. Salt hardens and toughens meat, and should be used on beef only when necessary for its preservation. No matter how well fatted beef may be, or how carefully and neatly butchered, steak must be cooked well to be eatable. A poor steak well cooked is better than a choice one poorly prepared. Broiling steak is a very simple process, and yet we rarely find a properly broiled steak on either public or private tables. The too common practice of pounding or chopping steak for the purpose of making it tender has the effect of depriving it of its juices, its very essence, leaving only the fibre of the cellular structure. The prime object in broiling a steak should be to preserve the juices in the steak itself, and not in the gravy. Pounding steak before cooking and then extracting its juices into the gravy to be used with it reminds one of grinding apples, pressing out the juice, and then pouring the cider over the pulp to season it to make it palatable. The gridiron was formerly used exclusively for broiling steak, but it is by no means necessary. An ordinary pan will answer quite as well. Place the pan on the stove until quite hot. Cut the steak of uniform thickness, from one-half to three-fourths of an inch, lay it in the pan, using care to have every point of it come in contact with the hot pan, and turn rapidly to avoid burning. Have butter, pepper and salt in a hot dish at hand; with a little of this baste the steak when nearly done to increase the flavor, if desired. The object in having the pan hot when commencing to broil the steak is to sear the outer surface to coagulate the albumen and thus prevent the escape of the juices. Rapid turning is necessary to prevent overcooking the outside before the interior is sufficiently done. When "rare done" the inside of the steak will be red but no blood will escape. At this stage it is more tender, better flavored and more digestible than if cooked more. The best steak will be tough if cooked slowly.

FRIED STEAK.

Cut the slices thin and of a uniform thickness, rub with salt and pepper on both sides and roll in flour. Place in a skillet of boiling lard. When nicely browned place on a hot dish and finish the gravy by throwing in a tablespoonful of flour. When it looks smooth add a cupful of water or milk and more salt, if needed. Pour over the steak.

HIDAWAY STEAK.

Sear a tenderloin slightly on a hot gridiron; place it in a pan and put it in the stove, pouring over it one pint of previously cooked tomatoes with a teaspoonful of finely minced onion in it.—*Mrs. W. W. Massie.*

ROLLED BEEFSTEAK.

Beat a large tender steak carefully and thoroughly. Sprinkle over salt, pepper, sage and minced onion, minced parsley, and bits of butter. Have ready some mealy Irish potatoes mashed fine and seasoned with a little butter and salt. Spread over all and roll up tightly; fasten the ends and sides securely with skewer pins; place in a pan with water and butter, or such gravy as may be on hand; simmer and baste as you would a roast duck; sift over it browned crackers pounded fine.

BOLOGNA SAUSAGE.

Take ten pounds of beef and four pounds of pork, two-thirds lean and one-third fat; chop very fine and mix well together; season with six ounces of fine salt, one ounce of black pepper, one half ounce of cayenne pepper, and salt to taste.

BEEF LIVER.

Cut the slices thin, as they require some time to cook; lay in salted water two hours, to extract the strong flavor. Fry in hot lard, and when done add butter, salt and pepper.

BEWITCHED LIVER.

Three pounds of calf's liver, chopped fine; one-fourth of a pound of salt pork, one cup of grated bread crumbs, two eggs well beaten, two teaspoonsful of salt, two teaspoonsful of black pepper. Mix all well together and put in a tin mould; set in a pot of cold water and let it boil two hours. Then set the mould in a cool oven to dry off a little. When thoroughly cold turn out.—*Marion Cabell Tyree.*

LIVER PUDDING.

Boil together a pound of hog's liver and half a pound of fat middling until tender. Then pass all through your sausage mill, and remove all skins and stringy parts. Season with salt and pepper and minced onion. Roll the cakes in flour and fry as sausages.—*Mrs. John Hollinshead.*

BEEF SAUSAGE.

Run beef, fat and lean mixed through the sausage mill; season with salt and pepper and dried sage. Fry in hot lard.

BEEF HASH.

Chop cold beef into small pieces; cover with water; add a pod of red pepper and slices of raw potato. When the potatoes are done add a half a cupful of milk, with a teaspoonful of flour stirred in. You may add minced onion also.

BAKED HASH.

Chop the meat very fine and put in a pan with some water; add salt and pepper, butter and bread crumbs to taste. Season with a little chopped onion, parsley and thyme, all minced fine; half a cupful of milk or cream, with one egg beaten in; grate some crumbs on top and bake till brown.

ROAST MUTTON.

Let the mutton lie an hour in salted water to extract the blood. Put on in cold water to cover and boil half an hour. The water should be salted and contain a pod of red pepper. Take out, lay in a pan with a pint of water. If the mutton is not fat add a tablespoonful of butter to the gravy. Baste often and serve with peas, horse-radish or mint sauce.

TO CORN MUTTON.

Mutton being less apt to keep than other meat, it is well when you have an over-supply to corn it exactly as you would beef.

TO GRILL A SHOULDER OF MUTTON.

Half boil it, score and cover it with egg crumbs and parsley. Broil it over a slow fire, or put it in the oven to brown. Serve with caper or mushroom sauce.

MUTTON CHOPS.

Beat them well, cut in pieces of equal size and lay them in melted butter; then broil on a hot gridiron, adding salt just before they are done. Pepper them plentifully.

MUTTON CHOPS.

Beat well, roll in flour, after being salted and peppered, and fry in hot lard.

MUTTON CHOPS.

Trim the chops, beat them well and chop into mincemeat, taking care not to separate the meat from the bones; chop both sides; sprinkle salt and pepper on both sides; have ready some bread crumbs and two eggs well beaten and dip the chop in egg and roll in crumbs; have in the frying pan two ounces of butter; when it melts put in the chops and fry slowly; never turn them till they look firm; flavor with onion and parsley, a dessert-spoonful of flour in an ounce of butter; brown the flour and roll in the butter.

SADDLE OF VENISON.

Put the venison on to bake with the side which is uppermost when it comes to the table next to the pan, then make the dressing thus: With the fingers crumble a small piece of light bread, which season highly with pepper and salt. When the meat is about half done, turn it over and cut on either side of the bone several pieces about two and a half inches long, which stuff with the dressing. Then pour all over the meat a half-cupful of catsup. Into a half-cupful of black molasses stir a tablespoonful of whole allspice and a teaspoonful of brown sugar; this too pour over the meat; then crumble light bread all over the upper surface, keeping the meat well basted all the while, and cooking slowly, for it burns readily. Just before taking the venison off put here and there, all over it, a little jelly.—*Mrs. C. S. Brent, in Blue Grass Cook Book.*

Veal is cooked in the same way as beef; the receipts for one being entirely suited to the other. So repetition is unnecessary.

ROAST TURKEY.

After having dressed the turkey and rubbed it well with salt and pepper, inside and out, tie a string to the neck and attach to a nail so it will lean against nothing. Do not cook for twenty-four hours, and forty-eight is better, if the weather will admit. Put it into a pan about three inches deep and sufficiently large so that it will not be cramped in any part. Rub it all over with butter and pour water to the depth of an inch in the pan. Baste frequently and thoroughly. If this is neglected the skin will parch and blister. When the turkey is half done take it out and stuff it with a dressing made as follows: Take a quart of crumbled biscuit and moisten with water; let it stand until all the lumps disappear and it is a perfect jelly; then add a teaspoonful of baking powder, half a cupful of melted butter, salt and pepper to taste, three raw eggs, white and yolks, a little powdered sage, two sprigs of fresh parsley and one small onion minced. Put into a stew-pan with about half a cupful of hot lard, or you can use butter. Stir constantly until it is thoroughly cooked, which you can tell by the disappearance of the raw taste. It must not be browned. You can omit the sage, parsley and onion if not liked. After the turkey is neatly stuffed if any dressing is left, you can make it into round cakes and fry brown in a little hot lard and place around the turkey. When you can take a fork and pierce through the breast easily, the fowl is done. While it is being cooked turn on the back and side that all parts may be equally done and nicely browned. For the gravy put the gizzard, heart and liver in a pint of water. They must be cut up in small pieces; add part of the dressings from the turkey when the meat is boiled until tender; use salt and pepper to taste and thicken with flour. You can add to the gravy, if liked, the pulverized yolks of three boiled eggs.—*Mrs. Ben Hamby.*

DRESSING FOR TURKEY.

Crumble four corn muffins and moisten with sweet milk; add the yolks of three hard boiled eggs, or you can use them raw; salt and pepper to taste, and a large tablespoonful of butter; cook in hot lard.

MUSH DRESSING.

Take a pint or more of boiling water salted, and add meal, dropping it slowly from the fingers, stir constantly until a fine thick mush is formed. Make it rich with butter and add pepper. When cold stuff the turkey.—*Mrs. G. J. Gable.*

BARBECUED TURKEY.

Make a steady fire in an open fire-place. Drive a long peg in the wall, and from this suspend the turkey with a stout string until it is directly in front of the hottest part of the fire. Place under it a large dish to catch the drippings, and with them baste the turkey quite often. Some like a little vinegar added to the drippings. If the turkey remains at a standstill, twist the string gently, so as to set it in motion. This mode of cooking was much used in olden times, and there has never been but one opinion concerning it, and that is that it is the best.

BOILED TURKEY.

Wash well with cold water, then put on in milk warm water, either tied in a coarse cloth dredged with flour or with a half pound of rice in the water. Keep well under

MEAT. 109

water and boil slowly three hours, adding salt just before it is done. When perfectly done and tender take out of the pot, sprinkle in the cavity a little pepper and salt and fill with oysters stewed just enough to plump them, and season with butter, pepper, salt and vinegar. Place in a dish and set in a steamer to keep hot. Strain the liquor in which the oysters were scalded, add drawn butter, chopped celery, parsley, and thyme. Pour over the turkey and serve. If not convenient to use oysters, use egg and butter sauce. Garnish with sliced lemons.

TURKEY HASH.

Cut the meat from the bones and pick it into small pieces. Boil the bones an hour, remove them, and add the meat; boil a half hour longer; add a tablespoonful of butter, a little minced onion, a sprig of parsley, some sliced potato and split biscuit. At the last add a cupful of milk, into which has been stirred a teaspoonful of flour. Let it boil up and serve.

BROILED CHICKEN.

Split the chicken down the back, wash it and rub it well with salt. Let it lie at least twelve hours. Rub it all over with a mop dipped in melted butter. Place it on a broiler not too hot, or it will scorch in stripes. Turn it over frequently, each time mopping with the melted butter. When an even brown all over remove to a hot dish, pepper it plentifully, and serve.—*Mrs. Robt. Irwin.*

FRIED CHICKEN.

Prepare the chicken as for boiling, and after having salted it keep in a cool place. When ready to cook cut up with a very sharp knife, dry the pieces in a soft towel. Then roll them in flour, and place in boiling lard. Placing chickens in cold lard or slightly warm is the cause of their being greasy and sodden. Do not cook too fast. You can never make good gravy if the lard is burnt at the bottom of the skillet. After removing the chicken add to the gravy a half cupful of water and the same of milk mixed with a teaspoonful of flour stirred in; or some prefer to add the flour to the gravy and when it looks smooth add the milk and water. You can use milk alone. The gravy will generally require more salt. Do not pour it over the chicken but take to table in a gravy boat or small bowl.—*Mrs. Wm. Barnes.*

SMOTHERED CHICKEN.

Cut up the chicken down the back and let it lie well salted and peppered for several hours. Put into a pan with a teacupful of water and a tablespoonful of butter. Baste frequently, turning it on the back and sides. When browned, remove to a hot dish and pour over the gravy. You can thicken the gravy with flour. Some add a beaten egg, letting it cook a little longer, pouring it around the chicken and sifting over browned crackers powdered.

BAKED CHICKEN.

Dress the chicken as you would a turkey; put it into a pan with a pint of water and a tablespoonful of butter. Baste frequently. When nearly done add the dressing. This is a nice way to cook chickens in late winter and early spring when they are too large for broiling or frying. The gravy is made just the same as turkey gravy.—*Mrs. C. C. Brumby.*

CHICKEN PIE.

Cut the chicken as for frying, cover with cold water, add salt, if the chicken has not lain in salt, one tablespoonful of butter, and plenty of pepper. Stew till the meat is tender, then remove and thicken the liquor with a little flour. Line a pan, bottom and sides, with paste, a rich biscuit dough will do. Put a layer of chicken at the bottom, then five or six dumplings, then another layer of chicken and dumplings, and pour over all the liquor. If you doubt its being rich enough add bits of butter. Put on the top crust, prick with a fork and bake very gradually. It is better to have the dumplings cooked before adding to the pie. You can use slices of broiled ham, hard boiled eggs, sliced potatoes, or boiled rice, just as your fancy dictates.—*Mrs. Wm. Bishop.*

CHICKEN PUDDING.

Ten eggs beaten very light, one quart of rich milk, one-fourth of a pound of melted butter, pepper and salt to taste. Stir in flour enough to make a thin, good batter. Put four young chickens nicely prepared and jointed in a saucepan with some salt and water and a bundle of thyme or parsley. Boil till nicely done, then take up the chickens and put in the batter. Put all in a deep dish and bake. Serve with gravy in a boat.—*Mrs. Dr. Coleman.*

TO ROAST GOOSE.

A goose must never be eaten the same day it is killed. If the weather is cold it should be kept a week. Before cooking let it lie several hours in weak salt and water to remove the strong taste. Then plunge it into boiling water for five minutes, if old. Fill the goose with a dressing made of mealy Irish potatoes boiled and mashed fine, a small lump of butter, a little salt or fresh pork chopped fine, a little minced onion, parsley, thyme, and a pound of chopped or powdered sage. Grease with sweet lard or butter. Lay in a pan with the giblets, neck, etc. Pour in two teacupsful of boiling water, set in a hot oven and baste frequently. Turn so that every part may be equally browned. Serve with gravy or onion sauce.—*Mrs. Samuel Tyree in Virginia Cook Book.*

ROAST DUCK.

Plunge in boiling water, then immediately into cold water, which makes them easier to pick. They are then dressed, stuffed, and baked exactly like turkeys.

WILD DUCK OR TURKEY.

Put them on a rack above a pan so that the gravy will drip through. This makes them as delicate as if roasted on a spit.

GUINEA FOWL.

Follow the directions for baked chicken.

TO BROIL PIGEONS.

Slit down the back, salt them and let them lie twelve hours. Rub them with butter and pepper, place a slice of fat bacon on each breast, cook the under side, then remove the bacon, dredge with flour, baste with butter and brown the breast.

QUAIL ON TOAST.

Broil the birds over live wood coals, basting often with butter. Take slices of bread two days old, toast in front of the fire, pour melted butter over, and on each slice lay a whole bird. It is an improvement to lay three broiled oysters in each one.—*Hotel Emery, Cincinnati, O.*

Woodchucks, snipes, robins and all small birds are broiled over live coals and dressed with butter and pepper. Tomato catsup, and horse-radish sauce, are liked by many as accompaniments.

STEWED SQUIRRELS.

Three fine squirrels skinned and cleaned, joint as you would chickens for fricasee; half a pound of fat salt pork, one onion if liked, twelve ears of corn cut from the cob, six large tomatoes, pared and sliced, three tablespoonsful of butter rolled in flour, parsley; enough water to cover squirrels. Put on squirrels, the pork; cut up small onion and parsley in the water and bring to a boil. When this has lasted ten minutes put in corn and stew until squirrels are tender. Then add the tomatoes cut up thin; and twenty

MEAT.

minutes later stir in butter and flour. Simmer ten minutes and serve in a large deep dish.

PIGEON PIE.

Clean, wash, and cut pigeons into quarters; wipe dry, and fry lightly in butter or drippings; sprinkle well with salt and pepper. Have ready a greased pudding dish and a good paste. Lay some pieces of pigeon in the bottom of the dish and cover with a mixture of chopped eggs and the **giblet**s boiled tender in a little water and then minced. More pigeons and another layer of the force-meat. Stir a tablespoonful of butter, rolled in flour, into the water in which the giblets were boiled. Season and pour enough into the pie to half cover the birds. Cover with a thick crust and slit in the middle. Bake one hour and glaze with beaten egg just before it is taken from the oven.

CAKE MAKING.

CAKE making should never be attempted unless all the ingredients are on hand. Put on a housekeeping apron, roll the sleeves above the elbows, and remove from the table everything not needed in making the cake. Have a receptacle for the shells, and a pan of hot soap-suds in which to throw every knife, fork, spoon and dish as soon as you have finished with them. A cake made with system is no Herculean task. It need not disarrange an entire dining room and kitchen and disturb the peace of a whole household as it often does. First, all the ingredients should be of the best quality. No art can disguise poor ones. In summer immerse your eggs in cold or ice water an hour before using. The whites will then froth more easily. The Dover egg beater saves much time and labor. It is well to have two, one for the whites, the other for the yolks. The flour and sugar should be sifted. Have an accurate pair of scales, and if the cake is measured use the same cup for each ingredient. If the receipt calls for baking powder or cream of tartar, sift it in the flour, and dissolve soda in milk. Cream the butter after the salt is worked out. Raisins should be seeded, currants stemmed, and then cleaned by rubbing in a coarse towel. Slice citron very thin, and then dust all your fruit with flour to prevent its sinking to the bottom. Every cake, except a sponge cake, should be thoroughly beaten, and a stout wooden paddle will save many spoons. Mixing the cake with the hands is a very popular way. When making sponge cake stir the flour in very lightly with a silver fork. Grease cake pans with butter or lard. Cut two pieces of white paper to fit the bottom and strips for the sides. Adjust them and grease again. Do not use chips or porous woods for the stove. They make a varying heat. Never attempt to make a cake while a meal is being prepared. Do not open the stove doors too often or too long at a time. Let the cake rise to its full capacity before beginning to brown, by protecting it with a paper cap. Cake pans are now made with covers to be kept on till the cake is fully risen. If the cake browns too rapidly on one side turn it around quickly and gently. You may know when it is done by piercing with a straw. If it comes out clean, take the cake from the stove. Black and fruit cakes must be baked slowly; white, pound and sponge cakes faster. Allow your black and fruit cakes to cool in the pan; all others must be taken out immediately, especially those baked in jelly tins. Turn your cakes out on a folded tablecloth and let them get thoroughly cold before removing to a plate or cake stand. This prevents a damp and sticky under-surface. Keep in a box or drawer devoid of other articles of food. Cake imbibes odors almost as readily as butter.

ANGEL'S FOOD CAKE.

Whites of eleven eggs, one goblet of flour, one and a half of granulated sugar. Sift flour and sugar each three times, and stir into the flour a teaspoonful of cream of tartar. First stir the sugar into the frothed whites, and then add the flour lightly. Pour into a pan that has never been greased. Do not open the stove for fifteen minutes. It will be done in forty minutes.—*Mrs. Mary Anne Atkinson.*

WHITE SPONGE CAKE.

Whites of twenty eggs, two goblets of flour, three of sugar, two teaspoonsful of lemon, one of cream of tartar. Barely stir flour in. Bake quickly.—*Mrs. L. D. Barnes.*

This is the premium cake at the Bourbon Fair.

BOILED SPONGE CAKE.

Seven eggs, half a pound of flour, one pound of sugar, half a tumblerful of water. Boil the sugar and water together, and when cooled to milk-warm stir in the beaten yolks, then the whites, flour last very lightly. Break the cake.—*Mrs. A. Y. Leake.*

A cake made by the above receipt took the premium in a contest at Phœnix Club Hall, November 8, 1884. Magnificent.

MRS. H. N. STARNES' SPONGE CAKE.

Twelve eggs, one pound of sugar, three fourths of a pound of flour, two teaspoonsful of Royal baking powder and a pinch of salt. Flavor with lemon.

CREAM SPONGE CAKE.

Beat the yolks of two eggs very light; pour over them one cupful of rich cream; add one teacupful of powdered sugar, and one and a half teacupsful of sifted flour, one heaping teaspoonful of baking powder and a pinch of salt. Flavor with vanilla.—*Mrs. C. Carroll, in Kentucky Home Cook Book.*

SPONGE CAKE.

Five eggs, one cupful of sugar, two of flour, two teaspoonsfuls of baking powder, grated rind and juice of a lemon.—*Miss Katie Howell.*

MISS CLIFF BAKER'S SPONGE CAKE.

One pint of flour, one pint of sugar, ten eggs. Beat the whites and yolks separately; add the sugar after being rolled and sifted to the yolks, then the frothed whites, and flour last, very lightly. Sift it in and stir with a fork.

SPONGE CAKE.

Ten eggs, leaving out six yolks; half a pound of flour, three-fourths of a pound of sugar.—*Mrs. Robt. Toombs.*

ALMOND SPONGE CAKE.

Beat fine with a wineglass of rose water, two ounces of almonds, half sweet and half bitter; one pound of sugar, ten eggs beaten separately; add lastly half a pound of flour.

GINGER SPONGE CAKE.

Half pint of molasses, one cupful of butter, one cupful of sour cream, one tablespoonful of ginger, one teaspoonful of soda, three eggs, five cupsful of flour, one teaspoonful of cinnamon.—*Miss Mary Redmon.*

ARROW ROOT SPONGE CAKE.

Sift together a half pound of arrow root and a pound of sugar. Beat the whites and yolks of seven eggs separately and then together, and stir them gradually into the arrow root and sugar. Flavor with mace, lemon, or rose water.—*Demorest's Monthly.*

PHŒNIX CLUB POUND CAKE.
Premium.

Eight eggs, one pound of flour, three-fourths of a pound of sugar, half a pound of butter, two teaspoonsful of Royal baking powder. Flavor with French brandy, essence of nutmeg and essence of lemon.—*Miss Ruby Lofton.*

OLD-FASHIONED POUND CAKE.

Twelve eggs, one pound of sugar, one pound of butter, one pound of flour.—*Miss Dora Hughes.*

POUND CAKE.

Nine eggs, one pound of flour, one pound of sugar, three-fourths of a pound of butter. Rub the butter into the flour with the hands, then add the yolks of the eggs and sugar beaten together, and lastly the whites. Pour in one-fourth of a teacupful of warm water with a pinch of soda dissolved in it. Flavor with best whisky.—*Mrs. W. W. Massie.*

CAKE MAKING.

WHITE POUND CAKE.

Sixteen whites of eggs, one pound of sugar, one pound of flour, three-fourths of a pound of butter. Cream the butter, stir in the sugar, then the flour and frothed whites alternately.—*Mrs. Geo. J. Gable.*

POUND CAKE.

Twenty ounces of sugar, fourteen ounces of flour, fourteen ounces of butter, and fifteen eggs.—*Mrs. Dr. Nelson.*

MRS. CLAY'S PREMIUM CAKE.

Fourteen eggs, whites only, one pound of sugar, three-fourths of a pound of flour, half a pound of butter. Whisky and lemon to taste.

WHITE CAKE.

Two cupsful of flour, one cupful of sugar, half a cupful of butter, three-fourths of a cupful of milk, a teaspoonful of Patapsco baking powder.—*Mrs. Arthur Davis.*

WHITE CAKE.

Whites of twelve eggs, one cupful of butter, two of sugar, four of flour.—*Mrs. Beri Riddell.*

ALPINE SNOW CAKE.

Fifteen whites of eggs, two cups of flour, two of corn starch, three of sugar, one of butter and one of sweet milk. Flavor with rose water. This receipt is from the "White House" cake and pastry department.

GOOD AND CHEAP WHITE CAKE.

Take one teacupful of buttermilk and dissolve in it one teaspoonful of soda; add the frothed whites of six eggs, a half cupful of butter, two cups of sugar and three of flour. —*"Aunt America."*

CORN STARCH CAKE.

Two cupsful of sugar, three-fourths of a cupful of butter, a cupful of corn starch dissolved in a cupful of sweet milk, two cupsful of flour, whites of seven eggs, two teaspoonsful of cream of tartar and a teaspoonful of soda mixed thoroughly with the flour; cream butter and sugar, add starch and milk, then add the whites and flour gradually. Flavor with lemon or rose.—*Mrs. W. P. Anderson.*

SILVER CAKE.

One pound of powdered sugar, three-fourths of a pound of flour, one half a pound of butter, whites of eleven eggs, one teaspoonful essence of bitter almond.

GOLD PERFECTION CAKE.

Eight eggs, one cupful of butter, two of sugar, three of flour and one of corn starch; two teaspoonsful of Royal baking powder dissolved in a cupful of sweet milk.—*Carrie Belle Lofton.*

GOLD CAKE.

One pound of flour, one pound of sugar, three-fourths of a pound of butter, yolks of eleven eggs, grated rind of an orange, juice of two lemons.—*Mrs. David Rule.*

GOLDEN CUP CAKE.

Half a cup of butter, one of sugar, two of flour, six eggs. Flavor with essence of nutmeg.—*"Bossy."*

SILVER AND GOLD CAKE,
(Marbleized.)

Make a golden cup cake by preceding receipt, and another just like it, only leaving out the yolks of the eggs. Pour into the pan alternately.

CROTON SPONGE CAKE.

Six eggs, half a pound of butter, one pound of sugar, one pound of flour, a teaspoonful of soda and two of cream of tartar in one cupful of sweet milk. Flavor with almonds blanched and beaten.—*Mrs. Hill.*

ONE, TWO, THREE, FOUR CAKE.

One cup of butter, two of sugar, three of flour, four eggs, a teaspoonful of baking powder. There is no better or simpler cake than this to eat with sauce, or to bake in jelly tins for stock cake.

CUP CAKE.

Six eggs, one cupful of butter, one cupful of sour cream, two cupsful of sugar, three cupsful of flour, one-half teaspoonful of soda and one teaspoonful of cream of tartar.

A GOOD CUP CAKE.

Four cupsful of flour, two of sugar, one of butter, one of buttermilk, five eggs and one teaspoonful of soda. When cold ice it and cut in squares.

SMALL CUP CAKE.

One-half cupful of butter, one cup of sugar, two of flour, half a cupful of sour cream, and half a teaspoonful of soda. You can use sweet milk and a pinch of powdered ammonia dissolved in it.—*Rachel Lowe.*

ONE EGG CAKE.

One cupful of butter, one and a half of sugar, three of flour, one of sweet milk, one egg, a teaspoonful of soda, two teaspoonsful of cream of tartar in the flour, a cup of raisins chopped fine.

LEMON JELLY CAKE.

One cup of butter, two of sugar, three of flour, four eggs, one teaspoonful of baking powder. Bake in jelly tins. Filling: Take the juice and rind of four lemons, three tablespoonsful of butter, a cupful of sugar, and four eggs. Set on the stove and stir constantly till thick and spread thickly between the cakes.—*Mrs. Dr. Buttolph.*

ORANGE CAKE.

Two cupsful of sugar, yolks of five eggs, whites of two, half a cupful of cold water, two and a half cupsful of flour, two teaspoonsful of baking powder, the juice and grated rind of an orange and a pinch of salt. Bake in jelly tins. Beat the whites of two eggs to a stiff froth, add seven large tablespoonsful of powdered sugar, the grated rind and juice of an orange. Spread between the layers.—*Miss Nannie Scott.*

ROMAN SASH CAKE.

Make a white cake batter and divide into five equal parts. Let the first remain white, add beaten yolks to the second, color the third green with spinach coloring (see receipt), the fourth pink with Price's cake coloring, and the fifth with black molasses and ground spices. Put a layer of icing between each.—*Hollingsworth Confectioner.*

COCOANUT CAKE.

Make a white cake batter and bake in jelly tins. Filling: Take two cupsful of sugar, with water enough to dissolve, and boil it almost to candy. Pour it hot over the frothed whites of three eggs and a grated cocoanut. Beat well and spread between cakes.—*Miss Sabine Alston.*

COCOANUT CAKE.

Three cupsful of white sugar, one cup of butter, the whites of six eggs, five cupsful of sifted flour, one cupful of milk, one cocoanut grated fine, two teaspoonsful of baking powder mixed in the flour.—*Mrs. R. Hirsch.*

PINEAPPLE CAKE.

Make a sponge cake and bake in jelly tins. Filling: Take half a pint of pineapple juice, a cupful of sugar, two eggs and two tablespoonsful of butter. Boil till thick.—*Miss Etta Brown.*

WHITE AND PINK MARBLE CAKE.

Make a white cake batter and divide into two equal parts. Color half of it with Price's cake coloring and pour into the pan alternately. Equal parts of alum, cream of tartar, and cochineal pounded fine and dissolved in water, makes a beautiful coloring for cake.

WATERMELON CAKE.

Make a white cake batter and color half of it pink and add raisins. Pour the white in the pan first and then the pink.—*Miss Willie Price.*

A NICE FLAVORING FOR CAKE.

One teaspoonful of lemon acid pulverized, and one tablespoonful of brandy mixed.—*Mrs. Cunningham.*

CHOCOLATE CAKE.

Eight eggs, one cupful of butter, two of sugar, two of flour, one of cornstarch. Add two teaspoonsful of baking powder dissolved in half a cupful of hot milk. Bake in jelly tins. Filling: One-quarter of a cake of chocolate, one cupful of milk, one cupful of molasses, one cupful of water, a piece of butter the size of an egg. Boil till thick. Another filling: Take whites of three eggs beaten stiff, one and a half cupsful of powdered sugar, six tablespoonsful of grated chocolate, a teaspoonful of vanilla. Do not cook.—*Miss Kate Agricola.*

MARBLED CHOCOLATE CAKE.

Make a batter as for white cake; take out one cupful, add to it five tablespoonsful of grated chocolate moistened with milk and flavored with vanilla. Pour a layer of the white batter in the pan, drop the chocolate batter with a spoon in spots, and pour the remainder of the white batter over it.—*Dixie Cook Book.*

EGG-NOGG CAKE.

Make a pound cake or sponge cake batter and bake in jelly tins. Filling: Take three eggs, beat them well, pour over half a pint of whisky and half a pint of thick cream mixed. Sweeten to taste, and when it begins to boil thicken with cornstarch. Let it become cold before using.—*Mrs. Dr. Campbell.*

BLANC MANGE CAKE.

Make a gold cake batter and bake in jelly tins. Filling: Put a pint of fresh milk on the stove, add three or four well-beaten eggs, sweeten to taste, flavor with vanilla. When it begins to boil, add three heaping tablespoonsful of cornstarch, rubbed to a paste in a little milk. When cold and stiff, spread between cakes.—*Mrs. Louis Tennent.*

NUTMEG CAKE.

Take one cupful of butter, one cupful of brown sugar, one cupful of black molasses, half a cupful of sweet milk, four cupsful of flour, two teaspoonsful of baking powder. You can use sour cream or buttermilk and soda. It is better to have the flour browned. Grate in a whole nutmeg, or use essence of nutmeg. By the addition of a pound of currants, a pound of raisins, a little sliced citron and brandy, you have a very fine fruit cake.—*Mrs. John Hollinshead.*

SPICED CAKE.

Yellows of seven eggs, two teacupsful of brown sugar, one teacupful of molasses, one teacupful of butter, five teacupsful of flour, one teacupful of sour cream, one teaspoonful of soda, spices to taste.—*Mrs. H. C. Buckner, in Blue Grass Cook Book.*

COFFEE CAKE.

Four eggs, one cupful of butter, one cupful of brown sugar, one cupful of molasses, one cupful of strong coffee, four cupsful of flour, one cupful of raisins, one teaspoonful of soda, spices to taste. Add whisky or blackberry cordial. —*Miss Flora Lanehan.*

AN INEXPENSIVE BLACK CAKE.

One cup of butter, one of brown sugar, one of black molasses, three of browned flour, six eggs, two teaspoonsful of baking powder. Add a half pound of raisins, a half pound of currants, a fourth of a pound of citron, whisky and spices to taste. Good, and easily made.—*Mrs. Ben White.*

BLACK CAKE.

One pound of flour, one pound of sugar, one and one quarter pounds of butter, thirteen eggs, three pounds of raisins, two pounds of currants, one pound of citron, one wineglass of brandy, two of wine, one grated nutmeg, one teaspoonful of cinnamon, one half teaspoonful of mace and cloves, each. Just before putting into the stove, stir in a small teacupful of vinegar with a teaspoonful of soda.—*Mrs. H. C. Buckner, in Blue Grass Cook Book.*

This cake will be as good in ten years as the day it was baked. You will never find a better receipt.

WEDDING CAKE.

Four dozen eggs, four pounds of sugar, four of flour, four of butter, twelve of raisins, eight of currants, two of citron, a pint of brandy, a fourth of an ounce of cloves, an ounce of cinnamon, four of nutmeg.—*Vienna Bakery, Philadelphia.*

CURRANT CAKE.

The whites of fourteen eggs, one pound of flour, three-fourths of a pound of sugar, half a pound of butter, two teaspoonsful of baking powder; add one and a half pounds of currants.—*Mrs. James Buttolph.*

QUEEN'S CAKE.

One pound of butter, one pound of sugar, one pound of flour, one gill of cream, one gill of wine, one gill of brandy, one pound of fruit, eight eggs, and one nutmeg.— *Mrs. Martha Berrien Duncan.*

LOAF CAKE.

Nine pounds of flour, five pints of sugar, four pints of butter, five pints of fruit, fifteen eggs, half a pint of wine, half a pint of brandy, two quarts of milk, and a pint of yeast; spices to taste.—*Mrs. Martha Berrien Duncan.*

CURRANT CAKE.

A cupful of butter and a cupful of sugar rubbed to a cream. Add four eggs well beaten, and two cupsful of flour; stir in last a large cupful of currants, washed, dried and floured.— *Mrs. George J. Gable.*

BLACK AND WHITE MARBLE CAKE.

White part: Whites of seven eggs, half a cupful of butter, one cupful of sugar, half cupful of sweet milk, a teaspoonful of baking powder, two cupsful of flour. Dark part: Yolks of five eggs, a cupful of brown sugar, half a cupful of molasses, half a cupful of sweet milk and two of flour, with a teaspoonful of baking powder. Add half an ounce each of powdered cinnamon, cloves and allspice, and a fourth of a pound of citron cut in slices. Mix the white and dark batter alternately in the pan.—*Mrs. Lattimer.*

WHITE FRUIT CAKE.

One pound of sugar, half a pound of butter, three-fourths of a pound of flour, three-fourths of a pound of grated cocoanut, one pound of almonds blanched and beaten, one pound of citron cut fine, sixteen eggs, whites only.—*Mrs. T. C. Nisbet.*

BLUE GRASS FRUIT CAKE.

Three-fourths of a pound of butter, three-fourths of a pound of sugar, three-fourths of a pound of flour, eight eggs, one gill of cream, one teaspoonful of cinnamon and nutmeg mixed, half a gill of brandy, one pound of currants, and one pound of raisins.

FRUIT CAKE.

One cup of butter, one of brown sugar, half a pint of molasses, two eggs, a cup of sour milk, a teaspoonful of soda, a pound of flour, one of currants, one and a half of raisins. Flavor to taste. This has been thoroughly tested, and is a great favorite.

MOCK FRUIT CAKE.

Five eggs, five cups of flour, three cups of sugar, two cups of butter, one cup of buttermilk, one teaspoonful of soda in the buttermilk, spices to taste, half a wineglass of wine, one wineglass of syrup. Do not beat your batter after you have put in soda, but stir in citron, dried apples, plums, cherries, peaches, or any other fruit.—*Mrs. H. N. Starnes.*

FRUIT AND FEATHER CAKE.

Six eggs, two scant cupsful of sugar, butter twice the size of an egg, two cupsful of flour, two teaspoonsful of cream of tartar, one teaspoonful of soda. Take out a little less than half, and into this stir half a pound of currants, half a pound of raisins, two tablespoonsful of citron, and half as much candied orange or lemon peel, one teaspoonful of powdered nutmeg, one of cinnamon, half a glass of brandy, one teacupful of molasses, and two teacupsful of flour. Bake in jelly tins first the plain, then the fruit cake, and cover each with jelly.—*Miss Nannie Scott.*

HICKORY NUT CAKE.

A cup of butter, two of sugar, three of flour, one of sweet milk, whites of seven and yolks of two eggs, a teaspoonful of soda and two of cream of tartar, one pint of hickorynut meats, rolled and sprinkled with flour; beat the whites to a froth.

TEA CAKE.

One cupful of strong tea, one cupful of butter, two cupsful of sugar, three eggs, one and a half pints of flour, one and a half teaspoonsful of baking powder, one cupful of raisins, and a half cupful of chopped citron; spices to taste.

MOLASSES CAKE.

One cupful of butter, one cupful of brown sugar, a half cupful of molasses, one cupful of milk, one and a half pints of flour, one and a half teaspoonsful of baking powder, one egg. Cheap and good.

DRIED APPLE CAKE.

Soak two cupsful of dried apples in warm water overnight, drain off the water through a sieve, chop the apples slightly, then simmer for one and a half hours in two cups of molasses; add one cup of sugar, one cup of sweet milk one-fourth of a cup of butter, flour to make a stiff batter, and a heaping teaspoonful of baking powder in flour. Spices to taste.—*Mrs. John Roberts.*

SOFT GINGER CAKE.

Five cupsful of sifted flour, two cupsful of brown sugar, one of molasses, one of butter, one or two of sour milk or clabber, five eggs, one tablespoonful of ginger, one of allspice, one of cinnamon, one teaspoonful of cloves, one teaspoonful of soda in flour.—*Mrs. Nellie Screven.*

SOFT GINGER CAKE.

A half cupful of butter, one cupful of sugar, one cupful of molasses, four cupsful of flour, one cupful of sweet milk, a teaspoonful of baking powder, one tablespoonful of ginger.—*Mrs. Robt. Goodman.*

SUPERIOR GINGER LOAF.

Five cupsful of flour, one cupful of brown sugar, two cupsful of molasses, two cupsful of sour cream, one cupful of butter, six eggs, two tablespoonsful of ginger, two of cinnamon, two teaspoonsful of mace, one of cloves, one of soda, one pound of currants, one pound of raisins.—*Mrs. John Ray.*

DUTCH CAKE.

Three pints of milk; put flour and yeast with it sufficient to raise it as a sponge. Let it stand until morning, then add one pound of sugar, one of butter, one of flour, cinnamon, nutmeg, and rosewater to taste.—*Mrs. Tom Irvine.*

HONEY CAKE.

Half a cupful of butter, one cupful of sugar, one cupful of honey, one pint of flour, one teaspoonful of baking powder, two eggs.—*Royal Pastry Cook.*

COCOANUT CAKE.

Whites of sixteen eggs, one pound of sugar, one pound of flour, three-fourths of a pound of butter. Filling: Take the whites of six eggs, beat to a froth, and add sugar till a stiff icing is formed. Flavor with lemon and vanilla. Spread the cakes thickly with this icing, then sprinkle on fresh grated cocoanut, then a sifting of loaf sugar powdered. Continue until all the cakes are used. Then pour the remainder of the icing and mixed cocoanut over the whole cake.—*Mrs. Dr. Adair.*

WHITE MOUNTAIN CAKE.

One pound of granulated sugar, half a pound of butter, one pound of flour, one cupful of milk, the whites of six eggs, two teaspoonsful of baking powder. For icing, one pound of sugar, four eggs; flavor to taste. Bake in jelly tins with icing between. This cake can be heartily recommended after an acquaintance of years.

LADY CAKE.

Three-fourths of a pound of flour, one pound of sugar, half a pound and two ounces of butter, the whites of fourteen eggs, half an ounce of bitter almonds or peach kernels. Pound the almonds in white liquor, cream the butter and sugar together, and add the flour and eggs alternately.—*Mrs. H. N. Starnes.*

COMPOSITION CAKE.

Twelve eggs, three-fourths of a pound of butter, one pound of flour, one pound of sugar, one gill of brandy, one cup of wine, one ounce of mixed spices.—*Mrs. Stoddard Johnson.*

TEXAS CAKE.

Whites of twelve eggs, five small cups of flour, three of sugar, one of butter, one of sweet milk, one of soda, one of cream of tartar; soda in the milk, cream of tartar in the flour.—*Mrs. Wm. Phillips, Jr.*

MARIETTA CAKE.

Whites of twelve eggs, one cup of butter, two of sugar, two of flour, one of cornstarch, two teaspoonsful of baking powder. Bake in jelly tins. For the filling make a rich syrup and when it is almost candy beat in the frothed whites of four eggs. When cool stir in finely chopped figs, seeded raisins, chopped and thinly sliced citron. Spread between the layers.

CINCINNATI CAKE.

Pour over one pound of fat salt pork, free from lean and rind, one pint of boiling water; let stand until nearly cold, add two cupsful of brown sugar, one of molasses, one tablespoonful each of cloves and nutmeg, two of cinnamon, two pounds of raisins, fourth of a pound of citron, half a glass of brandy, three teaspoonsful of baking powder, and seven cupsful of sifted flour. Bake slowly two and a half hours. This is excellent and requires neither butter nor eggs.

KELLY ISLAND CAKE.

One cupful of butter, two of sugar, three of flour, four eggs, half a cupful of milk, three teaspoonsful of baking powder; bake in jelly tins. For filling, stir together a grated lemon, a large grated tart apple, an egg, a cupful of sugar, and boil four minutes.

PEACH CAKE.

Bake a pound or a white cake in jelly tins. Chop ripe peaches very fine, spread on the cakes, and pour frothed cream, sweetened and flavored, over.

SILVER OR WHITE CAKE.

One pound of flour, one pound of sugar, three-fourths of a pound of butter, whites of sixteen eggs, one teaspoonful heaped of baking powder. Flavor with vanilla or lemon. Cream the butter well, add the sugar and mix well with the butter. Beat to a stiff froth the whites of eight of the eggs, and put them to the sugar and butter, and stir them in well; add the flour gradually until it is all in, and then the well beaten whites of eight more eggs. Mix well, and put in the flavoring and then the baking powder, made smooth and fine. Mix thoroughly. Grease the pan with a little lard; cut paper to fit the bottom of the pan, grease that too; dust the whole of the inside with flour and shake off as much of the flour as you can. Put in the batter and place it in a moderate oven; put paper over the cake and above the paper put a piece of sheet iron. Keep up a regular heat about the same as for a loaf of bread. Turn the cake around carefully quite often. If the fire is right it will bake in about an hour.—*Mrs. Dick.*

This is the cake that attracted so much attention at Dr. Buttolph's silver wedding anniversary a few years since.

GOLD CAKE.

Yolks of eight eggs and one and a half cups of sugar beaten thoroughly; add a half cup of butter and three large kitchen spoonsful of milk. In three cupsful of flour put one teaspoonful of baking powder. Any flavoring you like.—*Mrs. J. W. Baker.*

All receipts for sponge cake will direct you to stir the flour in lightly, but do not go to extremes and not stir it in thoroughly. If you do you will find the bottom of the cake a jelly without any flour, streaks of egg and lumps of flour all through it. Stir from the bottom of the bowl and directly it is poured in the pan set it in the stove.

In preparing currants it is sometimes difficult to know when *all* the stems have been removed. Place them on white paper or a towel and draw them towards you. The contrast in color will enable you to detect any remaining stems very readily.

GNADINGER'S TEA CAKES.

One-half pound of butter, one pound of sugar, two pounds of flour, four eggs, half an ounce of carbonate of ammonia, half a pint of water, dust with sugar, and bake This has been the most popular of all Mr. Gnadinger's small cakes.

LADY FINGERS.

Make a sponge cake by Mrs. A. Y. Leake's receipt, and drop it from a spoon in oval shapes on buttered white paper. Have them as near the same size as possible. Spread the under side of each with icing, and lay two together. You can use jelly if preferred.

NICE TEA CAKES.

Make a baking-powder biscuit dough (see receipt), only use nearly twice the amount of lard. Add a little sugar and grated nutmeg. Handle but little, cut in squares, and bake quickly.

CREAM TEA CAKES.

Dissolve one ounce of ammonia in a pint of milk overnight; five eggs, four cups of sugar, two of butter; mix soft. When baked, drop a teaspoonful of icing on the top of each, and in the centre of the icing press a large raisin.—*Put in-Bay House.*

MORAINES.

Half pound of almonds, ten yellows, a half pound of butter, twelve ounces of sugar, two ounces of citron, half a pound of flour, one pint of cream. Mash the almonds with the eggs in a mortar, mix with all the above ingredients; beat the ten whites to a stiff froth, mix all well together. Bake in small fluted moulds, in a moderate oven.—*C. E. F. Hegman, in Blue Grass Cook Book.*

CREAM CAKE.

One pint of milk, half a pound of butter, twelve ounces of flour, ten eggs. Place the milk and butter in a stew pan; when it boils, stir in the flour. Keep it on the fire, and stir constantly till the dough loosens from the bottom of the pan, then add eggs. Bake in a hot oven in buttered pans. Cut open, and fill with lemon cream.—*C. E. F. Hegman.*

NICE FRIED CAKES.

Take one pint of buttermilk, one egg, one cupful of white sugar, one tablespoonful of butter, a little ginger, one teaspoonful of soda; knead as soft as you can roll. Fry in boiling lard.

COCOANUT TEA CAKES.

Take one pound of sugar, one teacupful of butter. seven eggs beaten separately, two grated cocoanuts.

GERMAN TEA CAKES.

Take one pound of sugar, one pound of butter, one pound of flour, one tablespoonful of whisky, two raw eggs, ten hard-boiled yolks mash till the lumps disappear; then add the butter, sugar, whiskey and flour. Roll thin, sprinkle sugar over the dough, cut and bake quickly. A little more flour may be needed but the dough must not be stiff.—*Mrs. W. W. Massie.*

RICH JUMBLES.

Take two pounds of flour, one pound of sugar, three-fourths cupful of butter, four eggs beaten very light, one-half cupful of cream one teaspoonful of baking powder. Flavor with a little nutmeg and a few drops of bitter almond.—*Mrs. J. H. Robinson, in Kentucky Home Cook Book.*

COOKIES.

(Good and Simple.)

One cupful of butter, two cupsful of sugar, three eggs, five tablespoonsful of sour milk, five cupsful of flour, half a teaspoonful of soda. Flavor with nutmeg.—*Mrs. N. B. Moore.*

TEA CAKES WITHOUT EGGS.

One cupful of butter, two cupsful of sugar, one gill of brandy, half a grated nutmeg, one teaspoonful essence of lemon, one cupful of sour cream, or buttermilk, one small teaspoonful of soda.—*Mrs. Spalding in Augusta Cook Book.*

DAVIS JUMBLES

(Very fine)

One teacupful of grated loaf sugar, one teacupful of butter, one tablespoonful of thick cream, one egg, white only, fourth of a teaspoonful of soda; flour to roll out. Dip the cakes in grated sugar before baking.—*Mrs. J. W. Baker.*

SHORT BREAD.

One pound of flour, one-third of a pound of butter, half a pound of sugar. Roll thin and cut in cakes.—*Mrs. Chas. Harper.*

DOUGHNUTS.

Rub one cupful of butter and two cupsful of white sugar to a cream, add two eggs well beaten, two cupsful of sweet milk, and one cupful of yeast. Mix in flour enough to make a dough as soft as you can handle. Let it rise overnight in a warm place; roll the dough out about an inch thick, cut into small cakes, put a raisin in the center of each one and press it in the dough. Have a shallow kettle with about three pounds of lard; put it over the fire where it will melt; then set it forward, and when boiling hot lay in the cakes. In about ten minutes try one to see if it is done through. Drain them in a sieve and roll them in powdered sugar.—*Mrs. Warren K. Smith.*

FRENCH STRAWS.

Eight eggs, fourth of a teaspoonful of nutmeg, ten ounces of sugar, fourth of a teaspoonful of cinnamon. Beat the eggs very thick, add the sugar, spice, and enough flour to make a dough. Roll it half an inch thick, cut into strips two or three inches in length, give each one a twist, and drop in boiling lard. When cool sprinkle sugar over them.

GINGER SNAPS.

Half a pint of molasses, one teacupful of brown sugar, half a teaspoonful of soda, a little salt, two tablespoonsful of ginger, one cupful of lard. Warm the molasses, stir the soda into it, then the sugar; mix all together and roll out thin.—*Mrs. Geo. Davis.*

LEMON BISCUITS.

Ten ounces of sugar, fourteen ounces of flour, five ounces of butter, three eggs, a little soda and cream of tartar, fifteen drops of oil of lemon, and water enough to make a stiff dough. Cut them and bake in a hot oven.—*Mrs. J. A. Massey*.

These small cakes are the ones that have been so popular at the festivals in Marietta.

ICING. (Plain.)

BEAT the whites of half a dozen eggs to a stiff froth; then take a stout wooden paddle and beat in icing sugar until stiff. Add a drop or two of Prussian blue, to make it blue-white. Spread on the cakes with a steel knife, dipped in hot water whenever it becomes cool. Let each coat dry before adding another. It may be put on in ornamental designs by using a tin funnel or one made of stiff white paper.—*Mrs. Humphrey Reid.*

This icing may be varied by adding Price's pink coloring to give it a rose tinge, or the yolks of two eggs to make it cream colored. It may also be made green with spinach. A cake with all these different icings arranged tastily, is beautiful. A little practice and a somewhat inventive genius are all that is necessary to insure success in this ornamental and much appreciated art.

CHEAP FROSTING.

Beat the whites of three eggs to a stiff froth and beat in granulated sugar till moderately stiff; not near so much so as icing, made of icing sugar. Do not spread on the cake but pour it over.—*Mrs. Hattie Baker.*

ICING.

Take the whites of eggs, *without beating*, and stir in icing sugar till very stiff. It requires more labor than any other kind of icing, but is the best in use.

This is the receipt of a professional of Mobile, Ala.

TO MAKE ICING.—EXCELLENT.

One pound of sugar, half a tumblerful of water, four eggs; boil the sugar and water to a candy, taking care not to stir; beat the whites of the eggs to a froth—not stiff—and pour the candy on it, a spoonful at a time. Stir until smooth and white.—*Mrs. W. P. C. Breckenridge.*

A cake iced, and with French candies arranged on top, and sides also, if preferred, presents a very beautiful appearance.

PASTRY.

THERE is no medium in pastry making. If it is not first class it is intolerable. Heavy pastry has caused more dyspepsia than any other article of diet. You may take exercise, use tonics, and read all the hygienic rules in existence, and yet if you eat a heavy indigestible pie once a week, your pains will go for naught. Puddings and pies are among our best desserts but are fast being relegated to obscurity because the process of making them is not thoroughly understood. A marble slab is neat and convenient in pastry making. No housekeeper who has once used one would willingly part with it. Explicit directions will be found in the receipts below.

PUFF PASTE.

One pound of butter, one pound of flour; sift the flour and then sift in something else a little additional flour for sprinkling and rolling; wash all the salt from the butter, then divide it into four parts; put one-fourth into the flour, and d vide the remainder into six pieces; mix with a knife the flour and butter into a stiff dough, sprinkle a little flour on the paste board, flour the rolling pin, and roll into a thin sheet; then put in little bits at equal distances one-sixth of the butter, fold the paste, flour it and roll again, and so on until the butter is consumed. Divide it into as many pieces as you wish pies; roll each piece and put into pans previously buttered; always roll from you.—*Mrs. Martin, in Blue Grass Cook Book.*

PLAIN BUT DELIGHTFUL PIE CRUST.

One quart of flour, a teaspoonful of salt, a large coffee cupful of lard, three teaspoonsful of baking powder. Mix with cold water, or ice-water if convenient. Handle but little.—*Mrs E. R. Tennent.*

DELICATE TART PASTE.

Yolks of three eggs, whites of one, one ounce of sugar, one ounce of butter, a little salt, flour enough to roll smoothly. Roll as thin as common pie crust. Bake in small tins. To keep paste from puffing up, prick it lightly, not piercing to the tins. Fill with jelly, preserves, fresh fruit, or anything you choose. Frost with the remaining two whites and one tablespoonful of sugar.—*Mrs. Dwight Pierce.*

EXCELLENT PASTRY.

Four cupsful of flour, one cupful of firm butter, one very small cupful of lard, one cupful of ice water, one teaspoonful of salt. Mix the butter and lard in the flour with a large flat knife, then add the ice water. Do not touch it with the hands. Take it up in a rough looking mass, roll it out quickly, not too thin. Cut it with a very sharp knife around the edges of the pastry pans. When intending to bake lemon puddings or cheese cakes, let the pastry bake four or five minutes before adding butter as this prevents the pastry from being heavy at the bottom. In summer it is best to put five cupsful of flour instead of four.—*Mrs. Margaret C. Cabell.*

PASTE FOR TWO PIES.

One cup of lard, salt, three cups of flour. Mix lightly; add one cup of water; mix, and roll out. Spread on little bits of butter and sprinkle a little flour. Roll up and roll out again. Repeat twice.—*Mrs. Dr. Rockwell.*

PIE CRUST FOR DYSPEPTICS.

One pint of cream, twelve good sized potatoes, boiled and mashed fine, flour to make a paste. Handle very lightly, and use no under crust.—*New Haven Cook Book*.

Brush your crust before it is baked with the white of an egg. It keeps the juice from seeping through and making the crust clammy. It also causes it to brown very beautifully.

PUDDINGS AND PIES.

COCOANUT PUDDING.

(Mrs. Chas. J. Jenkins's State Dinner Dessert.)

Two grated cocoanuts, with the milk, one pound of sugar, four eggs, one cupful of citron sliced, one cupful of raisins chopped, one wineglassful of brandy. Put the cocoanut and sugar on the fire, and let it clarify; then add the yolks of the eggs, fruit and brandy. Bake in pudding dish. Make a meringue of the whites, with a tablespoonful of sugar to each egg, and let it brown a little. Serve cold.

PLUM PUDDING.

Three dozen eggs, three pounds of baker's bread, stale and grated fine; three pounds of suet, three pounds of brown sugar, one pound of sliced citron, three pounds of currants, four pounds of seeded raisins, a half ounce of nutmeg and the same of mace, cloves and cinnamon, half a pint of wine, half a pint of French brandy. Mix and divide into six parts. Tie each part in a twilled cotton cloth, put them in boiling water, and let them boil four hours. Then hang them in the air to dry a day or two. Keep them in a cool dry place. When you wish to use one, boil an hour before dinner. Serve with rich sauce. It will keep six months, or a year.—*Mrs. Theo. M. Carson.*

PLUM PUDDING.

One teacupful of New Orleans molasses, one teacupful of suet pulverized, two teacupsful of sifted flour, two teaspoonsful of quick yeast, one teacupful of sweet milk, one pound of seeded and cut raisins, half a pound of currants. Steam it four hours. Keep boiling water high on mould. Sauce of sugar and butter flavored to taste.—*Mrs. Sue Miller.*

ECONOMICAL PLUM PUDDING.

Two pints of flour, two teacupsful of raisins, two of suet chopped fine, three of buttermilk, two of molasses, two teaspoonsful of soda; boil or steam four hours. Serve with sauce.

RAISIN PUDDING.

One pound of raisins, one pound of sugar, one half pound of butter, one pound of flour, seven eggs, beaten separately, one pint of milk or cream, one wineglassful of wine or brandy; flour the mould or bag, and butter it well; boil three or four hours. Serve with rich sauce.—*Mrs. H. C. Buckner, in Blue Grass Cook Book.*

MINCED PIES.

Two pounds of beef finely chopped, one pound of suet nicely shred; one dozen apples, pared and chopped small; two pounds of currants or raisins stoned and floured; three-quarters of a pound of sugar, with nutmeg, mace and cloves. Dried cherries are very nice; mix all together, stir with it sweet cider, French or peach brandy, slice in citron or preserved orange peel; some use cider and brandy, too—a quart of cider and a teacupful of brandy.—*Mrs. Martha Washington.*

MINCE MEAT.

One beef tongue chopped fine, twelve pints of apples chopped fine, three pints of currants, one pint of raisins, one pint of citron sliced very thin, two ounces of cinnamon, two ounces of mace, two tablespoonsful of cloves, one pint of brandy. Pulverize spices, mix all together, stir well, and pack in a jar with three-fourths of a pint of brandy, poured on top. Tie closely.—*Mrs Emily Tubman.*

MINCE MEAT FOR SIX PIES.

One pound of meat chopped fine, after being cooked, one pound of suet, two pounds of raisins, two pounds of chopped apples, four oranges, the peel of one-fourth of a pound of citron, one ounce of cinnamon, half an ounce of allspice, one grated nutmeg, two pounds of brown sugar.

RAISIN PIES.

One pound of raisins; boil one hour covered constantly with water; add one lemon chopped, one cup of sugar, two tablespoonsful of flour. Three pies.—*Hood's Cook Book.*

ORANGE JELLY PIE.

Take a pint of rich milk, the juice of three oranges, and the grated rind of one, yolks of three eggs; sweeten to taste and thicken with cornstarch. Bake in crust. Good.— *Mrs. Henry C. Lemon.*

ORANGE PUDDING.

Two oranges, juice of both and peel of one, juice of one lemon, half a pound of stale and crumbled lady fingers, two cups of milk, four eggs, half a cupful of sugar, one tablespoonful of cornstarch; wet with cold water.

LEMON CORN-STARCH PIE.

One cup of boiling water; dissolve in it two tablespoonsful of cornstarch. When reduced to a paste, add a small teacupful of sugar, one egg, and the juice of a lemon. Frost with the white of an egg.—*Mrs. J. I. Chamberlin.*

LEMON PUDDING.

The grated rind and juice of four lemons, one coffee-cupful of sugar, three tablespoonsful of butter, four eggs beaten light, stir constantly till as thick as honey; let it cool and place in pastry already baked.—*Mrs. E. R. Tennent.*

ONE-TWO-THREE-FOUR PUDDING.

One cup of butter, two of sugar, three of flour, four eggs, one cup of sweet milk, and two teaspoonsful of baking powder; flavor with nutmeg, and serve with sauce.

GEORGIA SWEET-POTATO PIE.

Boil, peel and mash in milk the potatoes; allow one pint of warm milk or cream to every pint of potatoes; three eggs, sugar and spice to taste; one crust; frost.—*Mrs. C. R. Upson.*

SWEET-POTATO PIE.

Two pounds of potatoes, steam entirely done and slice them; make a syrup of one teacupful of butter, two teacupsful of sugar, three-fourths of a teacupful of good wine, one dessert spoonful of allspice pounded fine, enough water to make one and a half pints of the syrup; boil for a short while, and line a deep pan with rich paste, and bake slightly; put in a layer of sliced potatoes and pour over some of the syrup, then another layer of potatoes and the rest of the syrup; cover with crust and bake.—*Mrs. Sam Brooks, in Blue Grass Cook Book.*

WHIPPED CREAM TARTS.

Make small crusts and bake; fill each with whipped cream, and drop on each a small piece of jelly.

HONEY PUDDING.

Half a pound of clear honey; add six ounces of butter beaten to a cream, four ounces of bread crumbs; beat all together for ten minutes with yolks of eight eggs; put into moulds and boil one and a half hours. Sauce.

IRISH-POTATO PUDDING.

Two teacupsful of sugar, two teacupsful of butter, one teacupful sweet cream, eight eggs, two and a half pints mashed potatoes, one nutmeg grated.

BLACKBERRY MUSH.

To two quarts of ripe berries, add one and a half pints of boiling water and one pound of sugar, cook a few minutes; then stir in a pint of flour; boil a few minutes longer, put in greased mould to cool and serve with cream or hard sauce.

SLICED APPLE PIE.

Pare and slice your apples thin, sprinkle a pint of sugar over a quart of apples, cover with water, and add a tablespoonful of butter. The butter seasons them highly, and prevents them from falling to pieces; put in a bit of cinnamon, mace, and grated nutmeg. Do not cook too long. Remove to a pan, lined with rich pastry, cover and bake. If there is too much juice to put in the pies pour into a small pitcher and use with the pies when served.—*Miss Mollie Downey.*

SUNDERLAND PUDDING.

Six eggs, three tablespoonsful of flour, one pint of milk, a pinch of salt, beat the yellows well and add flour, then the milk, the whites last. Serve with sauce.

PARADISE PUDDING.

Three eggs, three apples chopped fine, half a cupful of sugar, half a cupful of currants, two cupsful of bread crumbs grated, rind and juice of half a lemon, a little salt, half a cupful of milk. Sauce.

CATSKILL MOUNTAIN PUDDING.

One pint of sweet milk, two eggs, one quart of flour, one tablespoonful of butter, two tablespoonsful of sugar, half a teaspoonful of salt, two teaspoonsful of baking powder. Mix well. Bake in cups or boil in a mould. Serve with sauce.

STEAM PUDDING.

Half a cupful of butter, two cupsful of molasses, two cupsful of buttermilk, four cupsful of flour, one teaspoonful of soda.—*Miss Emma Scott.*

BUTTERMILK PUDDING.

Cream one tablespoonful of butter and one teacupful of sugar, four eggs, half a cupful of buttermilk, two tablespoonsful of cornstarch. Flavor with vanilla. Make a meringue of the whites and sprinkle with jelly.—*Miss Emma Scott.*

POOR FOLKS' PUDDING.

Two cupsful of blackberry jam, two cupsful of sugar, one of flour, six eggs, a cupful of butter, half a cupful of sour milk, one teaspoonful of soda, one teaspoonful of ground cinnamon, one of allspice, a little grated nutmeg. A wineglassful of whisky improves it greatly. Stewed dried apples with grated lemon peel may be used instead of the blackberries. It is good warm or cold, and is to be served with a milk and butter sauce. This is called Poor Folks' Pudding, but it is good enough for a millionaire. You have only to make it once and every member of the family will fall in love with it.—*Mrs. E. R. Tennent.*

SWEETENED APPLE DUMPLINGS.

One dozen tart apples sliced. Put in the pudding dish and cover with paste as for raised biscuits. Take one pint of water, one cup of sugar, and two tablespoonsful of butter. Pour over the crust and bake three-quarters of an hour. Serve with sauce or sugar and cream. Grate nutmeg on top.

RICE PUDDING.

Boil one pint of rice in one quart of rich cream. When done stir in a large teaspoonful of baking powder and sweeten with grated loaf sugar. Bake slightly in buttered

PUDDINGS AND PIES.

dish. Rice puddings made as above have long been great favorites at the Burnet House Restaurant, Cincinnati, Ohio. They have been sought after to the exclusion sometimes of far more showy and expensive dishes.

FROSTED RICE PUDDING.

One cup of rice boiled in one pint of water until dry; then add one pint of milk and boil again; add the juice and grated rind of one lemon, the yolks of four eggs and one-half cupful of sugar; stir well together and bake slowly for one hour. Beat the whites of four eggs to a stiff froth and add one cupful of powdered sugar; spread on the pudding and brown lightly.—*Miss Nannie Scott.*

RICE PUDDING.

Make a custard of a quart of milk, yolks of six eggs, a tablespoonful of butter, and sugar to taste. Stir in until thick boiled rice, salted as if for the table. You can add the grated rind of a lemon, grated nutmeg or vanilla. Beat the whites of three eggs to a froth and sweeten slightly for meringue. The pudding will be lighter if two teaspoonsful of baking powder are added.

TAPIOCA PUDDING.

Soak tapioca in water over night, substitute it for the rice and follow the receipt above.

CABINET PUDDING.

One quart of milk, four eggs, four tablespoonsful of sugar, half a teaspoonful of salt, one tablespoonful of butter, three pints of stale sponge cake, one cup of raisins chopped, citron and currants. Beat eggs, sugar, and salt together and add the milk. Butter a three pint pudding mould, sprinkle sides and bottom with the fruit and put in a layer of cake. Continue this until material is all used. Gradually pour on the custard. Let it stand two hours and steam one and one-quarter hours.—*Miss Parloa.*

FIG PUDDING.

Half a pound of bread crumbs, half a pound of figs, six ounces of brown sugar, two eggs, nutmeg, half a pound of suet chopped with figs, a little milk, two ounces of flour. Mix well; boil four hours; sauce.—*Mrs. Tillie Lansing.*

OLD FASHIONED GREEN APPLE PIE.

Pare and cut the apples in very small pieces; cover with water, cook to a pulp and press through a sieve; sweeten to taste and add a tablespoonful of butter and a little grated nutmeg. Do not have any top crust. Sift powdered loaf sugar over.—*Mrs. Nancy Offutt.*

CREAM PIE.

Bring a quart of cream to the boiling point, sweeten to taste, add a tablespoonful of cornstarch rubbed smooth in milk, the whites of five eggs and a tablespoonful of baking powder mixed well in the cornstarch. Bake in lower crust. —*Miss Sue Simpson.*

TOMATO PIE.

Slice very thin tomatoes which have just begun to turn. Lay them evenly in the paste and cover with sugar. Add a little lemon juice and grated peel and cinnamon. Cover with strips of paste and bake one hour.

MINUTE PUDDING.

Seven eggs beaten separately. Add to the yolks gradually ten tablespoonsful of sifted flour, alternately with a quart of milk and half a teaspoonful of salt. Beat till perfectly smooth; then add the whites; pour into a buttered dish and bake twenty minutes. Wine sauce.—*Mrs. Fanny Henry.*

EXCELLENT BATTER PUDDING.

One quart of flour, seven eggs, half a cupful of melted butter, one teaspoonful of salt, one teaspoonful of soda, dissolved in lukewarm water, two teaspoonsful of cream of tartar also dissolved, enough sweet milk to make a batter the consistency of sponge cake batter. Bake in a mould and eat with brandy sauce.—*Miss Smidt.*

STRAWBERRY SHORTCAKE.

Two heaping teaspoonsful of baking powder sifted into one quart of flour, scant half-teacupful of butter, two tablespoonsful of sugar, a little salt, enough sweet milk or water to make a soft dough. Roll out almost as thin as pie crust, place one layer in a baking pan and spread with a very little butter, upon which sprinkle some flour, then add another layer of crust, and spread as before; and so on until crust is all used. Bake about fifteen minutes in a quick oven and spread each layer with strawberries previously sweetened but not mashed. Serve warm with sugar and cream, or charlotte russe. Raspberry and peach shortcakes may be made in the same way.

PENNY PUDDING.

Beat five eggs very light; mix with five tablespoonsful of flour, one large spoonful of butter, and one pint of milk. Eat with sauce.

DELICIOUS PUDDING.

Beat the yolks of six eggs very light. Stir in alternately three tablespoonsful of flour and a pint of milk. Put a tablespoonful of melted butter and a teaspoonful of salt in the batter; then stir in the whites of the eggs beaten to a stiff froth. Butter the baking dish or cups, fill them a little more than half full, and bake quickly. Eat with some sauce. Make this pudding a half hour before dinner.

AUNT SALLY'S APPLE CUSTARD.

Stew half a dozen sour apples in half a cupful of water. Rub through a sieve and sweeten. Make custard of three pints of milk, six eggs, four tablespoonsful of sugar. Put apples in pudding dish. Pour custard over and bake half an hour.

APPLE CRUMB PUDDING.

Put in a pudding dish a layer of bread crumbs and then a layer of sliced apples. Sift on a little sugar and add a few lumps of butter. Continue so till dish is full, putting crumbs and butter on top. Bake slowly. Sauce.

BAKED APPLE DUMPLING.

Make a good soft biscuit crust and roll out. Cut into pieces, and on each piece place tender sour apples, pared and cored. Fill apples with sugar and spice; cover each apple with the crust. Bake and serve with sugar and cream. *Miss Ann Dabney.*

BAKED CHOCOLATE CUSTARD.

One quart of good milk, six eggs, yolks and whites beaten separately, one cup of sugar, six tablespoonsful of grated chocolate, vanilla flavoring. Bring the milk to a boil, stir in chocolate and simmer a few minutes. Beat yolks and sugar and stir into the milk. Have ready cups set in a pan of boiling water half submerged. Bake slowly twenty minutes. When cold frost with whites and a very little powdered sugar.—*Mrs. Gates Williams.*

SPICE CREAM PIE.

One pint of cream, white of one egg, one tablespoonful of cornstarch dissolved in a little milk. Spices and sugar to taste.—*Centaur Cook Book.*

QUEEN OF PUDDINGS.

One pint of fine bread crumbs, one quart of milk, one cupful of sugar, butter the size of an egg, yolks of four eggs, well beaten, grated rind of one lemon, salt. Bake like custard or until well done, but not watery; then spread over it a layer of jelly or preserves; beat the whites of the four eggs to a stiff froth; add one cup of powdered sugar; spread over jelly, just brown in oven. Cut out in slices when cold. Nice to make Saturday for Sunday dinner.—*Mrs. J. R. Hawley.*

HINGHAM PUDDING.

One cupful of molasses, two-thirds of a cupful of butter or suet, one cupful of water, three cupsful of flour, one cupful of raisins and currants, one teaspoonful of soda; steam three hours. It is as good when two or three weeks old as when fresh; put in and steam when wanted.

LEMON PUDDING.

Two teacupsful of powdered sugar, yolks of six eggs, one cup of sweet milk, three tablespoonsful of corn starch, or grated crackers, grated rind and juice of one lemon. Butter is no improvement. Bake with bottom crusts. Meringue; six tablespoonsful of white sugar and the whites of the six eggs, beaten as for icing. When the pies are baked place the meringue on top and brown a little. To be eaten perfect y cold.—*Mrs. J. W. Baker.*

I. X. L. PUDDING.

Cover the bottom of a well buttered baking dish with a thin layer of bread crumbs, and spread that with small lumps of butter about an inch or two apart, then a layer of finely minced apple, and a layer of sugar thickly sprinkled with ground cinnamon and allspice, letting the cinnamon predominate; then another layer of bread crumbs and butter, and so on till the mould is filled, letting the bread and butter form the top layer. Raisins are a great improvement, but not necessary. If the pan has been well buttered it will turn out nicely. Serve with rich wine sauce. —*Mrs. Haynes.*

DELICIOUS FRITTERS.

Take one quart of water and a piece of butter the size of a hen's egg, boil a few minutes; then stir in flour to make as thick as mashed potatoes; pour this into a bowl and beat six eggs into it, one at a time; add a little salt and nutmeg; then drop in hot lard.

ORANGE FRITTERS.

Remove the peel and seeds from the orange, mince it and sprinkle powdered sugar over; then stir it into common batter, and drop from a spoon into boiling lard.—*Mrs. Fannie Shipp.*

APPLE FRITTERS.

Four large sound apples peeled, cored, and cut into four slices; half a gill of wine, two tablespoonsful of sugar, one teaspoonful extract of nutmeg. Place slices of apple in bowl with sugar, wine and extract; cover with plate, set aside to steep two hours, then dip each slice in common batter, and fry to light brown in hot lard. Serve with sugar.

SUGARED APPLES.

Pare, core and slice your apples thin. Make a thick syrup, and when it is boiling, throw in your apples and cook till clear, but not ready to fall to pieces. A few whole spices will improve the flavor. Dip in common batter and throw them in hot lard. When lightly browned take them out and roll in granulated sugar. Serve hot.—*Mrs. Louisa Keiningham.*

BLACKBERRY FRITTERS.

One cupful of blackberries, one and a half cupsful of common batter. Mix berries in batter in bowl, and drop by tablespoonsful in plenty of hot lard. Serve with sauce. All berry fritters can be made as directed for the above.

SCOTCH PANCAKES.

One pint of milk, two tablespoonsful of butter, four eggs, two-thirds of a cupful of flour, one teaspoonful of baking powder, a pinch of salt. Sift flour, salt, and powder together; add milk, eggs, and butter melted, mix into thin batter. Have a small, round frying pan with a little butter melted in it; pour in a half cupful of batter, turn pan around to cover it with the batter, place on hot fire to brown, then hold it up in front of fire, and the pancake will rise right up. Spread each with marmalade or jelly; roll up, serve with sliced lemon or sugar.

POTATO CUSTARD.

Half a pound of mashed potatoes, sweet or Irish, one-fourth of a pound of butter, half a pound of sugar, three eggs, one teaspoonful of lemon extract. Cream the butter and sugar and add potato, and lastly the eggs well beaten. Any fruit may be substituted for the potato.—*Miss Nettie Kirkpatrick.*

TRANSPARENT PUDDING.

Eight eggs, four tablespoonsful of butter, eight tablespoonsful of sugar. Beat up the eggs, put them in a stewpan with the sugar and butter; season to taste. Set it on the stove and stir it constantly till it thickens; then pour in a bowl to cool. Line your dish with a rich paste, pour the pudd'ng in and bake in a moderate oven.—*Mrs. H. N. Starnes.*

ONE EGG PUDDING.

One egg, one cupful of sugar, one cupful of milk, two cupsful of flour, one tablespoonful of butter, two small teaspoonsful of baking powder. Or you can use sour milk and half a teaspoonful of soda. Serve with sauce.

SPONGE CAKE ROLL.

Five eggs beaten separately, add to the yolks two cupsful of sugar, and one cupful of buttermilk in which has been dissolved half a teaspoonful of soda; then stir in the whites, and lastly two cupsful of sifted flour. Spread quickly with jam or marmalade and roll. Serve with sauce.

SPONGE PUDDING.

One tumblerful of sugar and one of flour, five eggs beaten separately, two tablespoonsful of vinegar, or the juice of one lemon. Beat sugar and yolks together, adding the vinegar or lemon. Stir in the flour and whites alternately, barely mixing. Bake in a quick oven and serve hot with

SAUCE.

A piece of butter the size of an egg, one saucer of sugar, one tumbler nearly full of water. Put in a stew-pan, stir and let it simmer. Beat the yolk of one egg, pour the same slowly upon it, then beat hard. Return to stew-pan and stove to heat. Flavor with a wineglassful of wine. The egg may be omitted.--*Miss Mary Cheek.*

PUDDING WITHOUT MILK OR EGGS.

Put into a buttered baking dish alternate layers of grated bread and finely chopped apples, seasoned with brown sugar, bits of butter, and allspice. Pour over it a pint of wine and water mixed. Let the top layer be bread crumbs, and bake one hour.

ECONOMICAL BREAD PUDDING.

Soak one pound of stale bread in enough milk to make a pudding. When soft beat it up with two eggs, and three tablespoonsful of flour. Pour in a large lump of butter melted. Put in any sort of fruit and boil.

MOLASSES PUDDING.

Nine eggs, four cupsful of molasses, one cupful of butter. Bake in a paste.

MOLASSES PIE.

One teacupful of sugar, one teacupful of molasses, four eggs beaten separately, two tablespoonsful of butter, one teaspoonful of cinnamon, one of mace, half a one of cloves. Bake in a paste and frost.—*Mrs. Boulden.*

GINGER PUDDING.

Three eggs, one-half pint of molasses, one cupful of sugar, one cupful of lard, two tablespoonsful of ginger, one half teaspoonful of soda, or one teaspoonful of baking powder; make into a thick batter, put in a pan, and set in a steamer over a pot of boiling water; when done set in the oven to dry off. Serve with butter sauce.—*Mrs. George Davis in Blue Grass Cook Book.*

THICKENED MILK PUDDING.

One quart of milk; when it boils, stir in enough flour to make it thick like mush; add a piece of butter the size of a hen's egg. When cold add five eggs well beaten. Season to taste. Serve with sauce.

BUTTERMILK PIE.

Take the yolks of four eggs, one teacupful of sugar, one half cupful of flour, a half teaspoonful of soda, two tablespoonsful of butter, one pint of buttermilk. Flavor with nutmeg, lemon, or vanilla. Make a meringue and brown slightly. This quantity makes three pies and they are delicious.

BANANA PIE.

Slice raw bananas, add butter, sugar, allspice and vinegar or boiled cider; bake with two crusts.

VINEGAR PIE.

One egg, one large tablespoonful of flour, one teacupful of sugar. Beat well together; and add one tablespoonful of sharp vinegar, and one teacupful of cold water.

SOUTHERN TOMATO PIE.

For one pie, peel and slice green tomatoes, add four tablespoonsful of vinegar, one of butter, three of sugar. Flavor with nutmeg or cinnamon.

A KENTUCKY GIRL'S PUMPKIN PIE.

Cut pumpkin in halves, remove seeds, bake in a dripping pan, skin-side of pumpkin downward, with a slow fire until the pulp can readily be scraped from the skin. Mash fine, and while hot add to each quart of pumpkin two tablespoonsful of butter; when cold, sweeten to taste; add one pint of cream or new milk, yolks of three eggs well-beaten and strained, cinnamon and allspice to taste, ginger if preferred, one wineglassful of brandy; stir well, and just at the last add whites of eggs well whipped. The brandy may be omitted. Many like a tablespoonful of lemon extract and less spice. If lemon is used, omit brandy. Bake in deep pie plates, in a quick oven.—*Dixie Cook Book*.

RECEIPT OF A FAMOUS N. Y. RESTAURANT PUMPKIN PIE.

Take a large-sized pumpkin, firm, of deep color, wash and boil just as you would with the skin on; when thoroughly cooked, pass carefully through a sieve, clearing it of all lumps, seed, etc. Take one cup of brown sugar, one of molasses, mix well together. Beat well the whites and yolks of four eggs, and mix with the pumpkin; then add the molasses and sugar, a pinch of salt, four teaspoonsful of best ginger, one teaspoonful of ground cinnamon, one cup of milk. This is intended to make six pies. Should the pumpkin not be a large one, add less milk, so as not to get too thin. Bake in paste.

SAUCES FOR PUDDINGS.

COLD BUTTER SAUCE.

Take fresh butter just from the churn, salt it lightly, and cream it. To a cupful, add granulated sugar until it is thick. Cover, bake dumplings with it or spread it on cake, and grate orange peel or nutmeg over.—*Mrs. E. R. Tennent.*

CUSTARD SAUCE.

Take a pint of fresh milk and sweeten to taste. Beat three eggs light and stir in. When it comes to a boil add three teaspoonsful of cornstarch rubbed smooth in a little milk. Add, lastly, a dessert spoonful of butter, creamed and then flavor as you like.—*Miss Kate Bowie.*

COCOANUT SAUCE.

Two tablespoonsful of butter, a cup of sugar, a tablespoonful of flour, milk of one cocoanut with a small piece grated.

MOLASSES SAUCE.

Boil a pint of molasses and add three eggs well beaten. Boil a few minutes longer and season with nutmeg and lemon.

RICH SAUCE FOR PUDDINGS.

One pint of cream, half a pound of sugar, one tablespoonful of butter, one glass of wine. Spices to taste. Do not cook.

CHOCOLATE SAUCE.

Take a pint of fresh milk; sweeten to taste and add three well beaten eggs. When it comes to a boil, stir in a little cornstarch rubbed smooth in milk, four tablespoonsful of grated chocolate, and a teaspoonful of vanilla.—*Mrs. J. D. Chamberlain.*

Jamaica ginger flavors sauces very nicely. It does not discolor like powdered ginger and is stronger and better flavored.

STRAWBERRY SAUCE.

Take a cupful of strawberry preserves and mash into a perfect jelly. Make a sauce of a pint of cream, and a tablespoonful of butter thickened with cornstarch. Add the mashed strawberries and a little more sugar if needed. Grate nutmeg over.

WINE SAUCE.

One half pound of butter, yolks of two eggs beaten well and creamed with the butter; nine tablespoonsful of brown sugar, two glasses of wine. Let it simmer a short time and grate nutmeg over.

COLD SAUCE.

Whites of five eggs beaten to a stiff froth; sweeten to taste. Pour in some hot melted butter, stirring well. Flavor to taste.—*Miss Fannie Foster.*

PLAIN CREAM SAUCE.

One pint of cream, three tablespoonsful of brown sugar, and half a small nutmeg grated.

SAUCE.

Take a pint of boiling water and add a cupful of sugar and a tablespoonful of butter. Boil until clear. It is very much improved by adding a tablespoonful of any kind of jelly diluted with warm water and stirred in. Or add two tablespoonsful of strong cider vinegar.

SAUCE.

Take a half cupful of butter, two cupsful of sugar; mix well, add three-fourths of a cup of sweet cream, one tea-

spoonful of baking powder. Flavor with extract of lemon.
—*Mrs. McLelland.*

WINE SAUCE.

Take one and one half cupsful of butter, one and one-half cupsful of jelly, two-thirds of a cupful of port wine, one teaspoonful of allspice, two tablespoonsful of sugar. Stir until thick.

QUINCE SAUCE.

Set a glass of quince jelly near the fire until it becomes soft. Then beat it well with a very little warm water and add to a cupful of hot cream.—M*rs. Bettie Downey.*

MAPLE SUGAR SAUCE.

Melt over a slow fire in a small teacupful of water half a pint of maple sugar; let it simmer, removing all scum; add four tablespoonsful of butter mixed with a teaspoonful of flour and one of grated nutmeg.—*Dixie Cook Book.*

SAUCE FOR PUDDING.

Take half a cupful of butter, two cupsful of sugar, mix well together; one half cupful of sweet cream, one teaspoonful of Royal baking powder. Beat very hard and flavor with lemon extract or vanilla.

SWEETENED CREAM SAUCE.

One pint of cream, four tablespoonsful of sugar. Flavor.

GERMAN CUSTARD SAUCE.

Four eggs, yolks only, two ounces of powdered sugar, grated rind of a lemon, a glass of sherry and a little salt. Beat sharply over a slow fire until it assumes a light, frothy appearance.

ACID SAUCE.

One cup of sugar, one tablespoonful of cornstarch, one half teaspoonful of tartaric acid, one half cupful of water.

Mix cornstarch dry, with sugar to prevent lumping. Flavor if you choose.

GOOD PUDDING SAUCE.

One cup of sugar, one half cup of butter, stirred to a cream. Add one well beaten egg; beat all together. Add grated rind and juice of one lemon.

FANCY DESSERTS

ANGEL'S FOOD.

Take one box of Cox's gelatine; pour over it one pint of cold water; when thoroughly dissolved add a quart of hot water. Sweeten to taste, add stick cinnamon, whole cloves, and the juice of two lemons. Boil rapidly, pouring on the frothed white of an egg to gather up the impurities. Throw away, and then strain the jelly through a thick flannel bag. Add a half pint of best whisky or brandy. When about to congeal stir in a thick sweet cream frothed.—*Mrs. E. J. Ogden.*

BLANC MANGE. (Superior.)

To one quart of new milk add the beaten yolks of four eggs; sweeten to taste, and when it begins to boil stir in six even tablespoonsful of cornstarch rubbed smooth in a little milk. Stir constantly till it thickens, then pour into cups previously dipped in cold water. When cold turn out in a deep glass bowl. The custard to pour over is made just the same, only add three tablespoonsful of cornstarch instead of six. The blanc-mange and custard may be flavored with vanilla or almonds blanched and grated; essence of nutmeg and whisky also flavors it delightfully.—*Miss Peachie McGill.*

STRAWBERRY FLOAT.

Mash a quart of strawberries into a jelly. Sweeten to taste and add the frothed whites of six eggs. Serve with cream. This way of serving comes in nicely at the close of the season when the berries are small and do not look tempting when whole.—*Mrs. G. Pollock.*

AMBROSIA.

Grate one cocoanut—the white part only; sweeten to taste and place part of it in a glass bowl. Put in alternate layers of pulped orange and pineapple. Sprinkle sugar between each layer. Put a layer of cocoanut on top.—*Mrs. C. R. Upson.*

SYLLABUB.

One quart of cream, one gill of wine, juice of two lemons, or one teaspoonful extract of lemon, whites of six eggs; sugar to taste. Whip to a froth in a syllabub churn. Serve in glasses.—*Mrs. C. R. Upson.*

CHARLESTON SNOWBALLS.

Put quarter of a pound of rice in six gills of milk, with two ounces of sweet blanched almonds, two ounces of white sugar and a little salt. Boil till rice is tender. Put into small cups wet with cold water. When rice is cold turn out upon a dish in a circle. Make a border of rich preserves or jelly and pour a little cream into centre of circle.—*American Cookery.*

RICE CREAM.

One and a half pints of milk, three eggs, salt, a little corn starch. Flavor and sweeten to taste. Make like custard; and when done put in boiled rice.—*Mrs. Tuttle.*

PEACH JELLY.

Make a gelatine jelly and when it begins to congeal, stir in canned peaches, with the juice drained off.

COFFEE CUSTARD.

One pint of strong coffee, one pint of milk, boil together; six eggs beaten with one and a half cups of sugar. Serve with cake.—*Mrs. F. Perry.*

NORWEGIAN CUSTARD.

One cupful of cream, a half cupful of water, four eggs, two tablespoonsful of gelatine, four tablespoonsful of pulverized sugar, two tablespoonsful of wine. Dissolve the gelatine in the water, beat the yolks and sugar together, add the wine, beaten whites, and cream well whipped; then add the strained gelatine. Set to harden and serve with cream.—*Mrs. James Wallace.*

ORANGE FLOAT.

Make a custard of two cupsful of milk, yolks of four eggs, four tablespoonsful of white sugar and set aside to cool. Take the juice of two oranges and the rind of one, strain over two tablespoonsful of gelatine, and one cupful of sugar. Pour gently over this one pint of boiling water; stir until dissolved and set aside to cool. Beat the four whites stiff and stir into this one spoonful at a time. Put the grated rind into the custard, put into a glass bowl and heap the float upon it. It requires a good deal of beating.—*Mrs. Allen Bashford.*

VIENNA CREAM.

The whites of five eggs, five ounces of red currant jelly, five ounces of raspberry jelly, and two and a half ounces of sifted icing sugar. Put all into a bowl and beat until it rises into a stiff froth.—*Mrs Allen Bashford.*

LEMON JELLY.

Two large lemons, three teacupsful of sugar, four cupsful of water, five tablespoonsful of cornstarch, six eggs; slice the lemons and put them in the water; let them boil till the strength is extracted; then dip them out and strain the water; beat the yellows, butter and sugar together, and pour the water over them. Return to the fire, and when ready to boil stir in the starch. Beat the whites to a stiff froth and stir in lightly after it is taken from the stove.—*Miss Belle Croxton, in Blue Grass Cook Book.*

BOILED CUSTARD.

To every teacupful of milk add a tablespoonful of sugar, and one egg to every three cupsful of milk. Stir the sugar into the milk, put it on the fire and let it come to a boil, then pour it on the eggs, which must be well beaten; return it to the kettle and stir unt l thick enough. For every six cups of milk take a tab'espoonful of cornstarch and dissolve it thoroughly in a cupful of the unboiled milk, which add to the eggs before you pour on the hot milk. In warm weather the sugar may be left out until the custard is made; this prevents curdling. This makes nice ice cream. —*Mrs. H. N. Starnes.*

CHARLOTTE RUSSE.

Line a plain mould with sponge cake. Beat up one pint of cream with half a box of gelatine previously dissolved in milk enough to cover it, whites of five eggs, well beaten; put in the cream and stir until it begins to cool; then pour it in the mould. Flavor with vanilla and sweeten to taste. —*Miss Eddie Singer.*

CHARLOTTE RUSSE.

Yolks of four eggs, mix with one-fourth of a pound of fine white sugar; add a half pint of new milk; let it thicken, but not boil over the fire. Then add a half pint of very stiff, calfs foot jelly; strain all through a cloth. Set on the ice a dish containing one pint of very rich cream; whip it until it looks like a float; set aside, and put the custard on the ice, and stir with a paddle until it thickens. Add the cream very lightly. The mixture should look like sponge cake before it is baked. Put lady fingers in a deep dish, laying them closely around the edge and in the bottom. Pour the charlotte over it, and place on ice till wanted. It should retain the shape of the dish.—*Lyman's Housekeeping.*

A SIMPLE CHARLOTTE RUSSE.

Make a custard of one quart of milk, the yolks of four eggs, sweeten and flavor to taste. When it has boiled up, add a heaping teaspoonful of cornstarch rubbed smooth in a little milk. Boil half a box of Cox's gelatine in a pint of water. It is best to dissolve it thoroughly in enough water to cover before boiling. When both the gelatine and custard are cool stir the former into the latter. Set in a cool place, or on ice, and when ready to use stir into this mixture a pint or more of rich frothed cream. The juice of the orange, vanilla or extract of nutmeg are the best flavorings for Charlotte Russe.

JELLY CUSTARD

Fill the glasses two-thirds full of custard, and then heap up red raspberry and orange jelly alternately till glass is full.

ORANGE SOUFFLE.

One pint of milk, five eggs, one-fourth of a cup of granulated sugar, three tablespoonsful of powdered sugar, five Florida oranges, and a speck of salt. Put on the milk to boil. Beat yolks of five eggs and whites of two with the granulated sugar. Pour the milk gradually over this, stirring. Return to sauce pan, place in a basin of boiling water and stir till it begins to thicken. This will be about two minutes. Salt and set away to cool. Pare oranges, remove the seeds, cut fine and place in a glass dish. Pour on the cold custard. Frost with the remaining three whites and the powdered sugar.—*Miss Parloa.*

BAKED APPLES AND CREAM.

Remove the core from fair apples, fill with sugar, bake, and serve hot with cream.

CHOCOLATE CREAM.

Half a cup of grated chocolate, one cup of water. Boil together. Add one cup of sweet milk, and boil one heaping teaspoonful of cornstarch dissolved in a little milk; sweeten and flavor with vanilla.

RICE SNOW BALLS.

Boil one pint of rice in two quarts of water, with one teaspoonful of salt. Put into cups, and when perfectly cold turn them carefully into a deep dish. Make a custard of the yolks of three eggs, one pint of milk, one teaspoonful of corn starch, flavor; when cold pour over balls.—*Mrs. G. P. Fesenden.*

APPLE SNOW.

Boil six large apples pared and sliced in enough water to cover. Press through a sieve and sweeten. Do not add the sugar while cooking, as it hardens the fruit. Add half a grated nutmeg, half a teaspoonful of cinnamon, half a teaspoonful of mace and a pinch of ground cloves. Beat all thoroughly and stir in the frothed whites of four eggs. Serve with rich cream. The spices may be omitted.

ANOTHER APPLE SNOW.

Peel, core, and quarter a dozen Spitzenburg apples, and stew them gently with a cup of water, white sugar to sweeten, and a little cinnamon; when reduced nearly to a pulp, turn into a dish. Make a soft custard of a quart of milk, the yolks of four eggs, a little sugar, and extract of lemon. When it is cold lay it over the apples, and whip up the whites of the eggs with a quarter of a pound of sugar and heap lightly on the top.—*Mrs. Allie DeBard.*

SNOW PUDDING.

Dissolve one ounce of gelatine in one pint of water, beat up the whites of six eggs and after the gelatine has thor—

oughly dissolved, pour on it one pint of boiling water; then stir in one pound of sugar and the juice of four lemons; beat all together until it begins to thicken; then pour into a bowl; afterwards serve with sweetened cream seasoned with wine and nutmeg.—*Mrs. Dr. Powell.*

SNOW CREAM.

Whites of two eggs, one cupful of sugar, one cupful of fruit of any kind, oranges, peaches, or sour apples. Beat till smooth and stiff.—*Mrs. F. M. Stevens.*

FRUIT DESSERT.

Slice bananas and oranges; mix with chopped pineapple. Scatter powdered sugar over all.

CHOCOLATE CUSTARD.

One quart of milk, three ounces of chocolate. Boil together till thoroughly mixed. Let cool. Add four well beaten eggs. Sweeten and flavor to taste.—*Mrs. Winslow's Cook Book.*

DAINTY DESSERT.

Grate a fresh cocoanut; beat the whites of five eggs to a stiff froth. Add two large spoonsful of sugar and a pint of thick sweet cream. Beat all together till very light. Serve with cake and berries.

TAPIOCA AND FRUIT.

Soak one cupful of tapioca over night. In the morning cook in water till clear; sweeten and salt. Put a layer of any fruit, oranges, peaches, or berries in a dish, then a layer of tapioca, and so on till dish is full.—*Miss Osborn.*

CREAM PEACH DESSERT.

Whip one pint of cream to which a half cupful of sugar has been added. Take from six to twelve ripe peaches, pare and mash fine with a silver fork. Add one cupful of sugar and stir till it is dissolved. Dissolve half a box of gelatine in one cupful of water and strain into the fruit. Stir well and beat all into the whipped cream. Pour into moulds which have been dipped into cold water. Set in a cool place till next day. A grated pine apple can be used in place of the peaches.—*Mrs. Douglas.*

ORANGE JELLY BASKETS.

Take six oranges, cut the skin in such a manner as to form a round basket with a handle; cut notches in edge of basket for ornaments, carefully remove the pulp. For jelly, take half a box of gelatine, two cups of sugar, one cup of orange juice. Pour over this one and a half pints boiling water, boil till thoroughly dissolved, and fill baskets when cool. Set on ice.—*Capital City Club Restaurant.*

ECLAIR CUSTARD.

Line a deep bowl with stale sponge cake, partially saturate it with wine, pour on a rich custard, and put frothed whites on top.

COCOANUT CREAM. (NEW.)

Put one quart of new milk sweetened in a porcelain-lined kettle, let it come to a boil, grate one cocoanut and stir into the milk. Have six eggs beaten separately and then together, and a small piece of butter, all of which stir into the boiling milk; rub one tablespoonful of cornstarch, smooth in a little milk, and add to the custard just before pouring up.—*Mrs. Geo. J. Gable.*

GELATINE JELLY.

Take one package of Cox's gelatine and dissolve it in a pint of cold water; then add a quart of hot water, brown sugar to taste, lemon juice, stick cinnamon, mace and cloves tied in a bag; ginger also, if liked, and half a grated nutmeg. When it has boiled twenty minutes, strain several times through a thick flannel bag, and add half a pint of red wine. Set on ice to congeal.—*Mrs. Mary Duncan.*

GELATINE JELLY.

Soak one box of Cox's gelatine in a pint of cold water three hours, then add one pint of cooking wine, the rind and juice of one lemon, two pounds of white sugar, a little mace; stir these ingredients till the sugar dissolves, then add two quarts of boiling water, gently stirring till mixed, strain through a flannel bag twice. This is the best jelly I ever saw.—*Mrs. M. M. Dame.*

RASPBERRY FLOAT.

Crush a pint of ripe red raspberries with a gill of sugar; beat the whites of four eggs to a stiff froth, and add gradually a gill of powdered sugar; press the raspberries through a fine sieve to avoid the seeds, and by degrees beat in the juice with the eggs and sugar until so stiff it stands alone. —*Atlanta Constitution.*

MOONSHINE.

Take the whites of six eggs beaten to a stiff froth, stir in well six tablespoonsful of sugar, and one glassful of jelly. To be eaten with sweetened cream, flavored with vanilla.— *Miss Mary Hudnet.*

GATEAU DE POMMES.

Make a rich syrup of one and a half pounds of sugar with a pint of water. Two pounds of apples pared, cored and cut in small pieces. Boil them in the syrup with the juice and grate of a lemon till they are reduced to a smooth pulp. Pour into a mould; when cold turn out and serve with custard.—*Augusta Cook Book.*

COFFEE JELLY.

One pint of cold water, one package of gelatine, one quart of strong dripped coffee. Pour the water on the jelly, let it remain fifteen minutes, then pour on the boiling coffee; sweeten to taste then strain.

TIPSY SQUIRE.

Saturate with sherry wine a thin sponge cake. Ornament with blanched almonds, sticking them in with the points upwards and tastily arranged. Half fill a large glass bowl with good boiled custard, and carefully place the cake on top of the custard, taking care that the bowl used is of a circumference somewhat larger than that of the cake.—*Mrs. Hill.*

ANGEL'S FOOD.

Make a rich custard, pour into a bowl, put a layer of sliced cake on it; stir powdered sugar into quince jelly and drop it on the cake; then pour syllabub on the cake, and put on another layer of cake and jelly, and so on.—*Mrs. Albin Gilbert.*

ORANGE CREAM.

Half dozen oranges. Grate the peel into a pint and a half of hot water. Beat four eggs and add to the water. Sweeten, strain, and simmer till it becomes the consistency of cream. Serve with cake.

DELICIOUS BERRY DESSERT.

Whip one pint of cream to which half a cup of sugar has been added. Mash one pint of strawberries or raspberries very fine. Add one cup of sugar, and stir till dissolved. Dissolve half a box of gelatine in half a cup of water and strain into the fruit. Stir well and beat into the whipped cream. Pour into moulds which have been dipped into cold water and place where it will be cold till next day.—*Mrs. Douglas.*

COFFEE CUSTARD.

One pint of strong coffee, one pint of milk. Boil together; six eggs beaten with one and a half cups of sugar. serve with cake.—*Mrs. F. Perry.*

QUINCE DESSERT.

Use canned quinces or peel, slice, and stew quinces till they are very soft, strain through a colander. Sweeten them well and put them into a berry dish. While the quinces are cooling, make a custard of one pint of milk, yolks of three eggs, half a cup of sugar; let it cool and pour over the quinces. Make a meringue of the whites of three eggs, and into it beat a half cup of powdered sugar. Spread smoothly over the custard. Serve cold.—*Mrs. Ellis.*

FLOATING ISLANDS.

One quart of milk, five eggs, save out two whites for islands; five tablespoonsful of sugar; flavor; boil. Beat the two whites to a stiff froth. Slip over a pan of boiling water for an instant. Take off with a skimmer, and when cold put on custard for islands.—*New Haven Cook Book.*

FRUIT CREAM.

Mash ripe raspberries, or strawberries to a soft pulp, strain through a sieve and stir in thick sweet cream. Serve in goblets.

VELVET CREAM.

Place in a dish three tablespoonsful of orange or lemon juice, a little grated peel, a little marmalade chopped fine, and two spoonsful of strong whisky, brandy or wine. Place a pint of cream over the fire and dissolve a little sugar in it. Take from fire and keep stirring till about the warmth of new milk; strain through a fine colander upon the above mixture. Let it stand over night before serving.—*Mrs. Dr. Jas. Greer.*

BIRD EGG'S NEST.

Pare and core medium sized tart apples, leaving them whole, stick cloves into them; bake until they begin to soften, then fill each hollow with the white of an egg beaten stiff, sweetened a little and flavored. Return to oven. Do not bake so long as to lose form.—*Diamond Cook Book.*

RICE CUSTARD.

One pint of milk, half a pint of cream, one ounce of sifted ground rice, five or six bitter almonds, blanched and pounded, two tablespoonsful of rose water. Mix well, sweeten to taste, and stir well over the fire till it nearly boils. Add well beaten yolks of three eggs, stir and let it simmer for a minute. Serve in cups with powdered sugar on top.

CHARLOTTE RUSSE.

Take a box of Cox's gelatine, dissolve in one quart of cold water, boil and strain. Add half of it to a half gallon of rich custard and pour in a bowl, then take the whites of three eggs, beat to a stiff froth and beat in sugar till it looks like icing, then add a quart of frothed cream and the other half of the gelatine. Place this on top of the custard. Flavor both portions with wine, vanilla or lemon extract.—*Mrs. B. W. Wrenn.*

GELATINE JELLY.

Dissolve a box of Cox's gelatine in a pint of cold water, add the juice of six lemons, one pint of boiling water, and sugar till very sweet. Do not boil, but after sitting three hours, strain through a flannel bag and add a half a pint of best sherry wine. Do not use spices. This makes jelly as clear and sparkling as calves' foot and as good.—*Mrs. James Metcalfe.*

JELLIED APPLES.

Make a thick syrup and add to it a sliced lemon with seeds removed, throw in peeled and sliced apples and boil till tender. Remove to a deep dish, add a half a box of gelatine which has been dissolved in water, to the syrup, boil a few minutes, remove the lemon and pour over the apples. Set in a cool place to congeal.—*Mrs. Dana Bean.*

PEACH PYRAMID.

Cut a dozen fine peaches in halves, peel, take out the stones, crack half the seed and take out the kernel and blanch; make a clear boiling syrup of one pound of white sugar, and into it put the peaches and kernels; boil very gently for ten minutes, take out half the peaches, boil the rest for ten minutes longer and take out all the peaches and kernels; mix with the syrup left in the kettle, the strained juice of three lemons and one ounce of isinglass dissolved in a little water and strained; boil up once, fill a mould half full of this syrup or jelly, let it stand until "set," add part of the peaches and a little more jelly, and when this is "set" add the rest of the peaches and fill up the mould with jelly. This is a beautiful dish.

ORANGE CHARLOTTE.

Line a deep dish with sponge cake, then cut up enough oranges to fill the dish; cut them in thin slices, sprinkle sugar over them, pour a rich boiled custard over all, let it stand long enough to moisten the cake.—*Catholic Herald.*

 FRUITS.

A SHOWY FRUIT PIECE.

Take a watermelon and cut a slice off one end, so it will sit firmly on a waiter; then cut the other end in points; from each point suspend a large bunch of grapes; on top place a large ripe pear with the leaves; around the melon place small red apples, oranges, pears, plums, or any other fruit in season —*Mitchell House, Thomasville.*

HOW TO SERVE STRAWBERRIES.

It is a bad plan to let the berries lie in water while you are capping. They are softened and much of the flavor is lost. Either rinse and drain off the water, or dip them a few at a time in water. Some like to sprinkle sugar over at table, others prefer to let them lie in sugar, an hour or two before. It is now fashionable in New York hotels to bring them to table with caps on; to be dipped in grated loaf sugar.

TO PEEL PEACHES.

In peeling small peaches with a knife too much of the peach is wasted; but by having a wire cage similar to those made for popping corn, this waste is obviated. Fill the cage with peaches and dip it into boiling water for a moment; then into cold water for a moment, and empty out,—going on in the same way for all you wish to use. This toughens the skin and enables you to strip it off, saving much in labor as also the waste of the peach.—*Youman's Dictionary.*

TO SEED DAMSONS OR BLUE PLUMS.

Many persons find it very difficult to seed this fruit. With a sharp pen knife cut a slit lengthwise in each damson and set in the sun for an hour or two when the seed slips out without trouble.

Always allow a few of the leaves of any kind of fruit to remain when it is arranged for the table.

No painstaking hostess will ever place nuts on her table without plenty of nut crackers.

A finger bowl should be in reach of each person, or passed to them after partaking of fruit.

JELLIES.

In making jellies, the flavor and color of the fruit is best retained by boiling the juice quite a while before adding the sugar. In making jelly of sweet fruits a little tartaric acid added while cooking causes it to jelly quickly. Fit white paper dipped in brandy or whisky over the top to protect from mould.

APPLE JELLY.

Let your apples be pared and cored; put them in a preserving kettle with enough water to cover, boil them quickly until quite tender, strain them through a colander, then through a sieve, and lastly through a flannel bag. To every pint of juice, put a pound of loaf sugar with a little lemon juice and peel. Boil gently until jellied, which will be in an hour. Take off and put in glasses when hot.—*Mrs. H. N. Starnes.*

QUINCE JELLY.

Make the same as apple jelly, only do not pare or core the fruit. Very nice quince jelly is made from the parings and cores; or, you can boil the parings and cores in a very little water, and add it to apple juice and then proceed as usual.

CURRANT JELLY.

Gather the currants when just ripe, pick them carefully from the stem, press them thoroughly with the hands and strain without pressing through a flannel bag. One pound of sugar to one pint of juice. Put the juice in a kettle and let it almost come to a boil; skim several times, and then put in the sugar. Boil rapidly a few minutes. This makes the fairest jelly, but the quantity is not so great as when the currants are heated before straining.—*Mrs. Martin, in Blue Grass Cook Book.*

CURRANT JELLY WITHOUT COOKING.

Press the juice from the currants and strain it. To one pint of juice put one pound of white sugar, mix together until the sugar is dissolved, then put in jars, and seal them and expose them to a hot sun two or three days.—*Mrs. Dr. Bellamy.*

REMEDY FOR MOULDING IN JELLIES.

Fruit jellies may be preserved from moulding by covering the surface a quarter of an inch thick with finely pulverized white sugar. Thus protected they will keep for years.—*Mrs Meredith.*

VINEGAR JELLY. (NEW.)

To each pint of the purest cider vinegar add a pound of sugar, tie up a little stick cinnamon, cloves, and allspice in a bag and boil with it. When jellied pour into glasses. An excellent jelly for fowls.—*Mrs. Tennent.*

CRANBERRY JELLY.

Cover the fruit with water, and when it has boiled till soft, remove to a sieve and let the juice run through, but do not press it. Strain again through a flannel bag, and take a pound of sugar to a pint of juice.

BLACKBERRY JELLY.

Boil and strain the juice. To a quart of juice put a pound of sugar and boil till jellied.—*Mrs. H. N. Starnes.*

PEACH JELLY.

Pare, core and slice your peaches, cover them with water and add one-third of the peach kernels bruised, strain and take one pound of sugar to a pint of juice, and also the juice of one lemon. Let it boil twenty minutes before adding the sugar, which should be heated very hot. When it comes again to a boil remove.—*Mis Eva Moore.*

FOUR FRUIT JELLY.

Take equal quantities of ripe strawberries, raspberries, currants and red cherries. All should be fully ripe and the cherries must be stoned, taking care to preserve the juice that escapes in stoning and add it to the rest. Mix the fruit together, put it into a linen bag and squeeze it thoroughly; when it has ceased to drip, measure, and to every pint allow a pound and two ounces of the best loaf sugar. Mix the juice and sugar together, put them in a porcelain-lined preserving kettle and boil for half an hour, skimming frequently.—*Dixie Cook Book.*

GRAPE JELLY.

Put the fruit, previously washed, in a preserving kettle and let boil fifteen minutes. Pour into a jelly bag of flannel, and let the juice drip, but do not squeeze. Put a pint of sugar to a pint of juice and just before it is done add a teaspoonful of gum arabic.

CALVES' FEET JELLY.

Boil two calves' feet well cleaned in a gallon of water till reduced to a quart; then pour into a pan. When cold, skim off all fat, take jelly up clean, leave settlings at the bottom. Put jelly into sauce pan with pint of white wine, a half pound of loaf sugar, and juice of four lemons. Add the whites of six eggs well beaten; stir all well together, put on fire and let boil about fifteen minutes without stirring. Pour into a flannel bag and repeat straining till it runs clear.

CRAB APPLE JELLY.

Boil apples with just enough water to cover until they are tender. Mash with spoon and strain out juice. Take a pound of sugar to a pint of juice.—*Mrs. Kate Alexander*.

PRESERVES.

IF you wish to retain the color of the fruit use granulated or loaf sugar. Some persons do not care for fair or light colored preserves, in which case they may be made with brown sugar by dissolving in water, boiling and skimming well. Use an iron kettle porcelain-lined. It is better to cook but few preserves at a time. Do not have too fierce a fire. Stir them as little as possible, so as to prevent breaking the fruit. It is expensive to put preserves in air-tight cans. If you cannot afford this luxury, buy half gallon and gallon stone jars. If you wish to keep some time, tie over several layers of thick paper and paste to the jar securely. Label each jar with the kind of preserves and date of making. This will save endless confusion when they are needed for use.

MRS. TENNENT'S PREMIUM PEAR PRESERVES..

Take fine large pears, peel them very carefully, leave the stems on and drop them in a bucket of cold water. Take a pound of sugar to a pound of fruit. Put the fruit in a steamer over a vessel of boiling water and let it remain till tender. Put just enough water on the sugar to dissolve it, and when it has boiled twenty minutes add the pears, and set where it will keep very hot but not boil for three hours. Remove the pears to a dish and set in the sun for an hour. Then fill the jars with the fruit, strain the syrup through a flannel bag and pour over.

PEACH PRESERVES.

Pare clingstone peaches, halve them, take out the seeds and throw into cold water. Take a pound of sugar to a pound of fruit. Cover the seeds with water, and when they have boiled twenty minutes pour this water on the sugar. When the syrup is thick, add the peaches and cook till clear.—*The Shakers, Mercer County, Ky.*

STRAWBERRY PRESERVES.

Take a pound and a quarter of sugar to a pound of fruit. Pour over the sugar enough water to dissolve, and when it is boiling hot pour over the fruit and let it stand all night. The next morning pour off the juice, cook till thick, and then add the berries. When done, remove with a perforated skimmer, put into the jars; cook the syrup a little longer and pour over.—*Miss Lizzie Hale.*

Preserves made as above took premium at Macon Fair.

APPLE PRESERVES.

Pare and core your apples, and take a pound of sugar to a pound of fruit. Put the fruit in a steamer and let remain till tender. Then drop in the boiling syrup, to which raw ginger and lemon peel has been added.—*Mrs. Charles Redmon.*

Apple preserves made as above have taken the premium five years in succession at Bourbon Fair.

WATERMELON RIND PRESERVES.

Cut the rind into squares, stars, leaves, half moons, horse shoes or any shape you may fancy. Cover with water and boil till tender. Remove and add to the water as many pounds of sugar as there are pounds of fruit. Boil till thick replace melon, and add ginger.—*Miss Sallie Parrott.*

CHERRY PRESERVES.

Take a pound of sugar to a pound of fruit. Pour sugar over and let remain all night. Next day boil till thick. Leave in a few seeds.

FIG PRESERVES.

Let them lie all night in very weak salt water. Draw off the salt water in the morning; gash them across the top, and cover with fresh water. Make a syrup of three fourths of a pound of sugar to a pound of fruit. When it boils drop in the figs, a little ginger, and lemon peel. Cook till clear.—*Mrs. Dr. Cortelyou.*

FOX GRAPE PRESERVES.

Seed the grapes, then pour scalding water on them and let them stand till cold, then draw off the water. Put one pound of sugar to one pound of grapes, and boil gently about twenty minutes.

PEACH PRESERVES.

To fifteen pounds of clingstone peaches take seven and one half pounds of sugar; put two or three quarts of water in a bottle with one teaspoonful of pearlash; let it dissolve thoroughly. When the water is hot, throw a few peaches in this preparation; let them remain a few minutes. When taken out with a coarse towel wipe off the skins and throw them into cold water. To half the sugar, with as little water as possible to dissolve it, add a layer of peaches, and let boil from twenty to thirty minutes; then take them out and put on a flat dish to cool; gradually add the rest of the sugar. When all are done, boil the syrup till it becomes rather thick; add while in the kettle one half pint of alcohol. Put the peaches in jars, but do not cover till next day. In preserving peaches it is better not to peel them. Leave the seed in by all means.—*Miss Ellen Mitchell, in Blue Grass Cook Book.*

TO PRESERVE GREEN PEACHES.

Pare your peaches very thin and throw them into cold water; then take peach leaves and lay them in your kettle a layer of peaches, and a layer of leaves. When all are in, cover them with water, and cover the kettle. Let them cook very slowly until they are soft; then put them on dishes to cool. Put three-fourths of a pound of sugar to a pound of fruit; take some of the water in which they were scalded and make a thick syrup; let it boil up and skim it well; take off your syrup and when it is almost cold put in the peaches and let them cook slowly until done.—*Mrs. Martha Berrien Duncan.*

BRANDY PEACHES.

To one pound of fruit put one pound of sugar and a little water. Let the fruit boil until you can pierce with a straw; then put in the jars. Let the syrup boil until quite thick. Fill your jars half full of syrup and fill with brandy.—*Mrs. H. N. Starnes.*

BRANDY PEACHES.

Lay your peaches in a weak solution of soda and water until the furze can be easily rubbed off with a towel. To each pound of peaches allow a pound of loaf sugar. Place a layer of peaches in the jar, then a layer of sugar. Pour in the best white brandy. Set the jars in a flat bottomed kettle of cold water; let it remain until the peaches boil; then seal and keep in a dark closet.—*Mrs. Fannie Shipp.*

QUINCE PRESERVES.

Wipe the quinces off nicely, cover with water and parboil, then peel and core them and take a pound of sugar to a pound of fruit. Dissolve the sugar in the water the quinces were boiled in, and when it becomes thick, add the quinces and boil till tender—or, you can pare and core the fruit. Pour the sugar over and let remain over night. Next day cook till done.—*Mrs. Ed Guerrant.*

DAMSON, OR BLUE PLUM PRESERVES.

Make a slit in each damson lengthwise, lay them in the sun until the seeds come out easily, then take a pound of sugar to a pound of fruit, pour over and let remain all night. Next day pour off the juice, boil till thick, and add the fruit. Cook quite low.—*Mrs. Dr. Gibert.*

Raspberry, gooseberry and blackberry preserves should have a pound of sugar to a pound of fruit. Cook well.

CUCUMBER PRESERVES.

Take small fresh cucumbers and lay them in strong brine for four or five days, wash them, soak in clear water for a day, changing the water several times. Green them as for pickles, omitting the vinegar, being careful not to let them boil. When a nice green, drop them into ice-water; when perfectly cold make a slit in one side, and carefully take out the seed, filling them with chopped raisins and citron; sew them up closely with a thread, weigh them, and to every pound allow one pound of sugar. Dissolve the sugar with one pint of cold water, boil it quickly, skim closely, and drop in the cucumbers, boil slowly for half an hour, and lay them on a dish in the sun; boil the syrup until quite thick, adding a few slices of ginger and drop the cucumbers into the syrup again for a few moments. Put into glass, sealing when cold.—*Kentucky Home Cook Book.*

GRAPE PRESERVES.

Pulp the grapes and simmer the pulps in a preserving kettle, press through a sieve and add the skins. Allow a pound of sugar to a pound of fruit as weighed in the beginning, then stir all together. Boil thick as jelly.

GINGER PRESERVES.

For two weeks put the ginger every night and morning in fresh boiling water, take off the outside skin with a sharp knife; boil it in water until quite tender, slice it thin, prepare a syrup of one pound of sugar to half a pint of water, clarify it and then put the ginger into it. Boil it until it is clear.

TOMATO PRESERVES.

The day before preserving, peel and weigh eight pounds pale yellow, pear shaped or round tomatoes, not quite ripe, spread on dishes alternate layers of tomato and sugar, mixing with the latter the grated rind and juice of four lemons. In the morning, drain off the juice and boil to a thick syrup, drop in half the tomatoes and boil till transparent. Take up with a perforated spoon and put on dishes to cool, then carry the other half through exactly the same process, then strain the juice, wash the kettle and put in the juice again. When it boils hard, put in again the first boiled tomatoes, take them out when they become amber color and put in the rest. When they are all boiled to an amber color, and cooled on dishes, put them in half gallon glass jars, add the juice after it has been boiled to a thick jelly.—*Marion Cabell Tyree.*

CANDIED FRUIT.

Preserve the fruit, then dip into syrup boiled to a candied thickness and dry it. Grapes and some other fruits may be dipped in uncooked.

HONEY.

Four pounds of white sugar, one pint of water, one teaspoonful of alum, one teaspoonful of alcohol, and one and one-half drops of oil of roses. Boil until all are dissolved.—*Miss Kate Spears in Blue Grass Cook Book.*

TO PRESERVE ORANGE PEEL.

Squeeze the juice and make a syrup of it; soak the peel in fresh water, change the water twice a day as long as the water is bitter. Boil in water till a straw can penetrate it, then take a pound of sugar to a pound of peel.

APPLE DEVIL.

Peel and core about thirty good baking apples; slice them into a little cold water; add equal weight of lump or crushed sugar, the juice and peel of two lemons cut thin, two ounces of finely grated ginger, and one teaspoonful of cayenne pepper. Boil all together until the apples look quite clear. This will keep good for two or three years. It is to be eaten as a preserve. If required for a dish for dinner beat the whites of four eggs till very stiff. Sprinkle with a little crushed sugar while beating, and flavor with essence of lemon. When very firm pile up on some of the apple previously placed in a dish.— *Mrs. H. N. Starnes.*

COMMON PEACH JAM.

Take good ripe free stone peaches, pare them, and cut into small pieces seeing that none are in the least blemished. Cover the bottom of a stone jar with a thick layer of powdered sugar, good brown sugar will do; then put in a layer of cut peaches without any cooking, then another layer of sugar, then one of peaches and so on till the jar is filled, packing the contents down as closely as possible. The top layer must be of sugar spread on thickly. Cover the jar immediately and paste paper down over the cover. If the peaches are free from decay spots, and the sugar in sufficient abundance, the jam will keep many months.— *Mrs. B. L. McIntosh.*

TRANSPARENT MARMALADE.

Cut very pale Seville or Florida oranges into quarters; take out the pulp, put in basin, and pick out seeds and take off the peel. Put the peels in a little salt water and let stand over night; then boil them in clear water until tender. Cut into very thin slices and put into the pulp. To each pound of marmalade put one and a half pounds of white sugar, and boil for twenty minutes. If not clear and transparent in that time, boil for a few minutes longer. Keep stirring gently all the time, taking care not to break the slices. When cold put into jelly or sweetmeat glasses and tie down tightly with brandy paper.

APPLE MARMALADE.

Peel the apples and boil the peelings in enough water to cover. Strain and add the apples with three-fourths of a pound of sugar to a pound of fruit; also the juice of three oranges. Boil quite low, stirring all the time and put in air tight jars or store jars covered closely.—*Mrs. Humphrey Reid.*

Quince and pear marmalade may be made in the same way. All kinds of jams are made by taking three-fourths of a pound of sugar to a pound of fruit and stirring constantly until thick. If you intend to keep the jam a year or more, it is best to use pound for pound.

FINE BLACKBERRY JAM.

First weigh the fruit, and take three-fourths of a pound of sugar to a pound of fruit. Put in a preserving kettle without the sugar and boil half an hour. Then dip out all the juice possible and add sugar. Boil until thick, stirring constantly. The juice you dipped out, if strained and sugar added, will make good jelly.—*Mrs. Col. Charles Phillips.*

BLACKBERRY JAM.

Take a half or three-fourths of a pound of sugar to a pound of fruit. Put the fruit in a preserving kettle and let it boil twenty minutes; then press it through a sieve fine enough to retain the seeds, but which will allow the pulp and juice to pass through; then add the sugar and cook quite low.—*Mrs. Wm. Cumpstey.*

CHERRY PASTE.

Stone the cherries, boil them gently in their own juice for thirty minutes; press the whole through a sieve; reduce it to a very dry paste; then take it from the fire and weigh it; boil an equal quantity of sugar to the candying point; mix the fruit with it, and stir the paste without intermission over a moderate fire until it is again so dry as to form a ball around the spoon and to quit the preserving pan entirely; press it quickly into small moulds, and when it is cold, paper and store it like other preserves. This is the best preserve I have ever seen.—*Mrs. Humphrey Reid.*

PEACH CONSERVES.

Pare the peaches and cut them from the stone in thick slices. Make a syrup, allowing three-fourths of a pound of sugar to each pound of fruit. Boil the peaches and put them on dishes to dry. As they dry roll them in granulated sugar and pack in jars or boxes.

APPLE BUTTER.

Boil down a kettle full of cider to two-thirds the original quantity. Pare, core and slice juicy apples, and put as many into the cider as it will cover. Boil slowly, stirring often with a flat stick, and when the apples are tender to breaking take them out with a perforated skimmer. Put in a second supply of apples and stew them soft—as many as the cider will hold. Take from the fire, pour all together in a tub or large crock, cover and let stand twelve hours. Then return to the kettle and boil down, stirring all the while till it is of the consistency of soft soap and brown in color. You may spice to taste if you please. Keep in stone jars in a dry, cool place. It should keep all winter.—*Marion Harland.*

CANNING FRUITS AND VEGETABLES.

Many persons can never be induced to attempt the canning of fruits and vegetables, because they imagine there are mysterious secrets connected with the process known only to the manufactories, and a few fortunate outsiders. They are mistaken, and any one willing to exercise care and patience can succeed. First, you must see that your jars are free from flaws, the tops with no pieces clipped out, and the rubbers strong and well-fitting. The "Gem" jar grows in popularity every year. Set the jars in cold water with the rubbers on; gradually heat them through and through, then place one at a time in a plate, and put the plate in a steamer over a vessel of hot water. This keeps the jar from cooling before you have finished filling. Be sure your jar is running over with hot fruit, and quickly screw the covers on, which have also been lying in hot water. Let cool and give the cover another turn; then set the can on its head, and if no juice gets out no air can get in, and it is pretty sure to keep. Fruit should be watched for several weeks; try them occasionally to see if you cannot screw tops on a little tighter. Keep in a dark closet.

TO CAN PEACHES.

(San Francisco Method.)

Peel the peaches, take out the seed, and drop in cold water. When you are through, weigh them, and take a half pound of sugar to a pound of fruit, dissolve the sugar in water and bring to a boil; then add a pint of peach seeds, boil ten minutes and strain. Put the peaches in a steamer over a vessel of boiling water, and when tender place carefully in hot jars, pour syrup over and seal.

The fine display of canned fruits at the Centennial Exposition was prepared as follows: The fruits were selected with great care, of uniform size and shape, and all perfect. They were carefully peeled with a thin, sharp silver fruit-knife, which did not discolor them, and immediately plunged into cold water in an earthen or wooden vessel to prevent the air from darkening them. As soon as enough for one can was prepared, it was put up by laying the fruit, piece by piece, in the can and pouring syrup clear as crystal over it, and then after subjecting the whole to the usual heat, sealing up.

Some hot day try canning peaches cold. Fill jars full of quartered peaches and cover with cold water. Let it stand six hours till fruit is filled with water and then fill can again. Put on cover tight and treat as other canned goods.

CANNED CHERRIES.

Seed May cherries, or Morillos, and to a pound of fruit add half a pound of sugar; let it remain over night, and in the morning boil a half hour. Pour in hot jars and seal.

CANNED PEARS.

Peel the pears and drop them in cold water; do not remove the stems. Make a rich syrup of half a pound of sugar to a pound of fruit, with enough water to dissolve. When the syrup is boiling put in the pears and cook till tender; then place in jars and pour syrup over. If you wish them very fair, steam the fruit instead of boiling it in the syrup.

TO CAN GREEN GOOSEBERRIES.

Cook the berries in water until white, but not enough to break them; put in the cans with as little water as possible; fill up the can with boiling water and seal; when opened, pour off water and cook like fresh berries.

CANNED APPLES.

Pare, cut in halves and core. Drop the pieces in a vessel of cold water to prevent them turning dark. Make a syrup of one-third of a pound of sugar and one teacupful of water for each pound of apples. Cut oranges in slices about one-fourth of an inch thick, and allow two slices to each pound of fruit. Put the syrup and sliced oranges into a preserving kettle, boil carefully, removing all scum; then put in the apples and boil them until tender, being careful not to stir or break them. When done take out the pieces with a perforated skimmer, put in the cans, pour on the syrup, and seal at once.

TO CAN BLACKBERRIES.

Take a half pound of sugar to a pound of berries. Boil until the syrup is clear. Pour in jars and seal.

WARRANTED CANNED STRAWBERRIES.

Put four pounds of white sugar in a kettle, add a cupful of cold water, let boil till perfectly clear, then add four quarts of nice berries. Boil ten minutes, keeping them covered with syrup, but avoid stirring in order to preserve their good appearance. Take out berries with a small skimmer or strainer, place in a crock and let the syrup boil ten minutes longer; then pour it over berries, and when cool fill the cans, putting a tablespoonful of good brandy on top of each can; screw on lid tightly and put in a dry, dark place. This method is the only one whereby the peculiar flavor of the strawberries is preserved. To prevent the second handling put the hot berries in the cans, instead of the crock, till about three-fourths full. When syrup has boiled, fill each can with it, let stand till cool, then cover with the tablespoonful of brandy and screw on the lid. If after two or three weeks the least fermentation appears, put the cans in a boiler, fill with cold water nearly to the top of cans, loosen the lids but do not take them off, let water boil for a little while, then take out cans, tighten the covers, and the berries will keep over a year. Fully ripe cherries and currants prepared in the same way, one pound sugar to one of fruit, are delicious. They never need a second boiling if carefully prepared.—*Dixie Cook Book.*

CANNED CORN.

Dissolve an ounce of tartaric acid in half a teacupful of water, and take one tablespoonful to two quarts of corn; cook, and while boiling hot fill the cans, which should be tin. When used turn into a colander, rinse with cold water, add a little soda and sugar while cooking, and season with salt, pepper and butter.

CANNED TOMATOES.

Scald the tomatoes, peel them, draw off all the juice, bring slowly to a boil in a preserving kettle; boil ten minutes. Pour boiling hot into air tight cans and seal. It will improve the tomatoes to take hard parts out. If watery, dip out as much of the liquor as possible.—*Mrs. Josiah Sibley.*

PREMIUM CANNED OKRA.

Cook the okra as if for immediate use, fill the hot jars and pour the liquor over. Seal.—*Mrs. R. T. Nesbitt.*

PREMIUM CANNED PEAS.

Cover the peas with cold water, boil till tender but not shrunken, remove to hot jars and fill up with the liquor. Seal.—*Mrs. R. T. Nesbitt.*

TO CAN GREEN CORN FOR WINTER USE.

Scrape the corn from the cob, and in the bottom of a jar place an inch of salt, two inches of corn, salt again, and so on till full, placing two inches of salt on top. When wanted for the table soak over night in water, and prepare as green corn.—*Mrs. James Scott.*

CANNED CORN, TOMATOES AND OKRA.

Take two dozen ears of corn boiled on the cob, one peck of tomatoes peeled and chopped fine, one-fourth of a peck of small tender okra. After the corn is well cooked, cut it from the cob, boil the tomatoes half an hour, and the okra until tender, from which carefully drain the water, adding the okra and corn to the tomatoes. Season with salt and pepper, mix well together, put in the cans boiling hot, and have the cans soldered.

ICE CREAM.

In making ice-cream, nothing will take the place of thick sweet cream. It is far superior to all mixtures of milk, cornstarch, and yolks of egg. Really they do not deserve the name, being more on the order of custards. Cream, however, is often scarce, and cannot be bought "for love or money." In such cases milk can be used in making very agreeable frozen desserts. Get a freezer which your dealer can recommend, and use the coarsest salt with your ice,—a layer of each with salt sprinkled heavily on top. A coarse piece of carpet or blanket thrown on top of the ice and fastened, will retard its melting. Do this work of freezing in a cool cellar away from stove or sun heat. Never begin making a frozen dessert unless you are sure of an ample supply of ice. Nothing is more embarrassing than to be obliged to bring them to the table in a half finished state. Sixteen pounds of ice, with the exercise of judgment and care, ought to freeze three gallons of cream.

ICE CREAM.

Take the thickest and sweetest of Jersey cream. Whip to a froth, sweeten with loaf sugar, and freeze.—*Mrs. W. W. Massie.*

ICE CREAM.

Take one gallon of morning's milk. Remove the salt from one pound of butter, and rub to a cream. Beat into it the yolks of two eggs and a tablespoonful of cornstarch. When the milk comes to a boil, stir this in. When cool, flavor with vanilla, lemon extract, or anything preferred.

ICE CREAM.

One quart of milk, two eggs, one teaspoonful of corn starch, one teaspoonful of arrow-root. A small lump of butter.

WHITE ICE CREAM.

Three quarts of new milk, whites of four eggs beaten light, three tablespoonsful of arrow-root mixed in a little cold water and added to the eggs. Boil the milk and pour over the eggs. Then put on the fire and thicken a little. When nearly cold add a quart of cream. Sweeten and season to taste and freeze.--*Miss Hettie White.*

ICE CREAM WITHOUT CREAM.

One gallon of milk, yolks of two eggs, well beaten, whites of twelve eggs, well beaten. Sweeten and scald the milk and pour it on the eggs stirring well. Put it in the kettle again and let it come to a boil. Season to taste and freeze at once.

GELATINE ICE CREAM.

Take a pint of fresh milk and empty into it half a box of Cox's gelatine. Boil three pints of milk and pour on the gelatine, stirring hard. When cold, add a quart of frothed cream; sweeten, flavor, and freeze.---*Mrs. Sophronia Tucker.*

PEACH ICE CREAM.

Take nice soft peaches perfectly ripe. Pare and chop fine, make them very sweet and mash to a fine jam. To each quart of peaches add one pint of cream and one pint of rich milk. Mix well and freeze. If you cannot get cream, melt an ounce of Cox's gelatine in a cup of water. Boil the milk, pour it on the gelatine, and when cold, mix with the peaches.

ALMOND ICE CREAM.

Take two pounds of almonds; blanch and grate them and add to a half gallon of cream when it begins to freeze.

COCOANUT ICE CREAM.

Grate one cocoanut and add to a gallon of cream. A teaspoonful of vanilla improves it.

CHOCOLATE CREAM.

One quart of cream, one pint of milk, eight tablespoonsful of chocolate. Rub the chocolate to a paste in a little milk, and when the pint of milk boils, stir it in. When cool, add the quart of cream, flavor with vanilla and freeze.

ORANGE ICE CREAM.

Four oranges, one gallon of cream. Rub four or five lumps of sugar on the orange peel, squeeze the juice out, put the lumps of sugar in it and pour into the cream. Sweeten heavily with pulverized loaf sugar before freezing. —*Mrs. McGavock.*

STRAWBERRY ICE CREAM.

Four quarts of thick sweet cream, four quarts of strawberries. The berries must be mashed or bruised, caps and all, with a teacupful of granulated sugar to each quart. After standing several hours, strain through a thin coarse cloth. Put four teacupsful of white sugar to the cream, and then add the juice of the berries. Whip to froth the cream with a patent egg-whip or common egg-beater. Pour two-thirds of the cream into the freezer, reserving the rest to pour in after it begins to freeze. Raspberry cream may be made by the same receipt.—*Marion Cabell Tyree.*

BISQUE ICE CREAM.

One half gallon of freshly turned clabber, one-half gallon of rich sweet cream, one good vanilla bean boiled in one-half pint of milk, sugar to taste. Churn this five minutes before freezing. One can of condensed milk may be used with less clabber.

BUTTERMILK ICE CREAM.

Stir a little soda into a quart of buttermilk; add one quart of cream; make it very sweet; flavor and freeze. If the buttermilk is frothy and nice it makes an excellent ice.

CARAMEL.

Put in a stew pan one teacupful of nice brown sugar and half a teacupful of water. Stew over a hot fire till it burns a little. If too thick, make it the consistency of thin molasses by adding a little boiling water. Bottle and cork ready for use.

CARAMEL ICE CREAM.

One gallon of rich sweet cream, four teacupsful of powdered sugar, five tablespoonsful of caramel. Mix well and freeze hard.

LEMON ICE CREAM.

Squeeze the juice of a dozen lemons, make the juice quite thick with white sugar, stir into it very slowly three quarts of cream, and freeze.

PINE-APPLE ICE CREAM.

Three pints of cream, two large ripe pine-apples, two pounds of powdered sugar; slice the pine-apples thin, scatter the sugar between the slices, cover and let the fruit stand three hours; cut or chop it up in the syrup, and strain through a hair sieve or double bag of coarse lace; beat gradually into the cream and freeze as rapidly as possible.

TEA ICE CREAM.

Pour over four tablespoonsful of Old Hyson tea a pint of cream; scald in a custard kettle, or by placing the dish containing it in a vessel of boiling water, remove from the fire and let it stand five minutes; strain into a pint of cold cream, put on to scald again, and when hot mix with it four eggs and three-fourths of a pound of sugar well beaten together. Let cool and freeze.

KENTUCKY CREAM.

Make a half gallon of rich boiled custard, sweeten to taste, add two tablespoonsful of gelatine dissolved in half a cupful of cold milk. Let the custard cool, put it in a freezer, and as soon as it begins to freeze add one pound of raisins, one pint of strawberry preserves, one quart of whipped cream. Blanched almonds or grated cocoanut are additions. Some prefer currants to raisins, and some also add citron chopped fine.—*Mrs. Gov. J. B. McCreary.*

METROPOLITAN ICE CREAM.

One half gallon of rich cream; color with chocolate, flavor with vanilla to taste; one half gallon of cream, color with cochineal, flavor with rose; one half gallon of cream, flavor with lemon. Freeze each separately, then place in a mould alternate layers of each until filled. Put on ice and freeze again.—*Mrs. Matt Turney in Blue Grass Cook Book.*

FROZEN PUDDING.

Three quarts of rich custard, half a teacupful of seeded raisins, one pound of blanched almonds chopped, but not very fine. Mix and put into freezer; when beginning to freeze, stir in one quart of rich cream whipped, stir well every few minutes to prevent the fruit from falling to the bottom. Season with good whisky.

SHERBET.

Five quarts of water, five dozen lemons, add sugar till very sweet. When it begins to freeze, add the whites of twelve eggs beaten to a stiff froth and slightly sweetened. —*Kimball House.*

LEMON SHERBET.

Two quarts of water, two pounds of sugar, six lemons, whites of five eggs, one and a half pints of milk. Two-thirds of this is three pints of water, one and a half pounds of sugar, four lemons, one pint of milk, whites of three eggs.—*Miss Julia Ketner.*

ECONOMICAL LEMON SHERBET.

Dissolve three teaspoonsful of citric acid in one half teacupful of hot water, add one gallon of fresh water, four teacupsful of sugar, three teaspoonsful of lemon extract. When beginning to freeze, add the whites of two eggs well beaten.—*Mrs. Judge Payne.*

A NEW RECEIPT FOR LEMON SHERBET.

Make one and a half gallons of strong lemonade, grating the peel of three or four of the lemons before straining the juice into the water. Let it stand fifteen minutes, then make and add to it the following mixture: Pour a pint of cold water over one box of gelatine and let it stand half an hour, then pour over it one pint of boiling water, and let it stand till thoroughly dissolved. Beat the whites of eight eggs with two pounds of pulverized sugar till as thick as icing; then churn a quart of rich cream till it is reduced to a pint; then beat the froth of the cream into the egg and sugar. Pour in gradually the lemonade, beating all the time so as to mix thoroughly, and then freeze. Delicious.
—*Mrs. M. G. Whitlock.*

MILK SHERBET.

Four lemons to one gallon of milk. Grate the peel of the lemon on sugar and squeeze the juice on same. Sweeten the milk very sweet. Stir the grated rind, juice and sugar into the milk, and commence freezing immediately. Use as much cream as possible.—*Mrs. H. N. Starnes.*

ORANGE SHERBET.

One gallon of water, one and a half dozen oranges, three pounds of white sugar, the whites of nine eggs.

PINEAPPLE ICE.

Two cans of fresh pineapple, chop the fruit very fine, add the juice of four lemons, four teacupsful of sugar, a half gallon of boiling water. When cold add the whites of two eggs beaten to a stiff froth, and freeze till firm.—*Miss Kate James.*

This receipt is very popular.

MADEIRA WINE SHERBET.

Make a sweet sangaree of the best wine, mix with it the white of an egg and freeze.

CRESCENT CITY SHERBET.

Make a very strong and sweet lemonade; add whisky, wine or brandy to taste, and the whites of three eggs beaten stiff; freeze.

RASPBERRY ICE.

The juice of ripe raspberries and a little water; sweeten to taste. Add the juice of a lemon. Strain the mixture through a fine sieve into a freezer, and freeze. You can use the juice of raspberries or blackberries in the same way.

CITRON ICE.

Slice citron; pour on it a rich, hot lemonade, and freeze.

WATERMELON ICE.

Select a ripe and very red melon, scrape some of the pulp, and use all the water. A few of the seeds interspersed will add greatly to the appearance. Sweeten to the taste, and freeze as you would any other ice. If you wish it very light, add the whites of three eggs to one gallon of the icing just as it begins to congeal. Beat frequently and very hard with a large spoon.

GELATINE ICE.

Let one ounce of sparkling gelatine stand an hour in a pint of cold water ; then add three pints of boiling water, one and one half pounds of loaf sugar, one and one half pints of wine, juice of three lemons, rind of two lemons. Stir all these ingredients, and freeze before allowing to congeal. Delicious.—*Marion Cabell Tyree.*

BEVERAGES.

BLACKBERRY WINE.

To each gallon of ripe berries add one quart of boiling water; mash the berries and let them stand twenty-four hours; then express the juice, strain, and add two and a half pounds of sugar to each gallon. Place in a cask and let it stand until fermentation ceases, keeping the bung closed to prevent gnats and flies. Then strain, and stop tightly until cold weather, when you may draw it off and bottle it.—*Mrs. R. T. Nesbitt.*

This wine is recommended as being strictly first-class in every particular.

BLACKBERRY CORDIAL.

To two quarts of blackberry juice add half an ounce each of powdered nutmeg, cinnamon, and allspice, and one-fourth of an ounce of powdered cloves. Boil together to get strength of spices and to preserve berry juice. While hot add a pint of brandy, and sweeten with loaf sugar.—*Mrs. Berrien.*

BLACKBERRY WINE.

One bushel of berries; pour over them at night hot water enough to cover. Strain out in the morning; to one gallon of juice, add three pounds of sugar.—*Mrs. Hirsch.*

BLACKBERRY VINEGAR.

One gallon of fresh berries washed and picked. Pour over them a half gallon of good cider vinegar, let stand twenty-four hours; then strain. To each pint of juice add three-fourths of a pound of sugar; boil half an hour and skim carefully. When cold, bottle and cork tightly. When used pour the depth of an inch in the glass, fill with water, pounded ice and season with nutmeg. This is a temperance drink.—*Mrs. E. McCarney.*

CHERRY WINE.

Wash and stone large red cherries; mix with cold water one gallon to five pounds of cherries. Let it stand ten or twelve hours, thin, stir well and strain. Add three pounds of sugar to each gallon, and finish same as blackberry wine.

THE FAMOUS SOUTHERN PERSIMMON BEER.

Place carefully into a five or ten gallon keg a few pine tops for the double purpose of acting as a sort of filter and giving a sprucy flavor to the beer; make it draw well from a spigot bored about two inches from the bottom of the keg with a quarter or half an inch bit and fitted with a spile. Now put in persimmons well ripe (after frost) till the keg is one-fourth filled; fill up the keg with water (rain water is best). Then chip in a little bark of the sassafras root. Keep it in a warm place or near the fire, and in a few days it will have fermented and got clear, and you can draw off an agreeable, popular, and wholesome beverage. If it should not ferment well, a small quantity of yeast may be added.—*Dr. W. C. Bellamy.*

SWEET POTATO BEER

Is made in the same way, substituting boiled sweet potatoes for the persimmons.

CORN BEER.

Boil a gallon of corn till soft, and put in a five gallon keg. Add a gallon of molasses or of Louisiana or Florida syrup, a little yeast. Let it ferment and you have a fine beverage.

PERSIMMON BEER.

Take a barrel and lay broken sticks in the bottom, crossing them. On the crossed sticks place clean hay or straw. Put in a bushel of ripe persimmons, six buckets of cold water; cover it with a cloth, placing the barrel in a warm room. When the persimmons rise to the top, it will be fit for use.—*Mrs. Kennon.*

BEER.

Two quarts of wheat bran, two and a half gallons of water, a few hops, one pint of molasses, and one pint of yeast.

CHEAP AND GOOD GINGER BEER.

It may be made in three minutes and fit to drink in twelve hours, and need not cost but one cent a bottle. Take a spoonful of ginger, one of cream of tartar, one pint of yeast, one pint of molasses and six quarts of water. Mix together cold. Let it stand a few hours till it begins to ferment, then bottle it and set in a cool place.—*Col. S. J. Atkinson.*

CATAWBA WINE.

Cut the grapes off; throw away the green or imperfect ones. Dip each bunch in cold water and shake it around to get clean. Throw them in a tub and mash with a mallet. Do not crush the seeds. Let it stand twenty-four hours, then press the juice in tubs. Let it stand until the scum rises breaking in cracks. Skim it very thoroughly; adding two and a half pounds of sugar to a gallon of juice. Put the bung in loosely for a month, then tighten it and let it stand till spring. Strain, bottle and seal.—*M. Holtstein, Middle Bass Island, Lake Erie.*

MRS. EARLE'S GRAPE WINE.

Let the grapes be well ripened; mash them in a barrel with a beetle, stem and berries. Express the juice and put in a cask five-sixths full to ferment. Place one end of a siphon in the bung hole of the cask, the other being crooked over rests in a bucket of water. The fermentation commences in a day or two, and the carbonic acid escapes through the water. In ten or fourteen days the siphon may be removed, the cask filled up, and the bung driven in lightly. In cool weather draw off the wine, leaving the dregs at the bottom of the cask. Cleanse thoroughly and return the wine; if you choose, clarifying with beaten whites of four eggs mixed with some of the wine or with a handful of dissolved isinglass. The second fermentation occurs in the spring, about the time of the blossoming of the grapes; loosen the bung, and when it is over, the wine will be clear, and in two or three months safe to bottle; but that operation had best be deferred till November. The casks and all the vessels must be perfectly clean; keep the air from the new wine by having the cask constantly bung full, and there is no danger of spoiling. The juice should not be fermented on the hulls. These covered with water and allowed to stand four or five days, expressed and sweetened with about a pound of sugar to the gallon make a delightful vinegar with true vinous flavor and aroma. Avoid moving the casks or jugs which contain wine, as the shaking sets up another fermentation injurious to the quality of the wine. Professional wine makers allow three-fourths of a pound of sugar to the gallon of juice. Without their arrangements of deep cellars and uniform temperature that is too little. Two and a half pounds to the gallon makes a wine with more body, better keeping power and more of the alcoholic property.

CURRANT SHRUB.

The currants should be very ripe; squeeze them; to each quart, one pound of sugar. Put the currants in a kettle, boil ten minutes, skimming well; when cold allow one gill of brandy to each quart of juice. Bottle and seal. It improves with age.—*Capt. H. C. Buckner*.

STRAWBERRY WINE.

One gallon of juice, two and a half pounds of sugar, strain several times through a flannel bag and pour into a jug. Cover with gauze and let it remain till February.—*Miss Mary Davis*.

GOOSEBERRY WINE.

Gather the berries when ripe, mash them well and let stand from three to four days, then strain, and to nine pints of juice, add four pints of rain water; to this quantity put four pounds of brown sugar, let stand from five to six weeks, then strain and bottle.—*Mrs. Dudley*.

SCUPPERNONG WINE.

Gather the grapes when fully ripe, crush them, after which press the juice out as long as it will run. Put two pounds of best white sugar to each gallon of juice; fill a cask brimming full and leave the bung open. When fermentation ceases stop the bung tight. It will take about twenty days to ferment. Bore a spigot hole in the barrel with a gimlet, and try it frequently by taking spigot out to see if fermentation is entirely over.—*Mrs. R. T. Nesbitt*.

APPLE WINE.

To a gallon of new cider add a pound and a half of sugar, a quarter of a pound of raisins, and half a lemon. Put into a cask as soon as the sugar is dissolved.

APPLE WINE.

Take cider fresh from the press, and to each gallon add two pounds of good brown sugar; after dissolving the sugar, strain it and put in a new cask. One that has held whisky or brandy should not be used. Tack a piece of muslin, or perforated tin, over the bung and let it thus stand for a week. After this, put in the cork lightly and let it remain thus for two weeks longer, then fasten it tightly to exclude the air. The vessel should not be filled; at least one-eighth of the space should be left. It is not fit for use under two or three months; it should then be drawn off, bottled, and sealed. This makes wine equal to Catawba.—*Rev. D. P. Young in Blue Grass Cook Book.*

RAISIN WINE.

To two gallons of boiling water, add three pounds of finely chopped and seeded raisins, one pound of granulated sugar, the juice and grated rind of a lemon. Pour all in a stone jar, stir frequently, and in a week strain and bottle.

LEMON ICE FOAM.

Make a strong lemonade, fill a tumbler half full ; put in three tablespoonsful of finely crushed ice, and fill with thick sweet cream. Have a tin cup which fits tightly over the tumbler; shake back and forth rapidly till the whole is in a foaming state.—*Jack, Ward & Co.*

RASPBERRY AND MINT SANGAREE.

Take a glass half full of Bourbon whisky and dash it with champagne. Dissolve in it two or three teaspoonsful of sugar, and fill with ice water. On top of the glass lay a slice of lemon with sprigs of mint laid across. In the middle, put a little mound of crushed ice, and in an opening made in the ice lay three ripe raspberries. Use a straw.—*Howard, Lewis & Co.*

JAMAICA GINGER TEA.

(For a cold.)

Make a large cupful of hot lemonade; add a teaspoonful of Jamaica ginger, and whisky if liked.

SODA WATER.

Boil two pounds of white sugar and the whites of one and a half eggs well beaten with two teaspoonsful of flour; add two drachms of pulverized gum arabic boiled in two pints of soft water five minutes. Stir well while boiling; set it off to cool. When cool stir thoroughly into the syrup two and one-half ounces of supercarbonate of soda, and flavor with any extract desired. Keep this in a bottle by itself. Then dissolve two and one-half ounces of tartaric or citric acid in one quart of water and put in another bottle. This is the fountain. To mix, take a glass half full of ice water and pour from both bottles a large spoonful of the mixture in it.—*Ky. Home Cook Book.*

LEMON SYRUP.

Take one dozen lemons, and having pressed out their juice, separate the pulp from the skin. Boil the pulp a few minutes in a pint of water, add to this the juice previously extracted and strain. Add one pound of sugar to each pint of the juice, and boil it for ten minutes; bottle and seal. It keeps well and one tablespoonful in a goblet of water makes delicious drink.

EGG NOG.

Beat the whites and yolks of five eggs separately, and then together; add a quart of cream or milk, stirring well; then add whisky or brandy and sugar to taste, and grated nutmeg if liked. Never pour the whisky on to the beaten yolks alone. If it is strong it will curdle them.—*General Bolly Lewis.*

CIDER.

Cider may be kept fresh and sweet by simply heating it till it throws off steam, then put in hot bottles and seal immediately. Another way is to let cider stand until the taste just suits; then add two and a half ounces of salicylic acid to forty gallons of cider. This will retain the same flavor any length of time.

ROMAN PUNCH.

Make two quarts of lemonade very rich, shake well and freeze. Just before serving, add for each quart of ice half a pint of brandy and half a pint of Jamaica rum. Mix well and serve in high glasses, as this makes what is called a semi or half-ice.

RECEIPT FOR MAKING HOME BREWED ALE.

Steep sixteen pounds of ground malt in five gallons of water, nearly at boiling point one hour. Pour off the liquor and add three gallons more of hot water; straining through the malt, then add two gallons more of water; with these liquors, boil half a pound of choice hops three quarters of an hour. Molasses or sugar may be added if desired. Strain into a shallow vessel, and when blood warm put in one pint of yeast, let ferment about thirty hours, then put in keg, leaving the bung out. As it works over replenish the keg and when well fermented bung tight. This beer will be fit for use in from two to four days.—*Dole & Merrill.*

CONFECTIONERY.

COCOANUT DROPS.

Equal quantities of sugar and grated cocoanut, cook it on a slow fire and keep stirring until it begins to thicken, then let it get cool. Drop them on a pan and bake to a light brown.—*Mrs. J. A. Massey.*

KISSES.

Beat the whites of nine eggs to a stiff froth; mix with it fifteen tablespoonsful of finest white sugar, five or six drops of essence of lemon. Drop on white paper, sift sugar over them, and bake in a slow oven.—*Mrs. W. P. Stevens.*

CHOCOLATE CARAMELS.

One pound of sugar, one-fourth of a pound of chocolate, one cup of milk, and butter the size of a hen's egg. Boil thirty minutes.—*Mary Largimosino.*

CANDY WITHOUT COOKING.

The same quantity of water as the whites of two eggs before beating, which may be measured in tumblers. Put one teaspoonful of vanilla in water, beat the eggs very light, and add water and sugar alternately, a small quantity at a time; stir hard and continue to add sugar until stiff as dough, then work with the hands. Confectioner's sugar must be used. Make into small cakes about the size of a half dollar, and put an English walnut kernel in each side and press it in with the fingers. Set on ice to harden.—*Mrs. V. C. Gilman in Kentucky Home Cook Book.*

CONFECTIONERY.

TO CRYSTALIZE POP-CORN.

Put into an iron kettle one teacupful of water, and one teacupful of white sugar; boil until ready to candy, then throw in corn nicely popped, and stir briskly until the candy is equally distributed over the corn, set the kettle from the fire and stir until it has cooled a little and you have each grain separate and crystalized with sugar. Care must be taken not to have too hot a fire lest you scorch the corn when crystalized. Nuts prepared in this way are delicious.

COCOANUT CARAMELS.

Half a cake of Baker's chocolate, one quarter of a pound of butter, two pounds of brown sugar, one teacupful of rich milk; stew half an hour, or until thick, add a grated cocoanut, stir till it begins to boil again. Take from the fire, stir in a tablespoonful of vanilla, and pour into buttered dishes. When cool enough to handle, make into balls the size of walnuts and place on buttered dishes.

ALMOND MACAROONS.

One-half pound of almonds blanched and pounded, with a teaspoonful essence of lemon, till a smooth paste. Add an equal quantity of sifted white sugar and the whites of two eggs. Work well together with a spoon; dip your hands into water and work them into balls the size of a nutmeg; lay them on white paper an inch apart; dip your hands in water and smooth them, put them in a slow oven for three-quarters of an hour.—*Mrs. Mary G. Harding.*

DELICIOUS FRUIT CANDY.

Add chopped raisins and figs to a syrup made by stirring two pounds of sugar with the juice of two lemons, or if lemons are not at hand, with a cupful of vinegar flavored with essence of lemon.

WHITE CREAM CANDY.

Put eight pounds of fine white sugar in a pan, and add one teaspoonful of cream of tartar; pour over enough water to dissolve it, melt in water a little Prussian blue to color the sugar blue-white; pour into the above and boil till done. Then pour it on a marble-top stand that has been well oiled; turn the edges over in the middle and form into the shape of a ball, fasten it to a hook driven into the wall; pull the candy towards you, throwing it on the hook each time; continue until perfectly white, then pull out in a long roll and cut into sticks the required length. Flavor with vanilla.—*Philipp Nippert.*

CREAM CANDY.

Three pounds of white sugar, one pint of cream, a goblet of water, two tablespoonsful of vinegar, half a cupful of butter. Flavor with vanilla.—*Mrs. Kate Chambers.*

MOLASSES CANDY.

Boil the molasses slowly, stirring all the time; when nearly done add one teaspoonful of butter, one teaspoonful of brown sugar, a pinch of soda. Try it by dropping into water.

PEANUT CANDY.

Shell the pea-nuts and rub off the brown skins. Almost fill a pan or plate with them, and pour on the molasses candy made as above.

DIET FOR THE SICK.

ESSENCE OF BEEF.

Take of lean beef sliced a sufficient quantity to fill the body of a porter bottle, cork loosely, and place it in a pot of cold water, attaching the neck by means of a string to the handle of the pot. Boil for two hours, pour off the liquid and skim it. To this preparation may be added spices, salt, wine or brandy to taste.

A FINE BEEF PREPARATION.

Take three pounds of lean beef, mince it fine, cover with water, salt to taste and boil for an hour, adding more water if needed. Pour off the liquor, add as much browned flour as it will take ; make out into cakes ; put on white paper and dry in the sun. When needed dissolve in hot water and season to taste.—*Dr. Addis Emmett.*

DR. STEWART'S RECEIPT FOR CHICKEN SOUP.

With a hatchet or meat cleaver chop a chicken into fine pieces, bone and all. Put into a porcelain stew pan, cover with cold water and let simmer until the essence is extracted. Pour in a teacupful of rich unskimmed milk, and a tablespoonful of butter ; salt, pepper, and parsley to taste ; rice and noodles if liked. Thicken with cornstarch or flour rubbed smooth in a little milk. The most nourishing part of the fowl, the essence of the bone, is mostly lost in the way broth is ordinarily made ; hence the great advantage of chopping the bone.

CHICKEN WATER.

Take half a chicken, divest it of all fat, and break the bones. Add to this half a gallon of water, boil for an hour, strain and season with salt.

TO RELIEVE THIRST.

Take a crust of corn bread. Allow it to become very brown in the oven. Pour over cold water; let it sit an hour and drink occasionally. A little sweetened water is also very good.

APPLE WATER.

Slice two large apples and pour over the slices a pint of boiling water. Let it stand an hour, strain and sweeten with loaf sugar.

TOAST WATER.

Toast thoroughly a slice of stale bread, put it in a jug and pour over it a quart of water which has been boiled and cooked. In two hours pour off. A small piece of orange or lemon peel put into the jug with the bread, improves the flavor greatly.

BISCUIT JELLY.

White biscuit four ounces, to be boiled down in four pints of water to one-half, strained and evaporated to one pint; one pound of white sugar, four ounces of port wine, and one drachm of cinnamon water added and the whole well mixed.

PANADA.

Stale wheat bread one ounce, cinnamon one drachm, water one pint; cover up and let stand for an hour; boil for ten minutes, adding a little grated nutmeg and sugar.

CORN MEAL GRUEL.

Three tablespoonsful of sifted corn meal, moistened with a little cold water; pour it into a pint of boiling water; stir well; cook about ten minutes.

THICKENED MILK.

Take a pint of milk, and when it reaches the boiling point stir in a tablespoonful of cornstarch rubbed smooth in a little milk. Flour may be used instead of cornstarch. Sweeten, or season with salt.

RICE JELLY.

To a half pint of rice pour on a quart of boiling water, and when it cools rub it well between the hands. Strain, and boil rapidly.

BLACKBERRY JELLY.

Two quarts of blackberry juice, one pound of loaf sugar, half an ounce of nutmeg, half an ounce of cloves, half an ounce of cinnamon, half an ounce of allspice. Pulverize the spices, if whole. Boil all fifteen minutes. When cold, add one pint of brandy.

RICE CUSTARD.

Boil half a cupful of the best ground rice in a pint of milk until dissolved; then mix it with a quart of cream. Flavor with nutmeg, mace and a little brandy.

CHOCOLATE MILK.

Dissolve an ounce of scraped chocolate in a pint of boiling milk. Sweeten to taste.

MILK PUNCH.

Pour over a beaten egg five tablespoonsful of best whisky. Fill the glass with fresh milk and sweeten.

COLD CUSTARD.

Take the yolk and the white of an egg and a tablespoonful of sugar. Beat hard, and add half a pint of cold water, two teaspoonsful of rose water and a little grated nutmeg.

MULLED WINE.

Take quarter of an ounce of bruised cinnamon, half a nutmeg and ten bruised cloves. Infuse them in half a pint of boiling water for an hour; strain, and add half an ounce of white sugar. Pour the whole into a pint of hot port or sherry wine.

CALVES' FEET JELLY.

Take two calves' feet, and add to them one gallon of water and boil down to one quart; strain, and when cold remove all fat; then add the whites of six or eight eggs well beaten, a pint of wine, half a pound of loaf sugar, and the juice of four lemons. Boil, stirring constantly, and strain through a flannel bag.

REMEDIES.

CHALK MIXTURE.

For diarrhœa in children: Prepared chalk, one drachm; powdered sugar, one drachm; powdered gum arabic, one drachm; paregoric, half an ounce; tincture of catechu, half an ounce; water, four ounces. Mix. Dose, one teaspoonful every three hours.—*Dr. Gilbert Tennent.*

Hundreds of parents can testify to the efficacy of the above prescription. It has saved many a little life thought to be beyond the reach of medical aid.

Toothache may be speedily and delightfully ended by the application of a small bit of cotton saturated in a strong solution of ammonia to the affected tooth.

TO INSURE SLEEP.

If troubled with wakefulness follow these rules: Eat nothing hearty after sunset; calm your mind before retiring; go to bed at a regular hour; when you awake rise and dress at once, no matter how early in the morning; never sleep in the day. These five rules observed will insure sleep.

DOG BITE.

An aged forester has published the following in a Leipsic journal: "I do not wish to carry to my grave my much proved cure for the bites of mad dogs, but will publish the same as the last service I can offer to the world. Wash the wound perfectly clean with wine vinegar and tepid water, then dry it. Afterwards pour into the wound a few drops of muriatic acid, for mineral acids destroy the poison of the dog's saliva.

Poultices are generally better for the addition of a little sweet or castor oil and a few drops of laudanum.

TO RELIEVE CONSTIPATION.

Dissolve a teaspoonful of salt in a goblet of cold water, and drink each morning before breakfast. In a short while you will crave the salt water.

PREPARATION FOR IMPROVING THE SKIN.

Two ounces of blanched almonds, one pint of honey, whites of two eggs, half a pint of whisky, juice of two lemons.—*Mrs. W. W. Massie.*

TO DESTROY BED-BUGS.

Touch infested places with a strong feather dipped in corrosive sublimate. They will fall like leaves before the autumn blast.

TO DESTROY RED ANTS.

Break gum camphor into very fine crumbs, and scatter them on every shelf in the cupboard and pantry. The remedy is clean, easily applied, and withal effectual.

TO RELIEVE NERVOUS HEADACHE.

Wash well in strong soda water. This will also relieve severe colds.

FOR A BURN.

After burning or scalding the flesh, apply immediately equal parts of lime water and sweet oil. Pour on a cloth and bind.—*Dr. G. Tennent, Sr.*

COUGH MIXTURE.

Teaspoonful spirits of nitre, half a teaspoonful syrup of ipecac, half a teaspoonful of paregoric, and eight tablespoonsful of water. Dose, a teaspoonful three or four times a day. Rub the soles of the feet with five grains of quinine in teaspoonful of whisky morning and night.—*Dr. Ford.*

REMEDY FOR YELLOW THRUSH.

One teaspoonful of burnt alum, half a teaspoonful of powdered saltpetre, two tablespoonsful of powdered loaf sugar, two tablespoonsful of strained honey. Mix these all well together, add to them the white of an egg not frothed; then beat it a little. Let it simmer well, stirring constantly.—*Dr. Ford.*

A little calomel stirred in lard will cure scratches and pimples as if by magic.

CURE FOR TETTER.

Take sarsaparilla root, wash dry and cut up into small pieces, fill a bottle and pour on the best whisky. Dose, a tablespoonful three times a day.

CURE FOR CONSUMPTION.

Get the sawdust from rich pine wood, and cover with corn whisky. After forty eight hours, strain and take half a teaspoonful when the cough is troublesome. There are thousands of Georgians who have an unshaken faith in this remedy, and say it has restored to health many almost on the confines of another world.

A QUICK EMETIC.

Swallow raw eggs as rapidly as possible. Especially valuable in cases of poisoning.

POISON OAK CURE.

Bathe the affected parts long and well in sulphur and cream; in half an hour wash well in salt and water. Repeat twice a day. Three or four applications will cure.—*Mrs. Geo. Davis.*

NEURALGIA.

Two drops of laudanum in half teaspoonful of warm water dropped into the ears. It will give immediate relief.

CURE FOR DIARRHŒA.

One pint of brandy, one ounce of gum camphor, one ounce of opium, half an ounce of cayenne pepper. Dose for an adult: One teaspoonful in a little sweet milk.—*Mrs. A. L. Bean.*

A FINE RECEIPT FOR A COUGH.

Boil flaxseed in water until it becomes slimy; then strain and sweeten with rock candy powdered as fine as possible; season with the juice of fresh lemons. Take a wine-glassful when the cough is troublesome.

CROUP MIXTURE.

Teaspoonful of turpentine, teaspoonful of brown sugar, one tablespoonful of cold water. Mix in a cup, and each time before using stir well, and give half a teaspoonful every five minutes for seven doses. This medicine cannot be kept more than twenty-four hours, then fresh must be made.—*Dr. Ford.*

To stop bleeding at nose, press the thumbs at the back of the ear, lower part. Never known to fail.

To stop bleeding from a cut, bury the affected part in sugar, changing when it becomes bloody.

WASH FOR OLD SORES.

There is nothing better than diluted carbolic acid. It is the greatest purifier known.

REMEDY FOR THE HIVES.

Make a strong tea of peach tree leaves. Let it become cool and bathe the affected parts.

CURE FOR A WEN.

Bathe often in a strong solution of Turk Island salt.—*Dr. Gunn.*

TO REMOVE FRECKLES.

Take tansy leaves, bruise and soak in fresh buttermilk, bathe the face and avoid exposure to the sun.

FOR NAUSEA.

Take a handful of cloves, put in a teapot and pour boiling water over and steep. Sweeten, and when cold drink as required.—*Dr. Gilbert Tennent.*

REMEDIES FOR CROUP.

1st. Take a little powdered alum and dissolve in honey or molasses.

2d. Dissolve a pinch of soda in black molasses.

3d. Equal parts of syrup of squills and syrup of ipecac.

4th. A teaspoonful of goose-greese and one of honey or molasses.

5th. Wring a towel dry as possible out of cold water, bind to the throat and wrap a dry towel around the wet one.

6th. Saturate a cloth in lard or oil and spread over the breast. Grease the soles of the feet and behind the ears.

FOR A SNAKE BITE.

Drink strong whisky without sugar or water. It is said that intoxication is impossible under the circumstances.

FOR SORES ON HORSES.

Wash with castile soap, rinse in clear cold water, and then touch firmly but gently with a rag dipped in oil of spike and glycerine equal parts. Magical.

FOR INTENSE ITCHING.

Bathe in salt and water, dry with a towel and rub with sweet oil.

CURE FOR RHEUMATISM.

Three ounces of chloroform, four ounces of alcohol, five ounces of ether; mix the chloroform and ether first, and in fifteen minutes add the alcohol; then pour on a damp cloth and apply.

VAPOR BATH.

All that is required is that the patient be seated on a chair with a vessel of hot water placed beside him, and the whole enveloped with a blanket to be thrown over his head if the vapor is to be breathed, or pinned around his neck where this is not the case. The steam soon surrounds his body and causes a copious perspiration; and should it cease too soon to be evolved, its generation may be restored by dropping a heated brick or stone into the water.

WARM BATH FOR CHILDREN.

If a child is taken with convulsions put it immediately in a hot bath and apply cold water to the head. Never attempt to dry the body with towels, but wrap it closely in a large soft blanket.

CURE FOR DRUNKENNESS.

It is alleged by one who has been cured of a consuming taste for alcoholic stimulant that a half ounce of ground quassia steeped in a pint of vinegar, a small teaspoonful of the decoction to be drank in a little water every time the thirst comes on, affords a certain cure. In a few days the liquor craving will have entirely disappeared. This is a cheap, simple and harmless remedy for a very serious and expensive passion.—*Paris True Kentuckian.*

TOOTHACHE DROPS.

One drachm of oil of cloves, three drachms of laudanum. Mix and put on cotton and apply to the tooth.

WASH FOR CHAPPED HANDS.

Twenty grains of powdered borax, two ounces of glycerine, one pint of boiling water, well mixed.

A POWERFUL APPETIZER.

Ten drops of tincture of iron, three times a day in half a cup of water, before meals. Take through a glass tube or quill to prevent discoloration of the teeth.

HOUSEHOLD.

JAPANESE CLEANSING FLUID.

One fourth of a pound of white castile soap, one-fourth of a pound of ammonia, one ounce of glycerine, one ounce of ether, one ounce of spirits of wine. Cut the soap fine and heat it in one quart of soft water until dissolved, then add four quarts more of water and all the other ingredients. This can be recommended as being one of the best cleansing fluids of the day. It is invaluable in restoring gentlemen's clothing when soiled and faded.—*Mrs. A. S. Edmonston.*

JELLY SOAP.

Six gallons of hot water, three pounds of hard soap, two tablespoonsful of spirits of ammonia, four tablespoonsful of spirits of turpentine, one pound of sal soda. This makes fifty pounds of soap; cheap and good; costs about twenty cents.—*Mrs. H. N. Starnes.*

SOFT SOAP.

Put the ashes in a barrel, or hopper, which is better. Pour water on every day; drain it off, and if not strong enough pour it back or boil it down till strong. Put straw in the barrels first, then pack ashes in. When the lye is strong enough to strip a feather, put in grease until the lye ceases to absorb it. Cook until the soap looks thick.—*Mrs. Harry Brent.*

TO REMOVE FRUIT STAINS.

Rub hard with whisky, alcohol or camphor before wetting. It will do no good after they are put in water.

TO REMOVE STAINS FROM MARBLE.

Take two ounces of common soda, one ounce of pumice stone and one ounce of finely-powdered chalk. Sift through a fine sieve, and with water mix to a paste. Rub the mixture well over the marble, and the stains will be removed. Wash the marble clean with soap and water. Sometimes the marble is stained yellow with iron rust; this can be removed with lemon juice.—*Mrs. H. N. Starnes.*

TO PRESERVE GARDEN SEEDS.

Put them in bottles, perfectly dry, and cork. They will then be safe from mice and other trespassers.

TO CLEAN SILVER.

Take Spanish whiting, and dampen with equal parts of spirits of ammonia and alcohol. Rub well, dry with soft flannels, and polish with chamois skin.—*Mrs. R. S. Nesbitt.*

TO WASH CALICOES THAT ARE NOT FAST COLORS.

One tablespoonful of spirits of turpentine, and one of alcohol, in enough water to wash dress.—*Mrs. J. W. Baker.*

An old artificial flower placed in the bottom of a lamp and the oil poured on, presents a very pretty appearance.

A FINE FURNITURE POLISH.

Equal parts of linseed oil, turpentine and alcohol. Apply with a cloth. This is used by the stock-keepers at the great Mitchell and Ramelsburg Furniture House, Cincinnati, Ohio.

FOR CLEANING STEEL KNIVES.

Buy a bath brick at your drug store, scrape with a knife, dampen, rub the knives well, and then again with a dry cloth. The best thing for the purpose now in use.

A CHEAP FLY TRAP.

Fill a large tumbler with soapsuds; take a crust of corn bread and punch a hole in the middle (a small one), then spread thickly with honey or molasses, placing the side thus treated to the water. Many will get in, but not one in fifty will get out.

MRS. JOHN B. GORDON'S FLOOR STAIN.

Dissolve in one gallon of hot water one-fourth of a pound of potash, one fourth of a pound of beeswax, one-fourth of a pound of burnt umber, one-fourth of a pound of yellow ochre; melt the wax before putting in the water; apply two coats with a brush. When thoroughly dry, rub with a stiff brush, and afterwards with a woolen cloth. The floor may be used the same day if perfectly dry. This quantity is sufficient for a very large floor.

It is a good plan, when a meal is finished, to take the knives, forks and spoons and wipe the grease from them with tissue or soft paper. They are much more easily cleaned, and the water is not so greasy for the articles that follow.

TO CLEAN BOTTLES IN LARGE NUMBERS.

To do this in the best and quickest manner rinse such as may particularly require it; put a little hay or a coarse cloth in a vessel and arrange them in it as compactly as possible; cover them with cold water, light the fire, and boil them gently for half an hour; take them out; let them cool; rinse them well, and when dry they will be ready for use. One or two may be broken in the process, but it is considered the most advantageous method of proceeding when they are very extensively used.—*Miss Eliza Acton.*

HOUSEHOLD CONVENIENCES.

A box for blacking and blacking brushes is indispensable. Also have a special drawer for shoes and slippers not in use.

Tack a piece of ticking inside your closet door and keep your patterns there. Some ladies spend as much time hunting up a pattern as others would require to make the garments.

Get a soft sheepskin for the big rocking chair in winter. You will soon feel that you have existed but not lived before you had it.

Have a separate bag for all kinds of scraps, and have them labeled. Always keep old linen in easy reach, in case of emergencies.

A small broom, with a handle six feet long, is very useful in reaching cobwebs.

No house should be without a small stepladder.

Keep a pair of tinners' shears, for cutting tin, zinc and wire.

You cannot afford to be without a medicine chest. Have it in the family room, under lock and key. The following medicines should always be found inside:

Arnica.
Turpentine.
Ammonia.
Spirits Camphor.
Paregoric.
Laudanum.
Quinine.
Sweet and Castor Oil.
Linseed Oil.
Lime Water.

Ground Quassia.
Pulverized Alum.
Black and Red Pepper.

The articles named are often needed suddenly, and it is not going too far to say that their timely use, in absence of a physician or a deferred visit, may save life. You can enlarge your stock as your means and inclination may suggest. In a drawer at the bottom of chest have flannel and linen clothes, mustard, mutton tallow, scissors, thread, sponges, healing soap, etc.

Frail vases are often easily upset. The touch of a feather duster will send them "where the woodbine twineth." Put a handful of pebbles in the bottom.

When the metal part of a lamp becomes detached, you can mend it with a little plaster of Paris dampened with water.

Nothing will remove an offensive odor from a room as quickly as burning brown paper. Take the heaviest kind, twist it hard so it will burn slowly, and light it. Place it on the hearth, and do not leave it until you have extinguished it. This will be found much more pleasant and effectual than burnt sugar, or anything else in use.

When fine feathers have been strewn over the floor after making ticks or pillows, dampen the carpet or floor with water slightly. You can then get the feathers together with light sweeping, and take them up in a wad.

TO REMOVE A TIGHT RING.

Bathe the finger in cold soap-suds for twenty minutes. It must be on tight, indeed, if it will not succumb to this treatment.

TO CLEANSE JEWELRY.

Wash it in warm water, in which a tablespoonful of ammonia has been added. Never rub it with chalk; it will settle in the interstices, and require much time to remove.

A GOOD WASH FOR THE SKIN.

Take two quarts of boiling water, add four large tablespoonsful of spirits of ammonia, four tablespoonsful of shaved castile soap, one teaspoonful of turpentine, a tablespoonful of sal soda and three of glycerine. A drop or two of oil of roses will take away the smell of the turpentine. You can leave out the turpentine if wished, but it is a very fine cleansing agent. This is one of the finest preparations for the skin ever known. Half a teaspoonful will lather a half gallon or more of water, and it is like oil to the touch. It leaves the skin soft and moist and nicely perfumed. It is cheaper and better than soap. [Original.] —*Mrs. E. R. Tennent.*

[The three receipts below were received too late for proper classification, but were deemed too valuable to be omitted.—A.]

ITALIAN CREAM.

Take a pint of cream, a pint of milk, yolks of eight eggs, and a little powdered sugar. Make a custard with the milk and eggs, flavoring it according to taste; whip the cream until very stiff; when all is quite cold, mix the custard with the cream and pour into a mould.—*Mrs. Jefferson Davis.*

WELSH RAREBIT.

One-half pound of fat, crumbly cheese, one ounce prime butter, one gill of milk, or if preferred, of old ale. Cut the cheese into small pieces, and melt over the fire in a shallow pan. Stir constantly, until the cheese is entirely amalgamated; pour over thick toast, slightly moistened with boiled milk; garnish with two poached eggs, celery top and parsley.—*Mrs. Jefferson Davis.*

EXCELLENT RECEIPT FOR CLEANING CARPETS.

Four pounds of laundry soap, one pound of sal soda, four ounces of spirits ammonia, four ounces of spirits turpentine, four gallons of water. Boil fifteen minutes. When ready for use, one gallon of the fluid to four gallons of water. Let the mixture get entirely cold, take a scrubbing brush filled with the mixture and scrub the carpet with it, and the colors will look like new.—*Mrs. Jefferson Davis.*

VESTIBULE AND HALL.

THE hall is the key-note to the whole house, therefore everything about it should be dark and solid. Light colors are frivolous and gilding is out of place. Dark, rich colors should be used for wall and ceiling decorations. Plain tinted walls are also in good taste. If possible have a tile or inlaid wood floor, but, if this cannot be had, stain the floor a deep wood brown, with the base-boards and mouldings to match; or, in place of the stained floor use a covering of wool or India matting, and on this lay a strip of carpet like that of the stairs. Rugs are very inviting for a wide hall, and are cleaner and healthier than carpets. The prettiest color for a rug or carpet is a crimson ground with small figures or moss-green that has a yellowish glint under the sunshine. The staircase should be well set in the hall, but not too near the door. It should be broad, if possible, with low, wide steps. The carpet should harmonize with the appointments of the hall, and should be made softer and more enduring by a pad beneath. If the hall is very narrow don't attempt a magnificence in the matter of hat rack and stand. A mirror, if you will, with pegs each side of it, and a wood slab below, only wide enough to hold a book or hat, with glove drawers; a small wood bracket on the other side will hold a salver or plate for visiting cards. But little furniture can be used in most halls, but if wide enough there should be two straight-backed solid chairs and a sofa. If there is a recessed window have a cushioned seat just filling the recess. An ancestral chest, if you are fortunate enough to possess one, is much prized for the hallway, and the more antique, the better. With its brass or bronze handles, its carved wood work, it looks as if it might have come over in the Mayflower and held the riches of the whole family. Those who have them not are having the designs copied and imitated in rich woods, and a goodly amount of money they cost, too. Some of them stand upon four square solid feet, others have lions' claws for support. Some have one or two drawers at the bottom, while a heavy carved lid shuts in the chest proper. Many of these odd chests, which had been degraded to hold carpenters' tools, or hid away in the garret as receptacles for rubbish, are being reclaimed, polished, and assigned to this place of honor. Here also may be assigned a few pictures—good ones—hung low down, and upon a level with the eye. If the hall is large and well lit this is one of the best of places for the family portraits, and, even if a small hall, it may be beautified by a few well selected pictures. If space is denied for the hall table or hat rack, a pair of horns, or even several of them, may be utilized, hung one above another, in graduated sizes. These make good hat racks as well as umbrella holders.

Umbrella stands may be bought, or made in many unique ways, and they are really necessary, to catch the drippings. If the halls have not stained glass windows, shades to match those of the other windows, may be used. White Holland, trimmed with antique lace or embroidered and fringed, or an æsthetic red in silk or Holland, is now very fashionable. The light filtering through these red draperies gives a warm, cheerful light to even the darkest and gloomiest hall. White shades are hardly artistic, and look glaring on the outside of the house, either in parlors or halls, unless of lace or swiss, and then their only charm is their purity. And now, if you have an old-fashioned Dutch clock to stand in the farthermost corner of the hall, a few growing palms or tropical plants, you will have the ideal hall of halls, even if not able to have bronze or marble pedestal figures and costly jars and vases.

PARLOR AND LIBRARY.

IN selecting furniture the first thought should be given to comfort. The best chairs and couches are those which one likes best and takes most comfort in, whatever may be the style or material. They should be graceful, of easy make, and covered with a good serviceable color and material. It is exceedingly uncomfortable to have furniture so frail that it is continually being broken or defaced, or so handsome that ordinary mortals are afraid to use it, or so delicate in color or material that every touch soils it. Solidity, richness and comfort are combined in the furniture of to day. The styles of Queen Anne are revived, the solid Eastlake designs are in favor, and the tapestry for upholstering furniture is in English, old Flemish, and old Italian styles. Eastlake drawing-room suites and parlor sets have ebony and gilt frames, though there are other styles in French marqueterie, inlaid walnut and gilt and carved French walnut frames. They are upholstered in all shades of satin, satin brocade, brocade rep, French raw silk, Ormoleu silk, silk-faced sateen, silk cortelain, crimson silk plush, embossed velvet, and flowered cashmere. Very elegant suites and sets in all styles and upholstered in these goods are in colors of blue, old gold and crimson, olive green and brown, drab, tan, amber, French grey, ashes of roses, and salmon.

An arm chair of rattan is now placed amongst the parlor furniture. The rattan is yellow, black or gilded, and is upholstered in gay plush. A little divan, furnishing two or three seats, covered with plush and softly tufted, forms a centre piece, and is a convenient and pretty addition to a parlor. Cabinets as antique and rare as money can buy, made of mahogany and ebony, and plentifully trimmed with brass, are used to collect pretty articles of bric-a-brac. These have beveled glass doors and sometimes are quaintly carved. Mantel mirrors are much smaller, have beveled edges, and are furnished with shelves.

One or two good upholstered easy chairs never seem out of place, even in the most elegant parlor, and here and there an occasional little cane-bottomed chair gives diversity to the looks of the room, where no two chairs should be alike. A span table near the bay window will allow of jardiniere holding a fern or india-rubber plant to stand in the sun. You can have nothing better than black and gold for this purpose. Marble-top tables are no longer in use. Inlaid or hand painted woods now decorate the tops, and an embroidered or heavily fringed scarf of plush or mummy cloth is thrown across the top with ends drooping over the edges. The newest tables have square corners and old-fashioned twisted legs. Pretty little tables have oval shaped tops, are elaborately mounted with brass, and inlaid in diamond and checker board designs.

Grand or square pianos must be entirely hidden by rich needle work coverings. The English cottage piano usually stands with the back towards the room, not against the wall, and this back is covered with handsome drapery.

Brass or Oriental China lamps are now the fashion for common use. Venetian chandeliers or large hanging brass lamps for receptions. For the artistic touches one needs to choose carefully and judiciously, or the rooms will look over-crowded. Upon the walls a few pictures. If you like the heads of saints, choose those of the old masters; if atmospheric effect, with glories of gold and crimson sunsets;

if cattle, where the dapple cows lie chewing their cud in contentment upon the banks of pleasant streams or in meadowland.

In this corner is placed an Eastlake, Queen Anne, Jacobin or Gothic style cabinet, inlaid in gold, gilt, and mosaic work; in that corner an easel with gilt designs, over which fling a piece of brocade of old gold and peacock blue in oriental mixture. A loosely held mass of dark olive, plum colored, or garnet satin may be placed against the wall in an alcove or the middle of a panel, and a light colored pitcher hung on it with a pretty knot passed through the handle and over a large gilt-headed nail. A bit of rich material— an old crepe shawl for instance—may be hung on a home-made easel draping a picture. A painted or embroidered silk curtain may hang beneath a bracket supporting a bust.

Persian embroidered "scarfs" or chair scarfs are now used instead of the obsolete tidy.

In the window recess place a pedestal to support a group of figures, a statuette or jardiniere filled with flowers or plants, natural—not artificial. An ottoman, upholstered in black satin and embroidered, will here find a place.

The centre of the mantel is usually occupied by a handsome clock and bronzes. At either end of the mantel a bust in bronze or bisque of Louis Quinze designs, representing shepherdesses, village girls crowned with flowers, and village lads with straw hats decked with ribbons.

There is still room for a plaque upon which may be exquisite groups of flowers, marine views, rural landscapes, or groups of figures in quaint or familiar costumes.

Plaques are brought out in charming relief when hung against a rich background of velvet or silk. Back of the statuette or busts are placed banners or fans in deep rich colors. On the tables and mantel are quaint card receivers, flower holders, ornaments in bisque, hammered brass and china.

The library has but few ornaments. Handsome pictures, one or two richly carved massive tables, a few straight-backed library chairs, and one Sleepy Hollow to curl up in and read on a stormy day or evening; soft rugs, a foot rest and a book-case with glass doors are all that is necessary.

THE FAMILY ROOM.

When the family room is entered, it should be so bright, so cheerful that sadness and depression give way. A sombre room will give any one the blues, and for this reason use all that is possible of the bright martial red; it arouses triumphant feelings, joy and gayety.

Get a carpet with scarlet predominating; a cream colored ground with deep scarlet roses is very pretty if one can afford a Brussels; if not, the new ingrains have beautiful designs and bright colors. Have a low divan couch with large square pillows. A rocker handsomely upholstered, a large, soft easy chair, a small sewing chair, a bamboo chair with broad flat arms, a Shaker or rush-bottomed chair of artistic design, are all comfortable and cheap. Numbers of small, oddly shaped tables, low and high, are placed about the room and used for books, work, photographs, etc. There should always be one large table covered with a quiet, rich, beautifully bordered cloth. If you have a couch that is stiff and ugly, try what a few yards of cretonne and soft cushions will do.

This room is also the place for the window-garden, the aquarium, fernery, bird-cage, and book-case, if you have no library.

An ordinary stone jar, such as pickles are kept in, may be painted a chocolate-brown or dark red, and decorated with ferns, flowers, birds and butterflies. Ginger jars, small stone jugs, whatever has a good or classical shape may be made a thing of beauty if harmony and taste are carefully observed.

There must be a bracket here and there, beneath a picture, where a pot of ivy can be placed to form a graceful framing to the portrait, perhaps, of some loved one, or for an engraving or pretty chromo.

A bunch of oats, with long even stems, tied with a band of wide satin ribbon, and suspended by the same under a picture, is a simple, pretty decoration within the reach of all.

A large pampas plume, with five or six long peafowl feathers, using the plume as a background for the feathers, all tied with a band of peacock blue or green ribbon, is fastened on the wall in a corner, or over the door, over or under a picture.

One or two bright tinted fans hung on the wall, a bunch of grasses tied with a bright bow of ribbon, or fastened on the picture cords, a large vase filled with autumn leaves, ferns, or grasses are also desirable ornamentations.

THE FAMILY DINING ROOM.

THE family dining-room is one which should receive especial attention. The first impression which it should make on the beholder, and the constant one upon its occupants, should be that of solid comfort. Let it not be fussy, airy or light; everything must be dark, solid and substantial. The colors should be deep rich ones that hold their own; the rich crimsons, the dark blues, the dull Pompeiian reds or olives, or any of the kindred tints that do not have a faded appearance. As for the walls of the dining room the rich warm colors are the best, and under no circumstances are light papers desirable. Solid colors are but little used, but instead are copies of old tapestries, Flemish and many other fabrics, of which the dominant shades are moss green, bronze, olive, etc. These are neither light nor very dark; they do not absorb the light, and form a good background for pictures, while, at the same time, they are dark enough in tone to prevent anything like a violent and crude contrast with the dark wood work and furniture. If one may have gilding in the paper anywhere it is in the dining room, and that is the sole place where it can be used to much purpose, for it adds to the desired idea of richness there. Everywhere else gilding is only to be used to enhance the effect of beauty, to throw up lights, to point out contrasts. Gilding is especially desirable if the room be on the dark side of the house, for it supplies a light of its own, independent of the sunlight, and a gilded background is frequently not amiss in setting off such pictures as one may put upon dining-room walls.

The next item of importance is the floor; here may be placed the rug with its border of bare floor or parquetry, or the entire floor laid in choice geometric designs of colored woods is equally suitable; or if laid in alternate strips of oak and walnut, or cherry and Southern pine, it is but little more expensive than common pine. Over any of these floors in winter the drugget is to be laid and dispensed with in summer or not, according to the taste. If, however, an entire carpet is preferred, remember that green, drab and red are the least desirable colors. For this room should be chosen carpets combining the colors of the wall paper in the dark rich shades belonging to Turkish and Persian designs.

Whatever the carpet is, the curtains should carry up this idea, and they need to fall in heavy folds, affording a rather subdued light. If hung on rods they may be pushed back to let in all the morning sunlight, which gives so much brightness to the breakfast room; at noon they may be arranged to keep out the garish light, and at night let fall to shut out the darkness and gloom without. The furniture of dining rooms is almost universally made of dark wood; the only exception is oak, and this is now generally darkened to a richer tint than that of the new wood.

The woods chiefly used are American walnut, dark oak, mahogany and stained wood. The painting of the woodwork corresponds in tone with that of the furniture. The cornice and wainscot are also dark, and would have a singularly bad effect if the walls were very light. The great object is to avoid all violent contrasts, which are contrary to good taste, and to choose shades that blend together and produce a harmonious whole.

The chairs are in the square, solid styles now so much in vogue with upholstering in embossed and gilded leather or in the plain leather which is most generally liked. Brass or silver nails are used profusely in upholstering leather furniture, and add to the solid and substantial appearance of the articles. Try the chairs thoroughly before you purchase, for the main object in the selection of dining-room chairs should always be solid comfort.

Extension tables are low and square-cornered, and are heavily carved. Buffets are very large, and are in Queen Anne style with quaint little cupboards for the display of decorated china and silver.

Sideboards are in square, massive styles, with shelves and niches for china and different kind of ware. The butler's tray and sideboard are much enlivened by heavy, rich-colored cloths worked in colors and dropping low over the sides, with heavy fringes showing handsomely against the dark woods.

Over the fireplace no arrangement will be found more picturesque than the narrow, high shelf and the tiny cupboards and racks above it, for the display of china too precious or too long-descended for daily use; in the centre, the mantel mirror, with beveled edges, and smaller bits of mirrors behind the open racks, also with beveled edges, whose jewel-like cut adds greatly to the brilliancy. On these open racks may stand many little oddities, hardly appropriate to other rooms, the odd mugs, brass or china candlesticks, porcelain pepper boxes, little old-fashioned pitchers and decanters, bits of coral, shells, jars and all those quaint little things that one inherits or else "picks up."

It has been the custom to have pictures of still life in the dining-room—of game and fish; but this is hardly a cheerful view, to see representations of the game and fish that one is soon to eat—in all the agonies of death. This room seems to be the most suitable place for family portraits —those of the last generation. Here they look down from their frames, welcoming each meal and the train of life it brings, and exercise as it were, a mute guardianship over thought and behavior. Here, also, may be placed mottoes, flower pictures, and some varieties of landscapes.

A screen is also quite necessary for the dining room, as the table is often, nearly always, placed so that some one must sit near the fire. The prettiest for this purpose is a three-leaf folding Japanese screen. Colored shades on the lamps, and a Japanese scroll on each side of the fire-place or on the door, give life and color. A few tall, growing plants, in large vases; a cheery hearth or bright stove; plenty of sunshine and good cheer, will make the dining-room the most pleasant in the house.

For the foregoing hints on house-furnishing, we are indebted to the "Household" of the *Detroit Free Press.*

THE KITCHEN.

IF a housekeeper cannot have a well furnished parlor and kitchen at the same time the preference should be given to the latter, and if needs be a parlor should be entirely dispensed with rather than be minus the comforts and conveniences of a well ordered kitchen. It should be closely built and plastered and connected with the main house. On many a tombstone in our cemeteries could be truthfully inscribed, "Died from exposure in an open kitchen." In winter stop up all doors and windows not absolutely needed; for the latter have red blinds or curtains made of plain or figured oil calico. They will add to the comfortable appearance of the room, and in summer serve to keep it darkened and free from flies. A carpet even though a very plain one is a great luxury and can be kept clean with care. However, if not convenient, or desirable, the floor may be oiled and then grease spots are removed with little trouble. Have a sofa covered with chintz or calico and a pillow filled with "excelsior;" also a rocking chair with cushion. This is for the housekeeper's comfort; for though it is a kitchen it is not necessary that one may have no time for comfort or rest. If the mistress is seldom in the kitchen, there is all the more reason for making the girl comfortable. Few servant girls will leave a mistress who makes their working place pleasant and shows a proper consideration for their comfort. Then when their work is done they can shut away all the unsightly implements of their service, and for a time forget that they are working for others, but feel as if they are in a home of their own. A side lamp should be placed on the wall out of the way. See that the

THE KITCHEN. 245

flue is in perfect order and tack a piece of zinc under the stove extending for two feet outside. Keep matches in a safe place out of the reach of children. Never lay them loosely on a table. A large box filled with wood and kindling should be in one corner of the room or just outside the door. *Do not place the wood-box near the stove.* A spark sometimes falls, or the stove gets intensely hot and the box or its contents may be ignited. It should be the last duty before retiring, to visit the kitchen and examine the fires. If this rule was followed in every house the number of disastrous conflagrations would be greatly lessened. A large table is required for the preparation of the meals, and nothing should be allowed to remain on it except the marble slab for pastry and bread making and a bucket of water. Set a large waiter (an old one will do) under the water bucket; this precaution will save you the disgusting spectacle of a sloppy floor or table. Several pounds of lard, a pound of butter, spices of all kinds, pepper and salt, should be placed in a safe near the table. Have a block for the preparation of your meats. If this work is done on your table it will soon be rendered unsightly. Hang a slate with pencil attached on your kitchen wall. When you find that you are in need of provisions, write the desired article on the slate; also if there is any duty connected with the household which must not be forgotten, make a note of it. It is a good plan in the afternoon to write down the bill of fare for next day. A small table with drawers should be in every kitchen; in the drawer keep a quire of foolscap paper, a pair of scissors, a pencil, a ball of cord, and your cook book. A kitchen is rendered much more attractive by having the utensils when not in use placed in a closet. If you are obliged to keep them in view have them systematically arranged on nails or hooks. The tinware should occupy one shelf; the earthenware another. Never employ any knives, spoons, dishes, or any articles in the kitchen which belong to the dining room. Spoons are sure to get scratched and a knife used for preparing an onion takes up its flavor which two or three cleanings will not remove. When a vessel is emptied of its contents place it back on the stove partly filled with water. When your meal is finished they will be waiting for you and will be more easily cleansed than if you had left them to dry. If your meals are taken in the kitchen throw a large table-cloth all over the kitchen table completely hiding from view the evidences of your work. It is not appetizing to be compelled to look at pans and biscuit board not cleaned and scraps of this and that.—*Mrs. E. R. Tennent.*

UTENSILS NECESSARY IN THE KITCHEN OF A SMALL FAMILY.

WOODEN-WARE.

Kitchen table, wash bench, wash tubs, (two sizes,) washboard, skirt board, bosom board, bread board, towel roll, potato masher, wooden spoons, clothes stick, flour barrel cover, flour sieve, chopping bowl, soap bowl, pails, lemon squeezer, clothes wringer, clothes pins, clothes basket, mop, wood boxes.

TIN-WARE.

Boiler for clothes, bread pan, two dish pans, preserving pan, four milk pans, two quart basins, two quart covered tin pails, one four quart covered tin pail, sauce pans with covers, (two sizes,) two tin cups, four jelly moulds, two pint moulds for rice, blanc mange, etc., one skimmer, two dippers, (different sizes,) two funnels, (one for jug and one for cruets,) one quart measure, also pint, half pint and gill measure, two scoops, bread pan, two round jelly cake pans, and two long pie pans, coffee pot, tea pot, colander, steamer, horseradish grater, nutmeg grater, small salt sieve, hair sieve for straining jellies, Davis egg-beater, cake turner cake cutters, apple corer, potato cutter, one dozen muffin rings, ice filter, flour dredge, tea canister, coffee canister, cake, bread, cracker and cheese boxes, crumb tray, dust pan.

IRON-WARE.

Range, pot with steamer to fit, soup kettle, porcelain preserving kettle, tea kettle, large and small frying-pans, dripping pans, gem pans, iron spoons of different sizes, gridirons, griddle, waffle irons, toasting rack, meat fork, jagging iron, can-opener, coffee mill, flat irons, hammer, tack hammer, screw-driver, ice pick.

STONE WARE.

Crocks of various sizes, bowls holding six quarts, two quarts and pint bowls, six earthen baking dishes, different sizes.

BRUSHES.

Table brush, two dust brushes, two crumb brushes, one blacking brush for stove, hearth brush, brooms.

THE LAUNDRY.

LAUNDRY CUSHION.

Sheets,	1	2	3	4	5	6	7	8	9	10	11	12
Pillow-cases,	1	2	3	4	5	6	7	8	9	10	11	12
Counterpanes,	1	2	3	4	5	6	7	8	9	10	11	12
Napkins,	1	2	3	4	5	6	7	8	9	10	11	12
Table cloths,	1	2	3	4	5	6	7	8	9	10	11	12
Towels,	1	2	3	4	5	6	7	8	9	10	11	12
Shirts,	1	2	3	4	5	6	7	8	9	10	11	12
Dresses,	1	2	3	4	5	6	7	8	9	10	11	12
Night-dresses,	1	2	3	4	5	6	7	8	9	10	11	12
Chemise,	1	2	3	4	5	6	7	8	9	10	11	12
Drawers,	1	2	3	4	5	6	7	8	9	10	11	12
Collars,	1	2	3	4	5	6	7	8	9	10	11	12
Cuffs,	1	2	3	4	5	6	7	8	9	10	11	12
Stockings,	1	2	3	4	5	6	7	8	9	10	11	12
Aprons,	1	2	3	4	5	6	7	8	9	10	11	12
Shirts,	1	2	3	4	5	6	7	8	9	10	11	12
Half-hose,	1	2	3	4	5	6	7	8	9	10	11	12

Every housekeeper should have a laundry cushion. No washing should go out, even if it is done at home, without a memorandum. It is no little trouble to get paper and write the name of each article and the number. A laundry cushion made according to design here presented will save time and annoyance. Say that you have six table-cloths in wash; you have only to stick a pin in the number six, opposite the word table-cloth, and so on. You can make this cushion at home by taking a piece of white cotton and penning the words and figures in indelible ink.

It will be much more satisfactory, however, and cost but little, to get a scrap of plain silk and have it printed. Stuff it with wool and make it as flat as possible, having the bottom and sides made of pasteboard covered with silk and made square at the corners like a shallow box.

You will find a crocheted bag hung on your bureau to receive soiled collars, cuffs and handkerchiefs, a great convenience. It is not well to throw them in a heap with the larger pieces for the reason that they are apt to be lost or overlooked. Sew a piece of narrow tape three inches long to each stocking and tie them together when sent to the washerwoman. You will then cease to be annoyed with "odd" stockings. Look over your napkins and table-cloths, and if they are stained with fruit, preserves or jelly, dip the stains immediately in whisky, camphor or alcohol. If stained with ink, dip in tallow or rub in sweet milk. Ink not dried can be entirely removed by sprinkling on pepper and salt. Iron rust can be removed with oxalic acid. Rub mildewed spots with buttermilk and lay in the sun. They may also be removed with lemon juice.

TO MAKE STARCH STIFF

Add a teaspoonful of Epsom salts to each bowl of starch before boiling.

TO GLAZE LINEN.

Add a teaspoonful of fine salt and one of scraped white soap to each pound of starch.

TO WASH MUSLINS, LINENS, OR PRINTS WITHOUT FADING.

Boil a quart of bran tied in a thin bag in four gallons of rain water. When it becomes tepid wash the material, reserving half the water for rinsing. This will starch and cleanse it thoroughly, and not injure the color. *Use no soap.*

Iron on the wrong side. In washing buff linens substitute hay for bran.—*Mrs. R. T. Nesbitt.*

CARE OF IRONS.

Keep them in a dry place where no water is likely to get to them. If rusty, rub with beeswax and salt. This makes them as smooth as a mirror. A polishing iron is very broad and heavy, and you should have a long narrow one for getting into gathers and pleats.

TO WASH BLACK CASHMERE.

Rub well in soap suds, warm, but not hot. If too hot, the goods will shrink; then rinse in warm, clear water. After this let it lie several hours in strong ammonia water. Wring out as dry as possible, place on a table with a blanket underneath, and rub lightly till nearly dry. Then iron on the wrong side with a very hot iron. A piece of black goods should be placed over the blanket and the rubbing should be done with a scrap of black.

TO RENOVATE BLACK SILK.

To a gallon of cold water, add four large sliced Irish potatoes. Let it stand over night, and in the morning wash the silk in the water, and iron on the wrong side. It is best to heat the water.

TO WASH WHITE LACES.

Squeeze, but do not rub them in warm suds; then rinse in clear, warm water. Dip in thin starch, squeeze out all you can and pin to a folded sheet. Do not iron, but press with the hand until thoroughly dry.

TO MAKE BROWN LACE.

It is often a difficult matter to buy deep cream or brown lace to trim suits. It can be made at home and never detected. Take white lace, and if soiled, wash thoroughly, lay it overnight in strong coffee. Dripped coffee is best for the purpose, as it is free from grounds. If made in the ordinary way, steam it. When taken out of the coffee squeeze hard and rub till dry with the hand.

TO WASH FLANNELS AND BLANKETS.

Wash them in warm soapsuds, but do not rinse—carry them through several waters. When nearly dry let two persons take hold of the blanket and shake as you would a carpet. No ironing will be necessary; it will eventually ruin them. All wool flannels should be shaken, also till smooth.

TO WASH TIDIES.

Wash in cold water, limestone water is preferable. Make a little suds with hard soap; rinse thoroughly and dry. Never put tidies worked with worsted in warm water.

EMBROIDERY.

Embroidery should be dipped in weak ammonia before using, in order to set the color, and articles embroidered or knit in worsted should never be washed with anything stronger than bran and water. A little ox gall mixed with the water will keep the colors from running, unless the work is rubbed or wrung.

Buggy grease or paint can be removed from articles that wash by rubbing in turpentine, and then washing in soap suds. If the goods is silk, or woolen, rub lightly with the turpentine, sponge with ammonia water and press with a hot iron.

GLOVE CLEANER.

Mix one-fourth of an ounce of carbonate of ammonia, one-fourth ounce of fluid chloroform, one-fourth ounce of sulphuric ether, one quart of distilled benzine. Pour out a small quantity in a saucer, put on glove and wash as if washing the hands, changing the solution until gloves are clean; take off, squeeze them, replace on hands, and with a clean cloth rub fingers, etc., until they are dry and perfectly fitted to the hand. This is an excellent clothes, ribbon and silk cleaner ; it is perfectly harmless to the most delicate tints. Apply with a soft sponge, rubbing gently until spots disappear. Care must be taken not to use it near the fire, as the benzine is very inflammable.

POULTRY.

It is impossible, in a work of this kind, to do the subject under consideration full justice, but the rearing of poultry is generally under the supervision of the housekeeper, and so indispensable to a good table that a few general rules are hereby given.

INCUBATION.

It is well to know in the beginning that hens are stubborn and inconsistent. If they choose their places for sitting you must acquiesce in the decision and place the eggs there. If two hens are found sitting in close proximity break up one or the other. You will frequently see three or more crowd on one nest while another is left without an occupant. For this reason it is best to have them separated. Barrels sawed half in two and boxes provided with clean straw placed in unfrequented localities, or partly obscured by spreading trees are favorite places. Never make a nest of cotton seed. The eggs are too much heated, and it is a wonder if one ever hatches. A damp situation is best and will insure good hatching in hot weather. Attempting to keep the nest and eggs dry has ruined many a brood. It is not so in nature. Every morning the hen leaves her nest and has to seek her precarious meal through the long wet grass which drenches her as if she had been ducked in a pond. With this saturated breast she returns and the eggs are duly moistened. But if the nest be dry, the hen kept dry, and the weather happens to be dry also, the moisture within the egg itself becomes dried to the consistency of glue, and the poor little chick, being unable to *move round* within the shell, cannot fracture it and perishes. Such a mishap will not occur if the ground under the nest be damp and cool. A good plan is to take a thick layer of fresh cut damp grass and cover with straw cut in two inch lengths. Do not set eggs which are more than two weeks old. If they are a month old it will be useless trouble. Every one should be marked with ink or pencil, so that if any be subsequently laid in the nest they may be at once detected and removed. Do not shake the eggs, and do not give to a hen more than she can comfortably cover. We have not only to consider how many chickens the hen can hatch, but how many she can *cover* when they are partly grown. If a hen be set in January she should not have more than seven or eight eggs, or the poor little things, as soon as they begin to get large, will have no shelter and die off. In April or May broods such a limitation is not needed, but even then eleven or twelve chickens are quite as many as a large and well feathered hen can properly nourish. The straw, as before stated, should be cut in two inch lengths; the reason is that the hen, during her twenty-four hours stay, gets her claws entangled in the long straws, and on leaving for her daily meal is very likely to drag one or two with her, fracturing them or even jerking them quite out of the nest. Should such a mishap occur, the eggs must be removed and clean straw substituted, and every sound egg at all soiled by the broken one be washed with a sponge and warm water gently but quickly, drying afterwards with a dry cloth. The hen, if very dirty, should have her breast cleansed and the whole replaced immediately, that the egg may not be chilled. A moderate hatch may still be expected, though the number of chicks is always more or less reduced by such an accident. The chickens break the shell at the end of the twenty-first day, on an average. Never attempt to assist a chick from the shell. To fuss about the nest frets the hen exceedingly, and even where the poor creature survived at the time, it never lived to maturity.

THE REARING AND FATTENING OF CHICKENS.

For twenty-four hours after hatching chickens require no food at all. It is best to let them remain undisturbed. It is a common practice to take those first hatched away from the hen and put them in a basket by the fire till the whole brood is out. When the eggs have varied much in age, this course must be adopted, for the hen, if she felt a few of the chicks moving beneath her, would not stay to hatch the rest. The nest should be examined and the shells removed. The first meal should consist of bread crumbs, moistened with milk and mixed with the hard boiled yolk of eggs. It would be better never to feed chickens or fowls of any kind on raw dough. It is very little trouble to mix the meal with a tablespoonful of cayenne pepper and water or buttermilk, and bake in the oven. An excellent food is made by bringing buttermilk to the boiling point and stirring in corn meal until thick. It is said to fatten fowls as if by magic. The hen should be confined in a coop which will allow the chickens to get in and out. She should be kept there for two weeks. A greater number of chickens are sacrificed every year by allowing them to wander through tall wet grass than are ever brought to the table. They are entirely unable to withstand such shocks. If the weather is cold or inclement, throw old pieces of rag carpet, bran sacks, or refuse oil cloth over the coops at night. Place a shallow pan of water near each coop and renew it frequently. When feeding fowls the bread is generally scratched about and much of it lost. This can be avoided by making a platform, raised two inches above the ground and surrounded by a raised border. Food must be given very often. For the first week, every hour is not too much; the next three weeks, every two hours; from one to two months old, every three hours, and after that, three times a day will be sufficient. Rice-grits makes a fine diet, and can be bought of general provision dealers. Oatmeal is extremely desirable, but it is too expensive to continue its use beyond the first week. Rice left over from a meal, small bits of ham, chopped lettuce, and many other scraps are heartily enjoyed, and you will be repaid for your trouble in collecting them. Never feed the chickens about the doors. Have a place remote from the house, and they will never come nearer. If you are troubled with chickens making a pleasure park of the house, walking into the parlor and viewing your mirrors and statuary, it is your own fault. The process of fattening should require but three weeks. It must be borne in mind that fat only is added by thus penning a chicken. The lean or flesh must be made before, and unless the chicken has attained the proper standard in this respect, it is useless to attempt to fatten it. Hence the importance of high feeding from the very shell. If extra weight and fat are wanted the birds may be "crammed" during the last ten days of the fattening period. The meal is to be rolled up the thickness of a finger, and then cut into pellets an inch and a half long. Each morsel must be dipped in water before it is put in the bird's throat. The quantity given can only be learned by experience.

HOUSES.

The first essential requisite to success in poultry keeping is a thoroughly good house for the birds to roost and lay in. This does not necessarily imply a large or costly one. It means simply that the fowl house must combine two absolute essentials—be both perfectly water-proof and well ventilated. Strive to keep out the rain and the wind also. Wood an inch thick will answer in any ordinary climate; the boards must be either tongued together or all the cracks between them caulked by driving in a string with a blunt chisel. The door should fit well, admitting no air except under the bottom: and, in short, every precaution taken to prevent draught. Planks alone make a good roofing. They should be laid horizontally, one plank overlapping the other, and the whole well tarred at first, and every autumn afterwards. The best flooring for the fowl house is concrete made with strong fresh slacked hydraulic lime and pounded "clinkers" put down hot, well trodden once a day for a week, and finally smoothed. The process is troublesome, but the result is a floor which is not only very clean in itself, but easily kept so. Cleanliness must be attended to. It is easily secured by laying a board under the perch, which can be scraped every morning. Or the droppings may be taken up daily with a small hoe and a housemaid's common dust pan, after which a handful of ashes or sand lightly sprinkled will make the house all that it should be. Near the fowl house have a heap of dry dust or sifted ashes for the fowls to roll in and cleanse themselves in their own peculiar manner, which should be removed as often as it becomes damp or foul from use.

The "run" for fowls should certainly be as large as can be afforded; an extensive range is not only better for their health, but saves both trouble and food, as they will to a great extent forage for themselves. Very few, however, can command this, and poultry may be kept almost anywhere by bearing in mind the one important point that the smaller the space in which they are confined the greater and more constant attention must be bestowed upon the cleanliness of the domain.

DISEASES OF POULTRY.

If fowls are kept clean and well sheltered from wind and wet; are not over fed, and have a due proportion of both soft and green food, with an abundant supply of clean water, they are apt to remain free from disease. You can do more to prevent disease than to cure it. To prescribe for a fowl is one of the most hopeless speculations you can engage in. It is now conceded by the best authorities that there is really no such disease as cholera; that the distressing symptoms are caused by mites; the remedies are therefore, self evident, CLEAN UP.

Kerosene mixed with their food is said to be an excellent remedy. The fowls will not object to it. Add Epsom salts to their drinking water. The American Agriculturist says that a strong solution of hyposulphate of soda given three times a day in teaspoonful doses is the best remedy.

A sprig of rue, a common garden herb, if placed in the drinking water is *the best* remedy for chicken cholera. I consider it infallible.—*Mr. T. H. Shockley.*

Gapes consist, so far as actual symptoms extend, in a number of small worms, which infest the windpipe and cause the chickens to gasp for breath. Give every day a morsel of camphor the size of a grain of wheat; or a little turpentine may be given in meal, taking care that the deficiencies in diet be amended. Roup is always caused by wet or very cold winds. It begins with a common cold, and terminates in an offensive discharge from the nostrils and eyes, often hanging in froth about these organs. It is highly contagious, and let all fowls affected by it be at once put by themselves, and have a separate drinking vessel. Mr. Tegetmeier's treatment is "to feed on oatmeal, mixed with ale and green food unlimited; washing the head with tepid water and giving daily one grain of sulphate of copper. Pip is no disease, and demands no treatment, being only analogous to a foul tongue in human beings. Cure the bad digestion, or whatever else is the real evil, and the thickening of the tongue will disappear too. For diarrhœa feed on warm barley meal; give some green food, but not very much; administer four times a day three drops of camphorated spirits on a pill of meal. Soft eggs are caused by overfeeding the hens, and the remedy is then self-evident. It may, however, occur from want of lime, which of course must be supplied; the best form being calcined, and powdered oyster shells. Insect vermin can only be troublesome from gross neglect, either of the fowls or of their habitations. In the one the remedy is a dust-bath mixed with powdered coke or sulphur; in the other an energetic limewashing of the houses.

We are indebted for much of the information in this department to "The Practical Poultry Keeper, by Wright," and to Capt. James Hughes, and Mr. Wm. Hames, of Marietta.

HOW TO SUCCEED WITH TURKEYS.

Few farmers who raise turkeys make suitable preparation for the business. These birds being but recently reclaimed from the forest, where they take care of themselves, many take it for granted that they are capable of doing well without care in a state of domestication; and being of a wild and roaming nature, assume that the more freedom they have the better it is for them. This is one of the half-truths that do great damage in the rearing of the birds. Turkeys should not be left to steal their nests in woods or swamps, and be allowed to lay and sit no one knows where, on account of the many enemies to which they themselves and their eggs and young are exposed. These enemies embrace the fox, raccoon, skunk, and the hawk, which is one of the greatest enemies of the young birds. While it is true that turkeys need to ramble through the summer, when they can get most of their living in the fields, and at the same time be of great benefit to the farm in ridding it of grasshoppers, bugs, worms, grubs, etc., injurious to growing crops, it is also true that they need restraint in the laying and hatching season, and for the first three weeks after the chicks leave the nest. None of our domestic birds are more susceptible of training, or take more kindly to the preparations that the wise housekeeper makes for their thrift and comfort. They require much attention during the laying and hatching season, and for a part of each day at least should be kept in a suitable yard or orchard by themselves, where convenient nests have been prepared for them. The success of the year depends largely on knowing where every bird is, where she lays, and especially where she sits. It is highly essential that turkey hens be tame and gentle; to accomplish this be kind and gentle with them; have but one person to attend to them during the hatching season, and when the chicks are young, as a stranger might do harm by causing fright. Be in no hurry to take the young from the nest. They require no food the first day. When the young are removed from the nest wash the old turkey on the underside of the wings, and on the body with a strong decoction of tobacco, to destroy vermin. When first taken off confine the young in a low yard, made by setting boards a foot wide or more on edge, and allow the old bird her liberty. Feed at first with dough made of coarse ground corn meal, finely chopped boiled eggs, and new milk. Feed little at a time and often; put sulphur in the feed occasionally; keep the young turkeys from getting wet, either by dew or rain, for the first month. Give them care and attention from the time the hen commences laying in the spring until the young are fit to slaughter, and they will be profitable.—*American Agriculturist.*

DUCKS.

Ducks will do well in a garden, or any other wide range where they can procure plenty of slugs and worms, with a pond in reach. Kept in this manner, they will not only be found profitable but very serviceable; keeping the place almost free of those slugs which are the gardener's great plague, and doing but little damage, except to strawberries, for which they have a great partiality, and which must be protected from their ravages.

They will keep themselves very nearly on what the hens refuse. Ducks should have a separate house with a brick or stone floor as it requires to be frequently washed down. Clean straw should be given them every alternate night. Other attention they need none beyond the precaution of keeping them in until they have laid every morning.

GUINEA FOWLS.

To commence breeding guinea fowls it is needful to procure some eggs and set them under a common hen; for if old hens be purchased they will wander off for miles as soon as they are set at liberty and never return. If hatched in the poultry yard, however, and regularly fed, they will remain; but must always have one meal regularly at night, or they will never roost at home. The hen lays freely from May or June till August. She is a very shy bird, and if eggs are taken from her nest with her knowledge she will forsake it altogether and seek another which she conceals with the most sedulous care. The nest should not be visited when she is in sight. Incubation is from twenty-six to thirty days. The chicks require food immediately, and should be fed and cared for in the same manner as young turkeys, though they may be allowed more liberty. They require more constant feeding than any other fowl, a few hours' abstinence being fatal to them.

GEESE.

Geese should be set in March or early April, as it is very difficult to rear the young in hot weather. The goose sits very steadily, but should be induced to come off once a day and take a bath. Besides this, she should have in reach a good supply of food and water, or hunger will compel her one by one to eat all her eggs. The goslings, when put out, should have a fresh turf daily for a few days and be fed on boiled oatmeal and rice, with water *from a pond,* in a very shallow dish, as they should not be allowed to swim for a fortnight. After two weeks they will be able to shift for themselves, only requiring to be protected from very heavy rain till fledged, and to have one or two feeds of grain daily in addition to what they can pick up. For fattening they should be penned up in a dark shed and fed on barley meal, being let out for several hours for a *last bath* before being killed, in order to clean their feathers.

FLOWERS.

THE only difficult part of making a garden is the deep digging and the enriching necessary to produce fine flowers. When the ground is very poor it should be spaded out and carted off, and its place filled with better. A mixture of leaf mould, barnyard manure, leached ashes, soot, and very little salt will make any clay hill or the pine barren blossom like a rose. Low wet lands require an addition of sand, where bulbous and tuberous rooted flowers are to be planted. There is no necessity for any one in the country to buy fertilizers, when with a little care a compost heap made of decayed leaves and chips, ashes, rich dirt from under woodpiles, bits of coal and soap suds, may always be ready to supply the wants of the garden. After the flower beds have been made sufficiently rich and light, they should be raked over until fine and smooth, and elevated in the middle so that the water will run off.

DESIGNS FOR FLOWER BEDS.

Much taste may be displayed in the selection of designs for flower beds. Fancy, complicated designs are pleasing, but unless such beds are carefully bordered, their outlines soon become marred. Long, sweeping curves are always effective. Circles are pretty and well suited for ribbon beds or masses of small flowers. Ribbon borders are made by having the outside of dusty miller, next foliage plants, and so on, as the fancy dictates, being careful to use nothing that grows high up off the ground. A beautiful bed is made of a border of dark foliage plants and in the centre a clump of scarlet geraniums. Plant a dozen together and keep them blooming by removing all dead leaves and decayed branches, and adding a drop or two of ammonia to the water they are sprinkled with. Oval, square, half circle and star beds, are all pretty. The walks should be from three to five feet wide. It is better to sacrifice a little more ground than to give a garden the contracted appearance always produced by narrow walks.

PLANTING THE SEED.

Nearly all kinds of flower seeds require transplanting, therefore it is best to plant in boxes, pots, or hot-beds. Old cigar boxes are easily handled, but first bore holes in the bottom of the boxes, and in them place either broken clam or oyster shells, or pieces of old flower pots, as a drainage, then take light, rich earth, and sift or rub it carefully in your hands, to be sure there are no lumps; some bake the earth to destroy any insects which may be in it, but it answers the same purpose to pour boiling water on it. After you have filled the boxes with this prepared earth sprinkle your seeds carefully over it, and sift over them light soil sufficient to cover them; moisten them with warm water, and place the box where there is but little light, and throw a piece of paper over the top. A warm place will start them best. Let them remain thus several days, till the seeds have a chance to swell, before you give them much light, and keep the earth moist; a sponge is excellent to water them, as it does not disturb the position of the seeds; also, use warm water; as soon as you see them sprouting, give them light and air, if not too cold. After the seedling plants are of sufficient size transplant them into small pots; you can easily plant them in the flower beds without disturbing the roots, and the plants will not need covering. First dig a hole and pour water into it, then carefully slip the plant, dirt and all, from the pots into the hole made for it, and press the earth tightly around it.

GERANIUMS.—To root them successfully, take coarse clean sand about three inches in depth, insert the cuttings about one to one and a half inches therein, press the sand firmly around them, and water freely at first, afterwards only water sparingly, and as soon as they commence to grow pinch back to make them stocky or throw out branches. If left to grow of their own accord or will, you will have plants very awkward in appearance. Put them now in pots, using soil made up of two thirds garden soil, one-third leaf mould, and a little sand to keep it porous. In the autumn change them into larger pots and get them into the windows before fires are made, and thereby acclimatize them. Geraniums treated in this way will bloom about the first of January, if in a sunny window, and continue to bloom all winter. Sometimes the leaves turn yellow and black. This is a sign they are having too much water. To get a nice symmetrical plant, when about four inches high pinch out the two uppermost leaves, which will cause the plant to throw out lateral branches. If you do not wish your geraniums tall, when you plant them out of doors and wish to cover a large space with them, just peg the branches very carefully down with a forked twig and you will have double the bloom from them in this position.

PANSIES.—Pansies prefer shade. A cool, moist situation suits them best, particularly in hot summer. For that reason never plant them in raised beds where the intense heat will rapidly absorb every particle of moisture. Choose rather a bed cut in the lawn, or, better still, the shady side of a house.

FUCHSIAS.—This plant requires frequent shifting into larger pots when growing. The pot must be shaded, for if set in a window, where the rays of the sun strike the side of the pot, the leaves will droop and the buds blight. A very warm, dry atmosphere is not favorable to their growth. The temperature should be from 55 to 68 degrees, with plenty of light and air, but not so much sun as geraniums and roses. They can be placed in the cellar in October. Do not water them; let them lose every leaf; late in January take them out and cut back severely. When they start to grow give them a good supply of water without keeping them soaking wet. They require good rich earth, with about one-fifth sand. Liquid manure once a week will greatly encourage their growth. If the plants drop their leaves, gradually cease watering, and put them to rest for the winter; and in the spring they will sprout again, much benefited for the season of rest.

Roses.—Do not have your pots too large. The rule is, one size larger than the plants have been grown in. The smaller the pot—provided, of course, it is large enough to contain the plant—the quicker and stronger the plant will grow. It is very difficult to get a small plant to live and grow in a large pot. A rose will not bloom much till the pot is well filled with roots; therefore small pots facilitate quick bloom. Have good, rich, mellow soil. That made from old, decomposed sods is best. If manure is used it should be old and thoroughly composted. Put in the plant and spread the roots out as naturally as possible; then fill in with fine earth, and press down firmly with the hand. When done, the pot should not be quite full; a little space is needed for water. When first potted, water thoroughly, and if the sun is strong, shade for a few days; then give full light and air. Though the plant should not be allowed to wither for want of water, the earth should get moderately dry before watering again. Very little water is needed until the plant starts to grow. Roses can be made to bloom in winter, provided their wants are studied and the proper treatment given. It is useless to dig up a rose plant in the fall, carefully pot it and expect it to bloom that winter, as some of our bedding plants—geraniums, for instance—will do. Roses intended for winter blooming must be grown in pots during the summer months, in order that they may gain working roots.

TUBE ROSES.—The best bulbs for flowering are those which are large and plump. Set them out in the latter part of May, first preparing the ground by deep spading and enriching with a liberal dressing of well-decayed manure; then plant the bulbs in rows, twelve inches apart in the row, setting them two or three inches deep. Keep the ground at all times free from weeds and well stirred by the use of a hoe. After the first frost has cut down the tops the bulbs should be lifted and set in the sun a day or two to dry, being careful to protect them from frost at night. When thoroughly dried they should be cleaned, removing the leaves and allowing two or three inches of the stalk to remain; then store in a warm closet till ready for planting. The tuberose is a native of a warm climate, and must have plenty of heat and moisture for its full development. With plenty of heat you cannot get too much moisture, but you can easily get too much moisture (which will cause the bulbs to rot) when you have not the necessary heat. A tuberose bulb, no matter how warm it has been kept, will not always bloom. Examine them carefully, and if there is sign of life in the large bulb, it is safe to bloom ; but be careful, for if you inadvertently break the centre shoot, it will be at the expense of the bulb, as it will surely decay.

HYACINTHS.—No bulb requires so rich soil as the hyacinth ; if planted in poor ground the flowers will do very well for the first year, but be trifling afterwards ; and if planted more shallow than four inches the heat of the sun will cause the bulbs to split and divide into innumerable small roots that will not bloom well for two or three years.

To grow hyacinths in glasses, fill the glasses so that the water will barely touch the root of the bulb. *Always use rain-water.* The water should be changed once in three weeks, using pure rain-water of the same temperature as you took them out of. A piece of charcoal in the water will cause it to keep sweet longer. A little ammonia dissolved in the water will give the flowers a much brighter color.

BEGONIAS.—Begonias require a warmer temperature than geraniums or roses, and our sitting-rooms, which in winter are too warm for many plants, are none too warm for begonias. An average of seventy degrees is about right. They thrive best in two parts good garden soil, one part well decayed manure, one part sand. In potting them put in about two inches of charcoal for drainage and fill the pot to within an inch of the top to allow watering. The ornamental-leaved class are cultivated for the beauty of the foliage, and are used only as pot plants or in wardian cases, being too tender to bear our summer sun. The leaves are large, variegated, and margined with a silvery metalic gloss. Care must be taken to keep the foliage free from dust, as the leaves of these varieties will not bear washing or showering, although they take an abundance of water at their roots. In this section are the famous rex begonia, which every flower lover longs to possess, and some others of most beautiful markings. Begonias are propagated from seeds, cuttings and leaves. Take a leaf of the rex variety and cut it into six or seven pieces; lay them on damp sand where they can get a little sun; punch holes through the veins with a pen-knife, and thus they root. Begonias are a little peculiar in their habits; they will not bear water on their leaves although they want abundance on their roots; neither do they like removal from one place to another; let them have a permanent position, say in the middle of the window garden. Moist, damp atmosphere suits them best, and the leaves must be carefully guarded from dust.

VERBENAS.—It does not seem generally known that verbenas raised from seed will produce larger flowers and more of them than those plants grown by a florist from a cutting. Nevertheless such is the case, and another thing to recommend these seedlings to favor is that they are nearly always fragrant.

If one desires to make a bed of verbenas in distinct colors then recourse must be had to the florist, for as he propagates from named varieties of which he knows their colors and habits, he is able to supply any shade. Seedlings cannot be relied upon to produce certain colors. It scarcely pays to propagate verbenas to keep over winter, since they are easily grown from seed sown during the winter, still there are some remarkably choice that are wanted for stock another season. To do this remove the young wood, take away the two leaves next *above* a joint, then with a very sharp knife cut straight across the slip immediately below the joint.

TULIPS.—They are of the easiest possible culture, and while any good garden soil will grow them, they do best in a well drained sandy-loam enriched with thoroughly well rotted manure. The proper season for planting them in beds is in the month of October and November. Plant them in circular beds, allowing five inches between each bulb of the early kind, and six inches for late varieties, covering all to the depth of three inches. All the care necessary after this is to throw some slight protection over the beds before winter sets in, to be removed in the spring.

CARNATIONS.—Carnations are among the most beautiful and valuable plants, being alike desirable for bedding out in summer and the decoration of the window garden in winter. They are of the easiest culture and beautifully formed, and variously colored flowers are produced in the greatest profusion. They should be planted as early as possible in the spring, being nearly hardy, and capable of enduring quite a severe frost without injury. Set out in beds at a distance of about one foot between each plant. Early in summer they will commence blooming and continue until they are checked by cold weather. If intended for winter blooming, remove all buds as fast as they appear until September, leaving those formed after that on the plants. In October the plants should be lifted, taking care to preserve some of the soil about the roots, and put into pots of suitable size; six inch pots will generally answer. They should be placed in a shady place for a few days, and will then be ready for removal to the window where they are to bloom. The carnation does not like a wet soil, and care should be taken not to water them too much, but the foliage should receive a thorough bath as often as once a week, for the prevention of red spiders. To grow carnations from seed sow early in boxes and transplant to the flower bed, and when they flower some of the finest may be treated for winter blooming, as above described. The propagation of the carnation by layers is a very simple process. When the plant is in full bloom lay around it some good, well rotted manure, which mix with the soil well; remove the lower leaves of the shoots selected, pass the pen-knife, slanting upwards half through the joint; fasten the shoot where so cut, about two inches under surface, with a small hooked peg, bending carefully, so as not to break it at the incision. Finish by pressing the earth around it with the fingers. Keep the soil moderately moist, and in a month or six weeks the layers may be severed from the parent plant and established for themselves.

LILIES.—The ground should be shaded very deeply, and an abundance of well-rotted manure worked in, but on no account use fresh manure on lily beds. If the soil is heavy or clayey, the addition of sharp sand will make it light and porous. Use plenty of sand and mix with the soil thoroughly. If the lilies are to be grown in beds, let them be about three feet wide, and as long as desired. Put the bulbs in deep; six inches is good, but eight is better, and a mulch of straw should be kept over them the first year. Whenever possible to do so, lily bulbs should be procured and planted in the fall of the year. After planting it will not be necessary to move them; in fact it will be better not to do so for three or four years. In moving them be very careful in lifting, not to break or bruise the roots at the base of the bulb; if these are injured it may cause the bulb not to bloom for the next season, or perhaps to decay. In growing the lily, to get the best result, select a dry spot, where no water will stand in the winter. Calla lilies usually bloom from autumn all through the winter, until spring. When the flowering season is over, the pot in which it is grown should be set out of doors under a tree or other shady place, and no water given it whatever. In August or September turn it out of the pot, remove all the small bulbs, and re-set the parent one in a four-inch pot. When you give water let it be luke-warm at first, and gradually increase the temperature until it is boiling hot.

PROPAGATING PLANTS.—One of the first necessary conditions is that the plant from which the cutting or slip is taken must be in vigorous health. One of the best guides to the proper condition is when the cutting breaks or snaps instead of bending. If it snaps off so as to break, it will root freely; if it bends, it is too old, and though it may root it will root much slower and make a weaker plant. The best conditions to root cuttings of the great majority of green-house plants is sixty-five degrees of bottom heat, and an atmospheric temperature of fifteen degrees less.

Sand is the best medium in which to place cuttings. From the time the cuttings are inserted until they are rooted, they should never be allowed to get dry; it is best to keep the sand soaked with water. Kept thus saturated, there is less chance of the cutting getting wilted; for if a cutting is once wilted its juices are expended. Permitting a moderate circulation of air in the propagating house prevents the germination of that spider-like web substance which is known as "fungus of the cutting bench." It is best to pot off the cuttings at once, when rooted. They should be placed in small pots from two to two and a half inches wide. In larger pots the soil dries out too slowly, and the tender root rots. A very good propagating bed on a small scale can be constructed by having the tinner make a tank, three or four inches deep, to hold water in. The sand is laid on the tank, and the water is heated by a small lamp, care being taken to make a passage to the open air for the escape of gas. The cost of the tank, if made of zinc will be about five dollars, and less if made of sheet iron. The glass case that goes over the whole is made on the plan of a miniature green house, and the top should be removable at pleasure, to admit air. A thermometer ought to be kept constantly imbedded in the sand, so that the bottom heat is never allowed to get above seventy-five degrees. Bottom heat—a technical term used in floriculture—is secured by the heat of a furnace, or by warm water, or by stable manure, or in some cases by steam. The "saucer system" is a simple method of propagating plants, and is the safest of all procedures in inexperienced hands. Common saucers or plates may be used to hold the sand in which the cuttings are placed. The sand is put in to the depth of an inch or so, and the cuttings inserted in it, close enough to touch each other. The sand is then watered until it becomes in the condition of mud, then placed on the shelf of the green-house or in the window-sill of the sitting room, fully exposed to the sun and never shaded. But one condition is essential to success: until the cuttings become rooted, the sand must be kept continually saturated. If once permitted to dry up, exposed to the sun as they are, the cuttings will quickly wilt, and the whole operation will be defeated. When the cuttings are rooted they should be potted in small pots and treated carefully by shading and watering.

POTTING AND RE-POTTING.—If possible never use any but the common clay pots, the fancy ones are a failure, as regards the health of the plants. Do not use saucers under the pots, as the water that may leak through has a tendency to draw the root to the bottom of the pot, and to perish or founder them. Gravel or broken crockery should be put in the bottom of the pot for drainage. You can have an improved flower pot made in this way. Get one with holes in the side instead of at the bottom. All cultivators know the difficulty experienced when the ordinary flower pot is placed on a bench, covered with sand or soil. The outlet often becomes completely closed by the washing of the soil through the outlet, and being closed by the sand the drainage becomes stopped as completely as if there was no orifice at all at the bottom of the pot. Again, worms breed quickly in the sand or soil, and seem to take a special pleasure in crawling under and through the holes in the bottom of the pots, to get at the rich soil which they contain. This improved pot is safe from the first difficulty, as the holes, being on the sides of the pot, cannot be clogged by the sand, while it is far less tempting to the worm, as a special effort must be made before the hole can be reached. Still another advantage is, that as these orifices are placed above the bottom, air is admitted more freely through to the roots, a matter which is very essential to the well-being of the plants. Sometimes plants become pot-bound. To know this turn the pot over with your hand on the top, tap the side or bottom, and if it comes out easy it is all right, but if it sticks it may be that it is full of roots, and needs to be changed to a larger pot. You can in this way also see if worms are infesting it, and remove them and save your choice plants. A plant needs repotting when the roots have formed a compact mass at the bottom of the pot. To ascertain this just set the pot in water that the ball of earth may be saturated. Now spread the fingers across the top of the pot, invert it, and a brisk tap of the rim on a shelf will make the ball come out. If it does need re-potting, carefully shake out the roots and shift them into a size or two larger, filling up the space with new soil. If you want flowers very early pack the soil into the pots as tightly as possible. Lily bulbs and roses should be potted tightly.

WINDOW GARDENS.

A window looking to the South is to be preferred; next to that an East or West window. Before cold weather comes carefully go over the entire frame and shut up every crack where the frost can obtain an entrance. A good plan is to have a plant stand mounted upon rollers so that every cold night it can be run away from the windows. Plants kept in the house over winter require attention paid to certain requisites—heat, light, ventilation and water. Too much heat is just as injurious to them as a deficiency. If the air is hot and dry the plants will soon be infested with the red spider, green fly and mealy bug, so try to maintain a temperature of seventy or seventy-five degrees by day, and fifteen degrees less at night.

To get the moist air, so essential to all plants, water must be evaporated on the stove. Light should be given at all times and as much as possible. Geraniums and heliotropes revel in the sunlight. Such charming window plants as the rex begonias are partial to shade, but can be put in among other plants. The same with fuchsias. Turn your plants frequently if you would have them symmetrical, and don't be afraid to pinch off the tops if you want them bushy. Ventilation should be given on every fine day. Do not allow a cold draught of air to blow on your plants, however. Watering should be done when the surface soil is dry, and only then.

Preparation for the winter garden should begin early in the summer. One cannot expect a rose or fuchsia which has given its lovely flowers during the summer to keep right along in flowers. Roses for winter blooming must be pot-grown and of varieties adapted to forcing. The leaves of plants need washing and syringing to remove the dust that gathers on them. Some plants, such as the rex begonia, do not like their leaves moistened. Others, like the camellia, require the leaves sponged off one by one. Always use soft tepid water, and attend to washing them at least once a week. The drainage of the pots should admit the surplus water to escape easily through the whole at the bottom of the pot. Never allow the water to stand in the saucers. One great error in window-gardening consists in attempting to grow too many plants. Better to have one full-grown plant than a dozen sickly enfeebled things which have neither beauty nor blossom.

GREEN-HOUSES AND COLD PITS.

A miniature green house may be arranged by means of a simple glass frame to fit the bay window. This being made, the size of the window, is fastened by hinges on the inside. By opening the sash top and bottom, the warm air of the apartment circulates among the flowers.

FOR A COLD PIT.—Select a spot with a southern exposure, protected from the north wind, if possible. The pit should be dug out about four feet deep, four wide and ten long, and then neatly bricked. The pit must be surrounded by a brick enclosure two feet high on the north side, sloping to one foot on the south side. Have three closely fitting sashes, with thick window glass to cover with. These may open on hinges or be made to slide. For protection against hail or snow, have at hand three light window shutters, larger than the frames, to place over them. Water the plants thoroughly on warm sunny days.

CONSERVATORY CHAT.

The most effectual remedy for green fly is fumigation with tobacco. Some plants will not bear fumigation without injury to the leaves, in which case sprinkle with tobacco water, afterwards syringe with clean water. A little turpentine diluted with water will destroy the mealy bug. Sprinkle your plants often, and you will not be troubled with red spiders; wherever the air is dry and close there is his delight. Alcohol, applied with camel's hair brush, will kill any insect it touches. Plants treated with these remedies must be syringed immediately with clear water. To kill white worms in flower pots, take common lime. This is a sure remedy for rose slugs: Make a tea of tobacco stems, and a soap suds of whale oil, or carbolic soap; mix and apply to the bush with a sprinkler, turning the bush so as to wet the under as well as the upper part of the leaves. Apply before sunrise two or three times. Angle worms at the root of plants can be made come to the surface by inserting a hair-pin or darning needle into the mould and then pouring lime water upon the soil. To destroy small green flies on roses in the greenhouse, put hot coals on the floor on which dampened tobacco stems are laid. To kill white worms, also fish worms, tie soot in a rag and dip and squeeze until the water is black. Give your plants some of this twice a week.

For fertilizing take the clippings from horses' hoofs, put

into a large vessel and fill with water. Apply with a watering-pot. Two or three weeks after the plants have been watered with this, the foliage will be changed from a green to a golden yellow, but it only lasts a short time, when it changes to a dark, glossy green. Plants under this manuring grow very strong; the flowers are very large and bright in color. Another splendid liquid manure is made by taking the droppings of the fowl house and pouring on several gallons of water. Dip off the water after it has set a week and apply with a sprinkler.

Frozen plants may be restored in this way: As soon as discovered pour cold water over the plant, wetting every leaf thoroughly. In a few moments it will be crystalized with a thick coating of ice. In this state place it in the dark, carefully covering with a newspaper. The ice will slowly melt, leaving the plant in its original state of health, but it must be left in a moderately cool place for several days.

Pots are just as good for shading young plants as some arrangements which admit more light and air, and at the same time turn off the sun's direct rays.

Never allow weeds to get the start; nip them in the bud.

All plants are benefited by having the ground stirred around them; there is no exception to this rule.

Seedlings in general should not be watered later than an hour or two before sun-down, as the damp surface is apt to produce a fungus which will cause the plants to damp off during the night.

Mildew is a disease caused by sudden changes of temperature and by a long continuance of damp, cloudy weather. The best remedies are sulphur and soot; sprinkle with water and apply one of the remedies.

To have roses bloom well keep old wood cut back; cover the bushes in winter with straw, cornstalks, or loose manure, and work iron filings into the soil around them, or break up old pieces of cast iron as fine as possible and put around next the roots.

A ROSE JAR.

A good way to preserve rose leaves, and one which may be kept for twenty years in all its sweetness is a scent or sweet jar. When the rose season comes in, gather from day to day the leaves from all varieties. The weather should be dry and sunny, and they should be gathered as soon as the dew has dried off. Strip the petals from the calyx, throwing out those decayed. When a half-peck has been collected, take a porcelain bowl and in it place alternate layers of the leaves and table salt, letting the last layer be of salt and cover with a plate that fits within the bowl. Let them remain for twelve hours, then turn, stir and mix them each day for a week. When the entire mass appears moist add three ounces of allspice to form the stock. Turn the mass thoroughly three more days, adding daily one-fourth of an ounce each of allspice and ground cinnamon. Put the mixture into the ornamental jar in which it is to be kept, and add the following ingredients—all coarsely powdered: cloves, cinnamon, nutmeg, mace, allspice, orange and lemon peel, anise seed and root, each one ounce; black pepper, one-fourth of an ounce; six grains of musk, and the same of oil of rose-geranium, lavender or rosemary; violets, orange flowers, myrtle leaves, clove pinks, jessamine, honeysuckle, mignonette, heliotrope and lemon verbena may be added as they bloom, and from year to year, always preparing the rose leaves as directed. The jar must be frequently stirred and shaken, and various perfumes and essential oils added as they are obtained. Never allow the mixture to freeze, and when it becomes dry moisten with any of the scented waters. Keep the jar tightly closed for a month after mixing them; open whenever the perfume is desired, and it will soon permeate the entire house, filling it with a delicious odor like the perfume from a thousand flowers.

PRESSED AUTUMN LEAVES.

The leaves must be gathered when perfectly dry—that is, no atmospheric damp upon them, or the leaf will shrivel, losing its bright color. Do not press the leaves, but use them fresh from the tree, and iron them with spermaceti, not wax, as the latter makes them dull-looking and does not bring out the colors. If properly done they will look brilliant; and it is surprising how long they will retain their beauty, in spite of light, dust and heat. Procure from the druggist smooth cakes of fine spermaceti. Put a board on the ironing table, as the grease spoils everything, and have as many thicknesses of cloth as for ordinary ironing. The iron must be just hot enough to "hiss" when touched with a wet finger; if too hot it scorches the leaves and ruins them. If the leaves are damp, wipe them first with a soft cloth, then pass the iron quickly over the spermaceti, then over the right side of the leaf; turn it over, and there will be sufficient sperm on the cloth to thoroughly saturate it; keep on ironing it, moving it to a new spot, until it is as dry as paper, stem and all. After doing as many leaves as you wish in this way, take a fresh iron at the same temperature, run it quickly over the spermaceti, and then as rapidly and as evenly as possible over the right side of your leaves. This gives them the final polish. Have a large newspaper spread conveniently to receive them when finished, and let them remain for an hour or so. Then place them carefully in boxes, away from the light, till ready for use. If they should curl, place them twenty-four hours after they are done in books under pressure, but not very heavy. If you find any spots that you have not touched, go over them again very carefully, with a little spermaceti on the point of your iron. With some artistic taste and an idea as to the blending and harmonizing of colors, one can almost have oil paintings made of these leaves. Walls with patches of leaves here and there, or a clump of fifteen or twenty lapped over each other, are not artistic. They should be put up separately, with the stems arranged in curves, as if it were a branch of leaves. Autumn leaves look very pretty with diamond dust sprinkled on them after they have been waxed. Put it on while they are warm. Both ferns and leaves can be arranged as vines on the wall or curtains, or as a cornice, by taking very fine wire and winding the stems, and then arranging them as a long vine. Another good way is to fasten them on with mucilage to a strip of muslin of suitable width, and then use it as a cornice for curtains, or border for lambrequins or brackets. A cluster of leaves put between two thicknesses of gauze, and the edge finished with ribbon, makes a pretty window transparency.—*May Perrin Goff.*

ADVICE TO YOUNG WIVES.

DON'T EXPECT TO BEGIN WHERE THE OLD FOLKS LEAVE OFF, but rather be willing to begin where they did, and gradually increase your comforts and luxuries. Many a young wife is rendered unhappy because she is unable to keep up the grandeur of her girlhood's home. If she marries a wealthy man, it is not unreasonable to expect it, but if her husband is poor, she should gracefully yield to the inevitable, and not allow the sacrifices she is compelled to make to cloud her young life. There is a poor prospect indeed ahead of the couple who commence housekeeping without having resolved to live within their means. Never buy a handsome carpet, curtains, or anything of the kind without you have the money to pay for them. The merchant will add a third to the cost because they are bought on credit, and perhaps when he grows impatient for collection you will be obliged to borrow the money and pay interest. You had better be compelled to look at your patched carpet and bare windows than to see the sheriff coming up the walk. Many persons are willing to economize, but they do not know how; they are brought to want and cannot see the cause of it; they cannot recall any great losses; nobody has cheated them; they have not been burnt out, yet here they are penniless. They do not recollect that it is "the LITTLE foxes that gnaw the vines." Bottles not corked, towels lost, soap left to melt in the water, crockery broken, pins and hair-pins scattered broadcast, bonnets left in the rain, as little as you may think of it, each helps to swell the wave which finally engulfs you.

Every wife should keep a memorandum of her expenditures. We are not advocating miserly habits, nor do we think any one should do without what they can afford; but the great question to be solved is, *What can I afford?* What is penuriousness for one would be extravagance for another; every one, rich or poor, should know *where* their money goes, and *for what.* A most excellent plan is to set aside on the first of the month a certain sum to be spent for family groceries, and firmly resolve that you will not spend more. If, therefore, you have company one day, and set a luxurious table, you will be reminded that next day you must economize. If you were running an account you would never think of it. The "credit system" is like a "wild train," rushing frantically onward, until finally it is smashed up, or leaps over a precipice, where it is obliged to stop. Every woman in good health, no matter where she lives, can make money. If on a farm, there are her garden, fowls, dairy, etc., all to bring in a revenue. If she lives in a city, she will find no limit to the demand for sewing, embroidery, and crocheting. If she is talented and well educated, her chances are still better. No honorable work is degrading. There are many persons not too lazy to work, but are ashamed of it. This brings to mind the case of the young man who hired a darkey to plow "next to the road," where people passed by, and he cultivated the back land, where he could not be seen. A friend who thinks less of you because you work would probably be the last one to assist you in times of distress. Any one who looks down upon laboring people should be allowed to enjoy their "gilded misery" to their hearts' content. Every wife should have this motto engraved on her heart, if not on her walls, "Beware of the first quarrel." Nothing renders a home so miserable as fault-finding and quarreling. If it is kept up it will end in bitterness and estrangement. Your husband is but human, and you also, as hard as he tried to make you believe you were an angel, so you must throw the mantle of charity around his faults, and hide them from the world. Wedded love, blessed with the prayers of friends, hallowed by the sanction of God, rosy with present joys, and radiant with future hopes, it dies not all at once. A hasty word casts a shadow upon it, and the shadow deepens with the sharp reply. A little thoughtlessness misconstrued, a little unintentional negligence, deemed real, a little word misinterpreted—through such small channels do dissension and sorrow enter the family circle. Love becomes reticent, confidence is chilled, and noiselessly but surely the work of separation goes on until the two are left as isolated as the pyramids—nothing remaining of the union but the legal form. Our ideal homes should be heart–homes, in which virtue lives and love flowers bloom, and where peace-offerings are daily brought to its altars. Children will leave such homes with regret, and come back to them in after-life as pilgrims to a holy shrine.

> "Cling to thy home! if there the meanest shed,
> Yield thee a hearth and shelter for thy head,
> And some poor plat with vegetables stored,
> Be all that heaven allots thee for thy board;
> Unsavory bread and herbs that scattered grow
> Wild on the river brink or mountain brow,
> Yet e'en this cheerless mansion shall provide,
> More heart's repose than all the world beside."

INDEX OF FOODS

Ammonia: Ammonium carbonate was a powdered leavening used much like baking powder.
Animal care. *See* Cows and Poultry.
Apples. *See* Fruits.
Ashes, cooking with
  Ash Cake, 15
  Curing Hams, 93
  Roasted Eggs, 72
  Roasted Green Corn, 85
  Roasted Potatoes, 79
Beans. *See* Legumes.
Beef, 98–105
  A Fine Beef Preparation (bouillon cakes), 213
  Advice for, 102–103
  Beef a la Mode, 98–99
  Beef Hash, 105
  Beef head, 101
  Beef hooves, 101
  Beef tail soup, 101
  Beef Tongue, 100
  Brine for Pickling Beef, 99
  Calves' Feet Jelly, 178, 216
  Chipped beef. *See* Jerked Beef, 100
  Clear Beef Soup, 33
  Corned Beef, 99, 100
  Dried Beef Gravy, 56
  Essence of Beef, 213
  Freshly butchered beef, 99, 100, 102
  Jerked Beef, 100
  Julienne Soup, 38
  Liver (fried), 104
  Liver, Bewitched (chopped, molded), 104
  Mince Meat for Six Pies, 143
  Minced Meat (tongue), 142
  Minced Pies (chopped beef, suet), 142
  Mock Turtle Soup (calf head), 35
  Pickle for Beef Tongue or Chipped Beef, 100
  Pompey's Head (meatloaf), 101
  Preserving beef, 99
  Rennet (calf stomach), 30
  Roast Beef, 98
  Sausage, 105
  Sausage, Bologna (beef, pork), 104
  Spiced Beef (Hunter's Round), 100
  Steak, Broiled, 102
  Steak, Fried, 103
  Steak, Hidaway (smothered in tomatoes), 103
  Steak, Rolled, 104
  To Stew Turnips with Meat, 88
  Veal, advice for, 107
  Veal, in soup, 33
  White Pudding (beef neck). *See* Scraffle, 102.
Berries. *See also* Beverages, Canning, Jellies, and Preserves.
  Blackberry cordial as cake flavoring, 124
  Blackberry Fritters, 152
  Blackberry Mush (molded pudding), 145
  Blackberry – Poor Folks' Pudding, 146
  Cranberry Sauce, 53
  Currant Cake, 124, 125
  Currants, in cakes, 131
  Currants – Cabinet Pudding, 147
  Currants – Hingham Pudding, 151
  Currants, Spiced, 69
  Delicious Berry Dessert, 170
  Fruit Cream, 171
  Raspberries. *See* Strawberry Shortcake, 149

INDEX OF FOODS.

Berries *(continued)*
  Strawberries, How to Serve, 174
  Strawberry Float, 161
  Strawberry Sauce, 158
  Strawberry Shortcake, 149
Beverages, 20-23, 200–216. *See also* Sickroom Foods.
  Advice for, 2, 20–22
  Ale (malt), 209
  Beer (wheat bran), 204
  Beer, Corn, 203
  Beer, Ginger, 204
  Beer, Persimmon, 203, 204
  Beer, Sweet Potato, 203
  Blackberry Vinegar (in water), 202
  Chocolate/cocoa, 23
  Cider, 208–209
  Coffee, ersatz creamer for, 22
  Coffee, Mrs. Tennent's Receipt, 20
  Coffee, Vienna, 20
  Cordial, Blackberry, 202
  Egg Nog, 208
  Lemon Ice Foam, 207
  Milk, Baked, 29
  Milk, Chocolate, 215
  Punch, Milk, 215
  Punch, Roman, 209
  Sangaree, Raspberry and Mint, 207
  Shrub, Currant, 205–206
  Soda Water, 208
  Syllabub, 162
  Syrup, Lemon (in water), 208
  Tea (hot), 22–23
  Tea, Iced, 23
  Tea, Jamaica Ginger (hot lemonade), 207
  Teatime. *See* Sally Lunn, 11
  Wine, Apple, 206–207
  Wine, Blackberry, 202
  Wine, Catawba, 204
  Wine, Cherry, 203
  Wine, Gooseberry, 206
  Wine, Grape, 204–205
  Wine, Raisin, 207
  Wine, Scuppernong, 206
  Wine, Strawberry, 206
Bread – Quick (without yeast), 8–18. *See also* Waffles.
  Ash Cake, Virginia, 15
  Battercakes. *See* Laplanders, 13
  Battercake advice, 13
  Battercakes, Buckwheat, 13, 14
  Battercakes, Corn 14
  Battercakes, Graham, 16
  Battercakes, Salt Rising, 14
  Battercakes, Scotch Pancakes, 153
  Battercakes, Wheat, 12
  Biscuit dressing. *See* Roast Turkey, 107–108.
  Biscuit Jelly (mush from biscuits), 214
  Biscuit, Baking Powder, 8
  Biscuit, Breakfast, 9
  Biscuit, Cream, 9
  Biscuit, Mrs. Nesbitt's Premium Cracker (beaten), 9
  Biscuit, Soda, 8
  Biscuit, Sour Cream, 10
  Biscuit, Sweet Potato, 10
  Biscuits, English (currant, coriander), 9
  Bread, Boston Brown (steamed), 17
  Bread, Clabber, 11
  Bread, Cracklin, 15
  Bread, Kentucky Corn Egg, 15
  Bread, Oatmeal, 16
  Bread, Passover (unleavened), 13
  Bread, Patrick, 10
  Bread, Pumpkin, 15
  Bread, Rice, 10
  Bread, Thomas, 10
  Bread, Victoria, 10
  Cakes for Soup, 34
  Corn Oysters (fried drop cakes), 86
  Crackers, Corn Starch, 18
  Dodgers, Old Fashioned Corn, 15
  Dressing for Turkey, 108

INDEX OF FOODS.

Gems, Graham, 16
Gems, Wheat, 12
Hoe Cake, Corn, 15
Laplanders, 13
Muffins. *See* Laplanders, 13
Muffins, Corn Meal, 14
Muffins, Cream, 12
Muffins, Wheat, 12
Pones (cornmeal), 15
Rolls, Sweet, 10
Scotch Pancakes, 153
Vanities (fried), 13
Bread – Yeasted, 3–8. *See also* Sandwiches, Toast, and Yeast.
Advice for, 2, 3–4, 18
Bread Made with Fleischman's Yeast, 5
Bread Pudding, 154
Bread, F. M. Jack's, 4
Bread, Graham, 15–16
Bread, Miss Magee's Premium Salt Rising, 7
Bread, Mrs. Tennent's Premium, 4
Bread, Nice Light, 8
Bread, Salt Rising, 7–8
Cracknells (sticks), 17–18
Rolls, Fleischman's Yeast, 5
Rolls, French, 13
Rolls, Mrs. J. I. Chamberlain's Premium, 5
Rolls, National Yeast Light, 5
Rolls, water bath during baking, 5
Rusk, Mrs. James Hughes', 17
Sally Lunn, 11
Wheat bran in bread, 8
Butter. *See also* Dairy production.
Churning, 26–28
Cold Butter Sauce, 157
Coloring, 29
Drawn Butter, 52
Preserving, 30
Serving advice, 1–2
Washing salt from, 28, 136

Cabbage. *See* Vegetables.
Cake, 114–131.
A Nice Flavoring for Cake (lemon, brandy), 122
Advice for, 114–115, 124, 131
Angel's Food Cake, 115
Apple – Dried Apple Cake, 127
Black and White Marble Cake, 125
Black Cake (spice), 124
Blanc Mange Cake (filled gold cake), 123
Chocolate Cake, 122
Chocolate – Marbled Chocolate Cake, 122
Cincinnati Cake (fat salt pork and spices), 129–130
Cocoanut, 121, 128
Coffee Cake (coffee flavored), 123–124
Composition Cake (brandy, spice), 129
Corn Starch Cake, 118
Cream Cake, 132
Cup Cake, 120
Cup – A Good Cup Cake, 120
Cup – Golden Cup Cake, 119
Cup – Small Cup Cake, 120
Currant Cake, 124, 125
Dutch Cake (yeast), 128
Egg-Nogg Cake, 123
Fruit and Feather Cake, 126
Fruit Cake, 115, 126. *See also* Black, Currant, Loaf, Nutmeg, Queen's, and Wedding.
Fruit cake – Blue Grass Fruit Cake, 126
Fruit Cake, Mock, 126
Fruit Cake, White, 125
Ginger – Soft Ginger Cake, 127
Ginger – Superior Ginger Loaf, 128
Gold Cake, 119, 131
Gold – Gold Perfection Cake, 119
Golden Cup Cake, 119

INDEX OF FOODS.

Cake *(continued)*
  Hickory Nut Cake, 126
  Honey Cake, 128
  Jelly Cake, Lemon, 120
  Kelly Island Cake (lemon, apple), 130
  Lady Cake (bitter almond), 129
  Loaf Cake (yeast), 125
  Marbled cakes, 119, 122, 125
  Marietta Cake, 129
  Molasses Cake, 127
  Mrs. Clay's Premium Cake (whisky, lemon), 118
  Nutmeg Cake, 123
  One Egg Cake, 120
  One, Two, Three, Four Cake, 120
  Orange Cake, 121
  Peach Cake, 130
  Pineapple, 121
  Pound Cake, 117, 118
  Pound Cake, Old-Fashioned, 117
  Pound Cake, Phoenix Club, 117
  Pound Cake, White, 118
  Queen's Cake (alcohol, nutmeg), 125
  Roman Sash Cake (multicolored), 121
  Shortcake, Strawberry, 149
  Silver and Gold Cake, 119
  Silver Cake, 119
  Silver or White Cake, 130
  Spiced Cake, 123
  Sponge Cake Roll, 153–154
  Sponge Cake, 116, 131
  Sponge Cake, Almond, 117
  Sponge Cake, Arrow Root, 117
  Sponge Cake, Boiled, 116
  Sponge Cake, Cream, 116
  Sponge Cake, Croton, 119
  Sponge Cake, Ginger, 117
  Sponge Cake, Mrs. Cliff Baker's, 116
  Sponge Cake, Mrs. H. N. Starnes', 116
  Sponge Cake, White, 115
  Tea Cake (flavored with tea), 127
  Texas Cake, 129
  Watermelon Cake (resembling a melon), 122
  Wedding Cake, 124
  White Cake, 118
  White cake – Alpine Snow Cake, 118
  White Mountain Cake, 128
Cakes (individual sweets), 131–135.
  Cookies (nutmeg), 133
  Doughnuts (fried), 134
  French Straws (fried), 134
  Ginger Snaps, 134
  Jumbles, Davis, 133
  Jumbles, Rich, 133
  Lady Fingers, 131
  Lemon Biscuits, 134
  Moraines (molded almond cakes), 132
  Nice Fried Cakes, 132
  Short Bread, 134
  Tea Cakes, Cocoanut, 132
  Tea Cakes, Cream, 132
  Tea Cakes, German, 133
  Tea Cakes, Gnadinger's, 131
  Tea Cakes, Nice (biscuit dough), 131–132
  Tea Cakes Without Eggs, 133
  Vanities (fried), 13
  Wafers, 17
  Wafers, Sweet, 17
Cake Fillings and Icings, 136–137.
  Apple. *See* Kelly Island Cake, 130
  Cheap Frosting (uncooked egg whites), 136
  Chocolate filling. *See* Chocolate Cake, 122
  Coconut filling,. *See* Cocoanut Cake, 121, 128
  Fig, raisin, and citron filling. *See* Marietta Cake, 129
  Icing (uncooked egg whites), 136
  Lemon jelly or curd. *See* Lemon Jelly Cake, 120
  Orange filling. *See* Orange Cake, 121

INDEX OF FOODS.

Pineapple filling. *See* Pineapple Cake, 121
To Make Icing (egg whites with boiled sugar), 137
Vanilla filling. *See* Blanc Mange Cake, 123
Candy. *See* Confectionery.
Canning, 189–193.
   Advice for, 189
   Apples, 191
   Blackberries, 191
   Cherries, 190
   Corn, 192, 193
   Gooseberries, 190
   Okra, 192, 193
   Peaches, 189
   Pears, 190
   Peas, 192
   Strawberries, 191–192
   Tomatoes, 192, 193
Catsup, 70–71.
   Baked Tomato Catsup, 70
   Cucumber Catsup, 71
   Tomato Soy, 70
   Walnut Catsup, 71. *See also* Worcestershire Sauce, 55
Chicken
   Baked Chicken, 110
   Broiled Chicken, 109
   Chicken Pudding, 111
   Dr. Stewart's Receipt for Chicken Soup, 36, 213
   French Salad Dressing (for chicken), 54
   Fried Chicken, 109
   Jellied Chicken, 48
   Pie, Chicken Corn, 86
   Pie, Chicken, 110
   Salad, Chicken, 47
   Salad, Mrs. Gen. Phillips' Chicken, 47
   Smothered Chicken, 110
   Virginia Brunswick Stew, 36
   Water, 214
Cochineal, 122, 198
Confectionery, 210–212
   Almond Macaroons, 211
   Candy Without Cooking, 210
   Caramels, Chocolate, 210
   Caramels, Cocoanut, 211
   Cocoanut Drops, 210
   Delicious Fruit Candy, 211
   Kisses (meringue), 210
   Molasses Candy, 212
   Peanut Candy, 212
   Pulled candy – White Cream Candy, 212
   Pulled candy – Cream Candy, 212
   To Crystalize Pop-Corn, 211
Corn. *See* Vegetables.
Cornmeal/Indian Meal
   Battercakes, 14
   Breakfast Bacon, 96
   Corn Hoe Cakes, 15
   Corn Meal Gruel, 214
   Corn Meal Muffins, 14
   Cracklin Bread (pones), 15
   Dressing for Turkey, 108
   Fried Mush, 19
   In bread, 10
   In yeast, 6–8
   Kentucky Corn Egg Bread, 15
   Mush Dressing, 108
   Pumpkin Bread, 15
   Salt Rising Bread, 8
   To Relieve Thirst (soaked corn bread), 214
   Virginia Ash Cakes, 15
Cows, Care of, 24–28
Dairy production, 24–31
Desserts. *See also* Cakes, Fritters, Ice Cream, Pies (sweet), Puddings, and Sauces (sweet).
Desserts – Fancy, 161–173.
   Advice for serving, 2
   Ambrosia (sweet fruit salad), 162
   Angel's Food (jellied cream), 161

Desserts – Fancy *(continued)*
- Angel's Food (quince), 170
- Apple Snow, 166
- Apples – Baked Apples and Cream, 165
- Apples – Bird Egg's Nest, 172
- Apples – Jellied, 172
- Blanc Mange (thickened milk), 161
- Calves' Feet Jelly, 178, 216
- Charleston Snowballs (rice), 162
- Charlotte Russe, 164, 165, 172
- Coffee Jelly, 169
- Cream Peach Dessert, 167
- Cream, Cocoanut, 168
- Cream, Fruit, 171
- Cream, Italian, 229
- Cream, Norwegian, 163
- Cream, Orange, 170
- Cream, Snow, 167
- Cream, Velvet (orange), 171
- Cream, Vienna, 163
- Custard, Boiled, 164
- Custard, Chocolate, 167
- Custard, Coffee, 171
- Custard, Éclair, 168
- Custard, Jelly (raspberry, orange), 165
- Custard, Rice Custard, 172
- Dainty Dessert (cocoanut), 167
- Delicious Berry Dessert, 170
- Floating Islands, 171
- Fruit Dessert, 167
- Gateau de Pommes (molded apple), 169
- Gelatine Jelly (lemon, spice, wine), 169, 172
- Gelatine Jelly (lemon, spice), 168
- Moonshine (egg whites, jelly), 169
- Orange Charlotte, 173
- Orange Cream, 170
- Orange Float, 163
- Orange Jelly Baskets, 168
- Orange Souffle, 165
- Peach – Cream Peach Dessert, 167
- Peach Jelly (gelatin), 162
- Peach Pyramid, 173
- Quince Dessert, 171
- Raspberry Float
- Rice Snow Balls, 166
- Snow Pudding, 166
- Strawberry Float, 161
- Syllabub, 162
- Tapioca and Fruit, 167
- Tipsy Squire (wine, cake, custard), 170

Desserts – Frozen, 194–201. *See also* Ice Cream.
- Citron Ice, 200
- Crescent City Sherbet (lemon, alcohol), 200
- Frozen desserts, advice for, 194
- Frozen Pudding (raisin, whisky), 198
- Gelatine Ice (wine, lemon), 201
- Lemon Ice Foam, 207
- Lemon Sherbet, 199
- Madeira Wine Sherbet, 200
- Milk Sherbet, 199
- Orange Sherbet, 200
- Pineapple Ice, 200
- Raspberry Ice, 200
- Roman Punch, 209
- Sherbet (lemon), 198
- Watermelon Ice, 200

Eggs, 72–76.
- A Nice Way to Serve Eggs (boiled), 73
- Advice on, 72
- Boiled Eggs, 72
- Breakfast Dish (meat, potatoes, egg), 76
- Coffee preparation (egg, eggshells), 21
- Common Egg Sauce, 56
- Deviled. *See* Egg Salad, 50 and Stuffed Eggs, 73
- Egg Salad, 50
- Fried Eggs, 73
- Omelet, Oyster, 43
- Omelette, Cheese, 75

INDEX OF FOODS.

Omelette, Cream, 76
Omelette, Tomato, 75
Pickled Eggs, 73
Poached Eggs and Oysters, 42
Poached Eggs, 73
Preserving eggs, 74
Roasted Eggs, 72
Scalloped Eggs, 73
Scrambled Eggs, 72
Stuffed Eggs, 73
Yolks mashed in soup, 34
Fish, 44–46
   Advice for, 44
   Bass, Boiled 45
   Codfish Balls, 46
   Cream Gravy for Baked Fish, 45
   Eels, To Fry, 45
   Fish Cake, 46
   Fish, To Broil, 44
   Fish, To Fry, 44, 45
   Herring, Baked, 46
   Rock, To Pickle, 45
   Salmon Salad, 48
   Salt Mackerel, 45
   Sauce for Fish, 45, 52. *See also* Mustard Sauce, 56
   Shad, Baked, 44
Fowl. *See also* Chicken and Turkey.
   Duck, Roast, 111
   Duck, Wild, 112
   Goose, To Roast, 111
   Guinea Fowl (baked), 112
   Partridge Soup, 35
   Pigeon Pie, 113
   Pigeons, To Broil, 112
   Quail on Toast, 112
   Robins, 112
   Snipe, 112
Fritters
   Apple Fritters, 152
   Apples, Sugared (fried), 152
   Blackberry Fritters, 152
   Delicious Fritters, 152
   Green Corn Fritters, 86
   Orange Fritters
   Parsnip Fritters, 87
Furnishings. *See* Household.
Fruits, 174–175. *See also* Berries, Beverages, Cakes, Canning, Desserts, Jellies, Ice Cream, Pies (sweet), and Preserves.
   A Showy Fruit Piece, 174
   Advice for arranging, 175
   Apple Crumb Pudding, 150
   Apple Fritters, 152
   Apple Sauce (for meat), 53
   Apple Water, 214
   Apples – Aunt Sally's Apple Custard, 150
   Apples – Baked Apple Dumpling, 150
   Apples – Paradise Pudding, 145
   Apples – Pudding without Milk or Eggs, 154
   Apples – Sugared Apples (fried), 152
   Apples – Sweetened Apple Dumplings, 146
   Apples, Fried, 87
   Cabinet Pudding (raisins, citron, currants), 147
   Candied Fruit, 185
   Fig Pudding, 148
   Lemon – Good Pudding Sauce, 160
   Lemon – Queen of Puddings, 150
   Lemon Biscuits, 134
   Lemon Pudding, 151
   Lemon, Sauce, 158–159
   Peach Shortcake. *See* Strawberry Shortcake, 149
   Peaches, Fried, 82
   Peaches, To Peel, 174
   Plums – To Seed Damsons or Blue Plums, 175
   Quince Sauce, 159
Game (wild). *See also* Fowl.
   Stewed Squirrels, 112. *See also* Virginia Brunswick Stew, 36.
   Turtle Soup, 35
   Venison Sauce, 52

INDEX OF FOODS.

Venison, Saddle, 106
Woodchucks (groundhogs), 112
Gardening, 263–280
  A Rose Jar (potpourri), 278–279
  Begonias, 268–269
  Carnations, 269–270
  Conservatory Chat, 276–278
  Designs for Flower Beds, 263–264
  Flowers on the dining table, 2
  Fuchsias, 265–266
  Geraniums, 265
  Green-Houses and Cold Pits, 275–276
  Hyacinths, 267–268
  Lilies, 270–271
  Pansies, 265
  Planting the Seed, 264
  Potting and Repotting, 273
  Pressed Autumn Leaves, 279–280
  Propagating Plants, 271–273
  Roses, 266–267
  To Preserve Garden Seeds, 225
  Tube Roses, 267
  Tulips, 269
  Verbenas, 269
  Window Gardens, 274–275
Grains. *See also* Cornmeal and Flour.
  Buckwheat Battercakes, 13, 14
  Cracked Wheat (porridge), 19
  Fried Hominy or Grits (corn), 19
  Oatmeal Bread, 16
  Oat Meal Porridge, 19
  Rye flour. *See* Boston Brown Bread, 17
Gravy
  Baked ham gravy, 94
  Chicken gravy, 109–111
  Cream Gravy for Fish, 45
  Dried Beef Gravy, 56
  Fried Steak gravy, 103
  Turkey gravy. *See* Roast Turkey, 107–108
Home Decorating and Management, 231–252.
  Parlor and Library, 234–237
  The Family Dining Room, 240–243
  The Family Room, 238–239
  The Kitchen, 244–247
  The Laundry, 248–252
  Utensils Necessary in the Kitchen of a Small Family, 246–247
  Vestibule and Hall, 231–233
Household, 224–230. *See also* Laundry.
  A Cheap Fly Trap, 226
  A Fine Furniture Polish, 225
  A Good Wash for the Skin, 229
  Excellent Receipt for Cleaning Carpets, 230
  For Cleaning Steel Knives, 225
  Household Conveniences, 227–228
  Mrs. John B. Gordon's Floor Stain, 226
  Removing grease from dirty silverware, 226
  Soap, Jelly, 224
  Soap, Soft, 224
  To Clean Bottles in Large Numbers, 226
  To Cleanse Jewelry, 228
  To Make Brown Lace, 250
  To Remove a Tight Ring, 228
  To Remove Stains from Marble, 225
Ice Cream, 192–198. *See also* Desserts – Frozen.
  Almond Ice Cream, 195
  Bisque Ice Cream (clabber, vanilla), 196
  Boiled Custard, 164
  Buttermilk Ice Cream, 197
  Caramel (topping), 197
  Caramel Ice Cream, 197
  Chocolate Cream, 196
  Cocoanut Ice Cream, 196
  Gelatine Ice Cream, 195
  Ice Cream without Cream (ice milk), 195
  Ice Cream, 194, 195
  Kentucky Cream, 198

INDEX OF FOODS.

Lemon Ice Cream, 197
Metropolitan Ice Cream (multiflavored), 198
Orange Ice Cream, 196
Peach Ice Cream, 195
Pine-Apple Ice Cream, 197
Raspberry, 196
Strawberry Ice Cream, 196
Tea Ice Cream, 197
White Ice Cream, 195
Indian meal. *See* cornmeal.
Infant foods, 29
Jam. *See* Preserves.
Jelly Tin: This was a round cake pan such as was used to make layered jelly cakes. *See* 246.
Jellies, 176–179. *See also* Desserts (fancy) and Preserves.
  Apple, 176
  Blackberry, 177
  Calves' Feet, 178
  Crab Apple, 179
  Cranberry, 177
  Currant Jelly Without Cooking, 177
  Currant, 176
  Four Fruit (berry and cherry), 178
  Grape, 178
  Peach, 178
  Quince, 176
  Remedy for Moulding [mold] in Jellies, 177
  Vinegar, 171
Laundry, 248–252
  Care of Irons, 250
  Glove Cleaner, 251–252
  Japanese Cleaning Fluid, 224
  To Glaze Linen, 249
  To Make Starch Stiff, 249
  To Remove Fruit Stains, 224
  To Renovate Black Silk, 250
  To Wash Black Cashmere, 250
  To Wash Calicoes That Are Not Fast Colors, 225

  To Wash Embroidery, 251
  To Wash Flannels and Blankets, 251
  To wash grease or paint out of fabric, 251
  To Wash Muslins, Linens, or Prints Without Fading, 249
  To Wash Tidies, 251
  To Wash White Laces, 250
Legumes. *See also* Vegetables.
  Bean Soup, 34
  Boston Baked Beans, 88
  Pea Soup, 34
Mold prevention, 64, 177, 249
Mutton, 105–106
  Chops, 106
  Roast, 105
  To Corn Mutton, 105
  To Grill a Shoulder of Mutton, 106
Noodles/pasta
  Boiled Macaroni (with cheese), 84
  Noodles for Soup, 35
  Scalloped Macaroni, 84
Nuts
  Advice for serving, 175, 170
  Almond Ice Cream, 195
  Almond Macaroons, 211
  Almonds, bitter, 117, 119, 129, 133
  Almonds – Moraines, 132
  Crystalized, 211
  Hickory Nut Cake, 126
  Peanut Candy, 212
  Walnut Catsup, 71. *See also* Worcestershire Sauce, 55
  Walnut Pickle, 63
Oysters, 40–43
  A Fine Oyster Pie, 42
  Baked Oyster Dumpling, 42
  Broiled Oysters, 41
  Cream Oysters, 40
  Dressing for Cove Oysters, 43
  Fried Oysters, 41
  Half-Fried Oysters, 41
  Omelet Oyster, 43

INDEX OF FOODS.

Oysters *(continued)*
  Oyster Salad, 49
  Oyster Soup, 40
  Oysters with Potatoes, 41
  Poached Eggs and Oysters, 42
  Raw Oysters, 43
  Roasted Oysters, 41
  Scalloped Oysters, 42
Pastry (paste/pie crust), 138–140.
  Advice for, 138
  Delicate Tart Paste, 139
  Excellent Pastry, 139
  Paste for Two Pies, 139
  Pie Crust for Dyspeptics (potato), 140
  Plain but Delightful Pie Crust, 139
  Puff Paste, 138
Pickles, 58–68
  Advice for, 58, 63
  Beets – Sweet Pickled Beets, 69
  Beets, Pickled, 65
  Brine for Pickling Beef, 99
  Cabbage Pickle, 60
  Cherries, Spiced, 68
  Chow-Chow (relish), 66
  Cucumber – Delicious Cucumber Pickle, 61
  Cucumber – Good Cucumber Pickle, 59
  Cucumber Mangoes, 64
  Cucumber Pickles, 59
  Cucumber Sweet Pickles, 68
  Currants, Spiced, 69
  Egg test for salinity, 61
  Eggs, Pickled, 73
  Fish – To Pickle Rock, 45
  French Pickle, 59
  Grapes, Spiced, 69
  Heyden Salad, 63
  Kentucky Pickle (relish), 67
  Lily Pickle, 65
  Mixed Pickles, 59
  Mustard Pickle, 62
  Onion Pickle, 60
  Onions, Pickled, 60
  Peach – Mrs. Kirk's Premium Pickle, 68
  Peach – Sweet Pickles-Spiced Peaches, 67
  Peach Pickles, 61
  Pickle for Beef Tongue or Chipped Beef, 100
  Premium Spanish Pickle (mixed vegetables), 64
  Pyfer Pickles, 66
  Raisins, Pickled, 68
  Sauer Kraut (fermented cabbage), 83
  Superior Mixed Pickle, 64
  Tomato – Green Tomato Pickle, 62
  Tomato – Ripe Tomato Pickle, 62
  Tomatoes, Spiced, 69
  Walnut Pickle, 63
  Watermelon Pickle, 67
Pies – Savory. *See also* Pastry.
  A Fine Oyster Pie, 42
  Backbone Pie (pork), 97
  Chicken Corn Pie, 86
  Chicken Pie, 110
  Pigeon Pie, 113
Pies – Sweet, 141–156. *See also* Pastry.
  Apple – Old Fashioned Green Apple Pie, 148
  Apple – Sliced Apple Pie, 145
  Apple – Sweetened Apple Dumplings, 146
  Banana Pie, 155
  Buttermilk Pie, 155
  Cream – Spice Cream Pie, 150
  Cream Pie, 148
  Lemon Corn-Starch Pie, 143
  Mince Meat for Six Pies, 143
  Minced Meat, 142
  Minced Pies, 142
  Molasses Pie, 155
  Orange Jelly Pie, 143
  Pumpkin – A Kentucky Girl's Pumpkin Pie, 156

INDEX OF FOODS.

Pumpkin – Receipt of a Famous N. Y. Restaurant Pumpkin Pie, 156
Raisin Pie, 143
Strawberry Shortcake (thin layered crust), 149
Sweet potato – Georgia Sweet-Potato Pie, 144
Sweet-Potato Pie, 144
Tomato – Southern Tomato Pie, 156
Tomato Pie, 148
Vinegar Pie, 155
Whipped Cream Tarts, 144
Pork/Ham, 92–98
   Backbone or Chine, 97
   Backbone Pie, 97
   Bacon, Breakfast Bacon, 96
   Barbecue. *See* Roast Pig, 95–96, and Roast Pork, 96
   Brains, Hog (fried), 97
   Brains, Stewed, 98
   Cincinnati Cake (salt pork), 129–130
   Cracklin Bread, 15
   Ham – Fried Eggs, 73
   Ham – To Boil a Ham in Cider, 93
   Ham – To Boil a Ham, 93
   Ham – To Glaze A Cold Ham, 94
   Ham Salad, 49
   Ham Sandwiches, 18
   Ham Toast, 18
   Ham, Baked 93–94
   Ham, Broiled, 94
   Ham, Fried, 94
   Ham, Mrs. Bledsoe's Premium, 93
   Ham, Preserving, 92, 93
   Ham, Stuffed, 94
   Ham, Virginia, 92
   Hams, Curing, 93
   Hog killing, 95
   Hog's head, 89, 98, 102
   Jowls and Greens, 89
   Liver Pudding, 104
   Liver, Bewitched (chopped, molded), 104
   Pig, Roast, 95–96
   Pig's Feet Souse, 97
   Pig's Feet, 97
   Pork Steaks or Chops, 96
   Roast Pork, 96
   Sausage Meat, 94
   Sausage, Bologna, 104
   Sausage, Smoked, 95
   Sausage, W. P. Stevens', 95
   Scraffle (head meat, also known as scrapple), 102
   Souse, Pig's Feet Souse (sliced hog "cheese"), 97
   Spare Rib, 96
   Stewed Squirrels (salt pork), 112
   Stuffed Cabbage (sausage, bacon), 80
   Sweet Breads (organ meat), 98
   To Stew Pig's Head and Jowl, 98
   To Stew Turnips with Meat, 88
Potatoes – Sweet
   Candied Sweet Potatoes, 79
   Fried Sweet Potatoes, 78
   Roast Sweet Potatoes, 78
   Sweet Potato Beer, 203
   Sweet Potato Biscuit, 10
   Sweet Potato Custard, 153
   To Preserve Sweet Potatoes for Winter, 79
Potatoes – White/Irish
   Boiled Potatoes, 77, 78
   Creamed Potatoes, 77
   Fried Potato Balls, 77
   Ingredient in yeast, 5–7
   Irish-Potato Pudding (dessert), 144
   Potato Custard (sweet), 153
   Potato Hash, 78
   Potato Puff (mashed and baked), 78
   Potato Snow (sieved), 77
   Potato Soup, 36
   Roasted Potatoes, 77
   Saratoga Chips (fried thin), 78
   White Soup, 38

INDEX OF FOODS.

Porridge (cooked grains). *See also* Sickroom Foods.
   Corn Meal Gruel, 214
   Corn Meal Mush, 19
   Fried Hominy or Grits (corn), 19
   Fried Mush (corn), 19
   Oat Meal Porridge, 19
   Rice Custard, 215
   Rice Jelly, 215
   Wheat, Cracked Wheat, 19
Poultry, care of, 253–262
Premium recipes, 4, 5, 7, 9, 60, 64, 68, 93, 115, 116, 117, 118, 180, 181, 192
Preserves, 180–188.
   Advice for, 180
   Apple Butter, 188
   Apple Devil, 186
   Apple Marmalade, 187
   Apple Preserves, 181
   Blackberry Jam, 187
   Candied Fruit, 185
   Cherry Preserves, 181
   Cucumber Preserves, 184
   Fig Preserves, 182
   Ginger Preserves, 184
   Grape – Fox Grape Preserves, 182
   Grape Preserves, 184
   Honey Preserves, 185
   Orange – To Preserve Orange Peel, 185
   Orange – Transparent Marmalade, 186
   Peach Conserves, 188
   Peach Preserves, 180, 182
   Peaches – Common Peach Jam, 186
   Peaches – To Preserves Green Peaches, 182
   Peaches, Brandy, 183
   Pear – Mrs. Tennent's Premium Pear Preserves, 180
   Pear marmalade. *See* Apple Marmalade, 187
   Plum – Damson or Blue Plum Preserves, 183
   Quince marmalade. *See* Apple Marmalade, 187
   Quince Preserves, 183
   Strawberry Preserves, 158, 181
   Tomato Preserves, 185
   Watermelon Rind Preserves, 181
Puddings – Sweet, 141–155. *See also* Sauces – Sweet.
   Apple – Aunt Sally's Apple Custard, 150
   Apple – Baked Apple Dumpling, 150
   Apple – Paradise Pudding, 145
   Apple – Pudding without Milk or Eggs, 154
   Apple Crumb Pudding, 150
   Baked Chocolate Custard, 150
   Blackberry – Poor Folks' Pudding, 146
   Blackberry Mush (molded), 145
   Bread Pudding, 154
   Buttermilk Pudding, 146
   Cabinet Pudding (raisins, citron, currants), 147
   Catskill Mountain Pudding (molded), 145
   Cocoanut Pudding, 141
   Custard, Baked Chocolate, 150
   Custard, Potato, 153
   Delicious Pudding, 149
   Economical Plum Pudding, 142
   Excellent Batter Pudding (molded), 149
   Fig Pudding, 148
   Ginger Pudding, 155
   Hingham Pudding (molasses, raisins, currants), 151
   Honey Pudding, 144
   Lemon – Queen of Puddings, 150
   Lemon Pudding, 143
   Minute Pudding, 148
   Molasses Pudding, 154
   One Egg Pudding, 153
   One-Two-Three-Four Pudding, 144
   Penny Pudding, 149

INDEX OF FOODS.

Plum Pudding, 141
Potato – Irish-Potato Pudding, 144
Potato Custard, 153
Raisin Pudding, 142
Rice – Frosted Rice Pudding, 147
Rice Pudding, 146, 147
Scotch Pancakes, 153
Sponge Pudding, 154
Steam Pudding (molasses), 146
Sunderland Pudding, 145
Tapioca Pudding, 147
Thickened Milk Pudding, 155
Transparent Pudding, 153
Puddings – Savory
   Chicken Pudding, 111
   Corn Pudding, 85, 86
   Liver Pudding (hog), 104
   White Pudding (beef). *See* Scraffle, 102.
Receipt: This is an outdated term for a recipe. For example, *see* Pineapple Ice, 200.
Remedies, 217–223
   A Fine Receipt for a Cough, 220
   A Powerful Appetizer, 223
   A Quick Emetic, 219
   Cough Mixture, 218–219
   Croup Mixture, 220
   Cure for a Wen, 221
   Cure for Consumption, 219
   Cure for Drunkenness, 222
   Cure for Rheumatism, 222
   Cure for Tetter, 219
   Diarrhea – Chalk Mixture for, 217
   Diarrhea – Cure for, 220
   Dog Bite, 217–218
   For a Burn, 218
   For a Snake Bite, 221
   For Intense Itching, 221
   For Nausea, 221
   For Sores on Horses, 221
   Neuralgia, 220
   Nosebleed, 220
   Poison Oak Cure, 219
   Preparation for Improving the Skin, 218
   Remedies for Croup, 221
   Remedy for the Hives, 220
   Remedy for Yellow Thrush, 219
   To Destroy Bed-Bugs, 218
   To Destroy Red Ants, 218
   To Insure Sleep, 217
   To Relieve Constipation, 218
   To Relieve Nervous Headache, 218
   To Remove Freckles, 221
   To Stop Bleeding, 220
   Toothache Drops, 222
   Toothache, 217
   Vapor Bath, 222
   Warm Bath for Children, 222
   Wash for Chapped Hands, 223
   Wash for Old Sores, 220
Rice
   Charleston Snowballs (dessert), 162
   Rice Bread, 10
   Rice Cream, 162
   Rice Custard, 172, 215
   Rice Jelly, 215
   Rice Pudding, 146, 147
   Rice Waffles, 12
   Snow Balls (dessert), 166
   Wheat Battercakes, 12
Salads – Protein, 47–50
   Chicken – Jellied Chicken, 48
   Chicken Salad, 47
   Chicken Salad, Mrs. Gen. Phillips', 47
   Egg Salad, 50
   Ham Salad, 49
   Lobster Salad, 48
   Oyster Salad, 49
   Salmon Salad, 48
   Turkey Salad, 47
Salads – Vegetable, 48–50
   Beet Salad, 48
   Cold Slaw, 49–50
   Potato Salad, 50

INDEX OF FOODS.

Salad Dressings, 51–57.
  Bottled Salad Dressing, 49
  French Salad Dressing, 54
  Salad Dressing, 54
  Sauce for Lettuce, 54
Sauces – Savory, 51–57. *See also* Catsups, Pickles, and Salad Dressings.
  Apple Sauce (for meats), 53
  Barbecue sauce. *See* Venison Sauce, 52
  Celery Vinegar, 53
  Chow-Chow (relish), 66
  Chutney Sauce, 55
  Common Egg Sauce, 56
  Cranberry Sauce, 53
  Cucumber Sauce, 51
  Drawn Butter, 52
  Dried Beef Gravy, 56
  Fish Sauce, 52
  Fish, Sauce for Fish, 45
  French Salad Dressing (for chicken), 54
  Green Tomato Sauce, 54
  Horse Radish Sauce, 54
  London Club Sauce, 52
  Mint Sauce, 57
  Mixed Sauce, 55
  Morcan's Tartan Sauce (for meats), 53
  Mustard Sauce (for meat, herring, and lobster), 56
  Mustard, Aromatic, 53
  Mustard, French, 56
  Onion Sauce, 52
  Pepper Sauce, 51
  Pepper Vinegar, 53
  Rich Dutch Sauce, 56
  Sauce for cold meats, 51
  Sauce for Lettuce, 54
  Sauce Remoulade (for meats), 51
  Soyer Sauce, 56
  Venison Sauce, 52
  Vinegar Jelly (for fowl), 177
  Worcestershire Sauce, 55

Sauces – Sweet, 157–160. *See also* Preserves.
  Acid Sauce (tartaric from grapes), 159
  Caramel, 197
  Chocolate Sauce, 157–158
  Cocoanut Sauce, 157
  Cold Butter Sauce, 157
  Cold Sauce, 158
  Cream Sauce, Plain, 158
  Cream Sauce, Sweetened, 159
  Custard – German Custard Sauce, 159
  Custard Sauce, 157
  Lemon – Good Pudding Sauce, 160
  Lemon Syrup, 208
  Lemon – Sauce, 158–159
  Maple Sugar Sauce, 159
  Molasses Sauce, 157
  Quince Sauce, 159
  Rich Sauce for Puddings, 157
  Sauce (butter, egg yolk, wine), 154
  Sauce (jelly, vinegar), 158
  Sauce for Pudding (lemon or vanilla), 159
  Strawberry Sauce, 158
  Sugar and butter sauce. *See* Plum Pudding, 141–142
  Wine Sauce, 158, 159
Seafood. *See also* Fish and Oysters.
  Clam Soup, 38
  Lobster Salad, 48
  Mustard Sauce (for herring and lobster), 56
Sickroom/Invalid Foods, 213–216
  Apple Water, 214
  Beef – A Fine Beef Preparation (bouillon cakes), 213
  Beef, Essence of, 213
  Chicken Water, 214
  Cold Custard, 215
  Corn Meal Gruel, 214
  Delicate Graham Bread for Invalids, 16
  Eggs, 72

INDEX OF FOODS.

Jelly, Blackberry, 215
Jelly, Calves' Feet, 216
Milk – For a Fevered Patient (iced), 29
Milk – To Prepare Milk for Infants, 29
Milk Punch, 215
Milk, Chocolate, 215
Milk, Thickened, 215
Mulled Wine, 216
Rice Custard, 215
Rice Jelly (porridge), 215
Soaked bread – Panada, 214
Soaked bread – To Relieve Thirst (corn bread), 214
Soaked bread – Toast Water, 214
Soaked bread, Biscuit Jelly, 214
Soup, Dr. Stewart's Receipt for, 36, 213
Soup, Partridge, 35
Soup, White (potato), 38
Soups and Stews, 32–39
    Advice for, 2, 32
    Bean Soup, 34
    Beef – Clear Beef Soup, 33
    Brunswick. *See* Virginia Brunswick Stew, 36
    Cakes for Soup (dumplings), 34
    Chicken – Virginia Brunswick Stew, 36
    Chicken, Dr. Stewart's Receipt for, 36, 213
    Clam Soup, 38
    French Soup (meat and vegetable), 39
    Green Corn Soup, 37
    Gumbo, 33
    Julienne Soup (beef and vegetable), 38
    Mock Turtle Soup (calf head), 35
    Noodles for Soup, 35
    Oyster Soup, 40
    Partridge Soup, 35
    Pea Soup, 34
    Potato – White Potato Soup, 38
    Potato Soup, 36
    Stock, 32
    Tomato – Delicious Soup, 33
    Tomato and Milk Soup, 37
    Turkey Bone Soup, 37
    Turtle Soup, 35
    Vegetable – Fine Vegetable Soup, 34
Tomatoes. *See* Vegetables.
Turkey, 107-109
    Barbecued Turkey, 108
    Boiled Turkey, 108
    Dressing for Turkey, 108. *See also* Roast Turkey, 107–108.
    Forcemeat balls, 37
    Mush Dressing (to stuff a turkey), 108
    Roast Turkey, 107
    Turkey Bone Soup, 37
    Turkey Hash, 109
    Turkey Salad, 47
    Wild turkey (roasted), 112
Vegetables, 77–91. *See also* Canning, Pickles, Potatoes, Salads, and Soup.
    Asparagus, 80
    Beet Salad, 48
    Beets, To Boil Beets, 89
    Broccoli. *See* Cauliflower, 90
    Cabbage – Ladies' Cabbage (boiled), 80
    Cabbage – Sauer Kraut (fermented), 83
    Cabbage Sprouts (boiled), 79
    Cabbage, Boiled, 79
    Cabbage, Scalloped, 80
    Cabbage, Stuffed (sausage, bacon), 80
    Carrots (boiled), 87
    Cashaw (mashed), 89
    Cauliflower (simmered), 90
    Celery (raw), 91
    Collards (boiled), 79
    Corn – Chicken Corn Pie, 86
    Corn – Green Corn Fritters, 86
    Corn – Green Corn Soup, 37
    Corn – Roasted Green Corn, 85
    Corn – Stewed Green Corn, 85

Vegetables *(continued)*
  Corn Oysters (fried drop cakes), 86
  Corn Pudding (baked), 85, 86
  Corn, Boiled, 85
  Cucumber Sauce, 51
  Cucumbers, Fried, 84
  Cucumbers, Raw, 84
  Egg Plant, Fried (breakfast), 84
  Greens, Jowls and Greens (boiled), 89
  Okra, Stew, 86
  Okra, To Fry, 86
  Onion Sauce, 52
  Onions – To Stew Young Onions, 82
  Onions, To Bake, 90
  Onions, To Fry, 90
  Parsnip Fritters, 87
  Parsnips, Stewed, 87
  Peas – Canned French Peas (boiled in can), 90
  Peas – To Boil Green Peas, 82
  Pepper Sauce, 51
  Pepper Vinegar, 53
  Pumpkin Bread, 15
  Pumpkin, A Kentucky Girl's Pumpkin Pie, 156
  Pumpkin, Receipt of a Famous N. Y. Restaurant Pumpkin Pie, 156
  Radish – Horse Radish Sauce, 54
  Radishes (raw), 90
  Salsify – To Cook Salsify (boiled), 87
  Soup, Fine Vegetable Soup, 34
  Spinach – To Cook Spinach (boiled and buttered), 89
  Squash – To Cook Squashes (boiled "to a jelly"), 82
  Squash, Baked, 83
  Succotash, 90
  Tomato and Milk Soup, 37
  Tomato Pie (sweet), 148
  Tomato Preserves (sweetened), 185
  Tomatoes – Green Tomato Sauce, 54
  Tomatoes – Southern Tomato Pie (sweet), 156
  Tomatoes, Baked, 81
  Tomatoes, Broiled, 81
  Tomatoes, Delicious Soup, 33
  Tomatoes, Fried Green, 82
  Tomatoes, Fried, 82
  Tomatoes, Raw, 81
  Tomatoes, Stewed, 81
  Turnips – To Stew Turnips With Meat, 88
  Turnips (boiled), 88
  Turnips used to prepare griddle, 13
  Vegetables for cows, 25
  Vegetables for soup, 32
Vinegar
  Blackberry Vinegar (beverage), 202
  Celery Vinegar, 53
  Pepper Vinegar, 53
  Spiced Vinegar, 58
  To Make Vinegar, 65
  Vinegar Jelly, 177
  Vinegar Pie, 155
Waiter: Outdated term for a tray.
Yeast: Form and strength of yeast varied in Tennent's day; trial and error will be necessary to determine how much is needed for modern readers.
Yeast
  Buttermilk Yeast, 6–7
  Good Yeast, 6
  Liquid Yeast, 6
  Receipt for Making the Yeast, 4
  Yeast Cakes, 5–6, 14
  Yeast longevity, 5
Yeast Powder: This is usually an outdated term for baking powder.
Waffles
  Rice Waffles, 12
  Waffles Made with Yeast, 12
  Waffles Without Eggs, 11
  Waffles without yeast. *See* Laplanders, 13

INDEX OF PROPER NAMES

Acton – xxiii, 226
Adair – xxiii, 128
Agricola – 122
Akin – xxiii, 75
Alexander – xxiii, 179
Alston – xxiii, 94, 121
American Agriculturalist – 258, 259–260
American Cookery – 162
Anderson – xxiii, 50, 67–68, 118
Arnold – xxiii, 9
Ashurst – xxiii, 10
Atkinson – xxiii, 63, 95, 100, 204, 115
Atlanta Constitution – xxiii, 29, 74, 167
Augusta Cook Book – 80, 133, 169.
Aunt America – 118
Aunt Polly – 15
Aunt Sally – 150
Auntie Barnes – 70

Baker – xxiv, 116, 131, 133, 136, 151, 225
Barbour – 42
Barlowe – xxiii
Barnes – xxiii, 115, 109–110
Bashford – xxiv, 163
Beall – xxiii, 15
Bean – xxiv, , 172–173, 220
Bell – xxiii, 66
Bellamy – xxiv, 177, 203
Berrien – xxiv, 202
Berry – xxiii, 66
Bishop – xxiii, 8, 110
Black – xxiii, 12, 36, 63
Bledsoe – xxiv, 93
Blue Grass Cook Book – 12, 16, 33, 36, 52, 61, 75, 86, 95, 98–99, 106–107, 123, 124, 132, 138, 142, 144, 155, 163, 176–177, 182, 185, 198, 206–207
Bossy – 119
Boulden – xxiv, 155

Bourbon Fair – 60, 115, 181
Bowie – xxiv, 157
Breckenridge – xxiv, 137
Brent – xxiv, 106–107, 224
Bridges – xxiv, 74
Brooks – xxiv, 144
Brown – xxiii, 58–59, 121
Brumby – xxiv, 110
Buckner – xxiii, 12, 85, 86, 123, 124, 142, 205–206
Burnet House (Cincinnati) – 146–147
Burnley – 40
Buttolph – xxiii, 12, 120, 124, 130

Cabell – xxiv, 139
Campbell, – xxiv, 8, 123
Capital City Club (Atlanta) – xxv, 168
Carroll – xxiv, 116
Carson – xxv, 141
Catholic Herald (New York) – xxiv, 173
Centaur Cook Book – 150
Centennial Exposition, 190
Chamberlain – xxiv, 5, 19, 143, 157–158
Chambers – xxv, 212
Cheek – xxiv, 50, 73, 84–85, 87, 154
Clay – xxv, 98–99, 118
Clifton – xxiv, 47
Coleman – xxiv, 111
Collier – xxiv, 42
Complete Home, The – xxx, 56, 80
Cortelyou – xxv, 182
Cox – xxiv, 63
Croxton – 163
Cumpstey – xxiv, 6–7, 187
Cunningham – xxiv, 122
Curtis – xxiv, 27

Dabney – xxiv, 150
Dairyman's Journal (New York) – xxiv

INDEX OF PROPER NAMES.

Dame – 169
Davis – xxiv, 118, 133, 134, 155, 219, 206, 229, 230
DeBard – xxiv, 166
Demorest's Monthly (New York) – xxiv, 117
Dep't of Agriculture – 25
Detroit Free Press – 240–243
Diamond Cook Book – xxiv, 172
Dick – xxiv, 59, 130
Dimmitt – xxiv, 57
Dixie Cook Book – 37, 49, 122, 156, 159, 178, 191–192
Dobbs – xxiv, 54, 101
Dole and Merrell (New York) – xxiv, 209
Dorsey – xxiv, 42
Douglas – 167, 170
Downey – xxiv, 49, 62–63, 145, 159
Dudley – xxiv, 206
Duffey – xxiv, 5
Duncan – xxiv, 30, 125, 168–169, 182–183

Earle – xxiv, 204
Edmonston – xxiv, 5–6, 18, 40, 80–81, 224
Edwards – xxiv, 60
Ellis – xxiv, 171
Emmett – 213

Falks – xxiv, 10
Fessenden – xxiv, 166
Ficklin – xxiv, 92
Ford – xxiv, 218, 220
Forest City Hotel (Cleveland) – xxiv, 54
Foster – xxvi, 158
Frey – xxiv, 15
Fulton Street Market (New York) – xxiv, 99

Gable – xxvi, 8, 38, 48, 52, 65, 90, 108, 118, 125, 168
Galt House (Louisville) – xxvi, 73–74
Garrett – xxvi, 33
Georgia Department of Agriculture – 99
Gibert – xxvi, 34, 184

Gilbert – xxvi, 170
Gilman – xxvi, 40, 210
Gnadinger – xxvi, 131
Goff – 279–280
Goodman – xxvi, 127
Gordon – xxvi, 226
Great Atlantic & Pacific Tea Company – xxvi, 22.
Greer – xxvi, 171
Guerrant – xxvi, 183
Gunn – xxvi, 70, 221

Hale – xxvii, 65, 181
Hamby – xxvi, 14, 107–108
Hames – 259
Hanley – xxvi, 61, 82, 84
Harding – xxvii, 211
Harland – xxvi, 78, 80, 188
Harper – xxvii, 134
Harrison – xxvi, 8
Hawley – 150–151
Haynes – xxvi, 151
Hazard – xxvi, 37
Heggie – xxvi, 13
Hegman – xxvii, 132
Hendricks – xxvi, 87
Henry – xxvii, 148
Hibler – xxvi, 10
Hill – xxvi, 11, 119, 170
Hirsch – xxvi, 35, 121, 202
Hollingsworth – xxvii
Hollingsworth Confectioner – 121
Hollinshead – xxvi, 105, 123
Holstein – xxvi
Holton – xxvi, 64
Holtstein – 204
Home Cook Book, The – 57
Home Guest (New York) – xxvi, 90
Hood's Cook Book – 143
Hotel Belle Vue (Munich) – 51
Hotel Emery (Cincinnati) – xxvi, 112
Howard & Lewis (Kentucky) – xxvii, 207

Howell – xxvi, 116
Hudnet – 169
Hughes – xxvi, 17, 26, 29–30, 100, 117
Hunt's Hotel (Cincinnati) – xxvi, 78
Hurt – 16

Inman – xxvii, 10
Irvine – 128
Irwin – xxvii, 109

Jack – xxvii, 4
Jack, Ward & Co. (Atlanta) – xxvii, 207
James – xxvii, 200
Jaynes – xxvii, 94–95
Jenkins – xxvii, 141
Johnson – xxvii, 129
Jones – xxvii, 10, 16

Keiningham – xxvii, 152
Kennon – xxvii, 204
Kentucky Home Cook Book – 6, 63, 64, 74, 88–89, 93, 116, 133, 184, 208, 210
Ketner – 199
Kilgour – 67
Kimball House (Atlanta) – 17, 198
Kirk – xxvii, 68
Kirkpatrick – xxvii, 153
Kolb – xxvii, 10

Lagomarsino – xxvii, 210
Lanehan – xxvii, 123–124
Lansing – xxvii, 148
Lattimer – xxvii, 125
Leake – 116, 131
Lemon – xxvii, 143
Lester – xxvii, 54
Lewis – 208
Lofton – xxvii, 117, 119
Lovelace -- 88
Lowe – 15, 120
Lyman – 164

Macon Fair – 181

Magee – xxvii, 7
Manget – xxvii, 76
Marlowe – xxvii, 49–50
Martin – 138, 176–177
Massa – xxvii, 41
Massey – xxvii, 134–135, 210
Massie – xxvii, 38–39, 48, 51, 59, 79, 103, 117, 133, 194, 218
McCarney – xxvii, 202–203
McCreary – xxvii, 198
McGavock – xxvii, 196
McGill – xxvii, 161
McIntosh – xxvii, 186
McLelland – xxvii, 158–159
Meade – xxvii, 53
Meredith – 177
Metcalfe – xxvii, 172
Miller – xxvii, 141–142
Mitchell – xxviii, 12, 52, 182
Mitchell & Ramelsburg (Cincinnati) – 225
Mitchell House (Thomasville) – xxvi, 174
Moore – xxvii, 9, 37, 48, 133, 178
Mrs. Winslow's Cook Book – 167

National Hotel (Dalton) – 14
Nelson, Mrs. Dr. – 118
Nesbett – xxvii
Nesbitt – 9, 13, 14, 65–66, 76, 100, 192, 202, 206, 225, 249–250
New Haven Cook Book – xxvii, 140, 171
Nippert – xxvii, 212
Nisbet – xxvii, 125

Oakman – xxvii, 21
Offutt – xxvii, 148
Ogden – xxvii, 161
Osburn – xxvii, 167

Palace Hotel (San Francisco) – xxvii, 47
Paris True Kentuckian – xxix, 222
Park – xxvii, 49
Parloa – xxvii, 147–148, 165

INDEX OF PROPER NAMES.

Parlor – xxvii, 14
Parrott – xxvii, 181
Payne – xxvii, 6, 59, 199
Perry – 162, 171
Philadelphia Centennial – 20
Phillips – xxvii, 47, 129, 187
Phoenix Agricultural Club – vii, 116, 117, 305
Pierce – xxvii, 139
Pinkerton – xxvii, 61, 93
Pitner –xxvii, 51
Pollock – xxvii, 161
Powell – xxix, 166–167
Preston – xxvii, 33
Price – xxix, 122
Puckett – xxvii, 86
Put-In-Bay House (Lake Erie) – xxix, 132

Ray – xxix, 128
Redmon – xxix, 52, 117, 181
Reed – xxix
Reid – 11, 136, 187, 187–188
Riddell– xxix, 7, 118
Robarts – xxix, 10, 18
Roberts – xxix, 93, 127
Robinson – xxix, 54, 133
Rockwell – xxix, 139
Rogers – xxix, 75
Royal Pastry Cook – xxix, 128
Rule – xxix, 119
Rusk – xxix, 85

Scott – xxix, 12, 68, 121, 126, 146, 147, 193
Scoville and Beerman (Atlanta) – xxix, 17
Screven – xxix, 127
Setz – xxx
Shakers, The (Kentucky) – xxix, 180–181
Shellman – xxix, 14
Shipp – xxix, 152, 183
Shirley House (Kentucky) – xxix, 14
Shockley – 12, 258
Sibley – xxx, 192

Simmes – xxix, 52
Simpson – 148
Singer – xxix, 164
Slade – xxix, 41
Smidt – xxx, 149
Smith – xxix, 134
Southern Cultivator (Atlanta) – xxx, 36
Spalding – 86, 133.
Spears – 185
St. Nicholas Hotel (Cincinnati) – xxix, 23
Starnes – xxix, 11, 34, 52, 62, 71, 116, 126, 129, 153, 164, 176, 177, 183, 186, 199, 224, 225
Stevens – xxx, 95, 167, 210
Stewart – xxix, 13, 36, 213
Strother – xxix, 101

Tabb – xxx, 6
Taggart – xxx, 97
Tarleton – xxx, 64
Tegetmeier – 258
Tennent – xxx, 4, 8, 20, 41, 68, 83, 123, 139, 143, 146, 157, 177, 180, 217, 218, 221, 229, 244–246
Tolleson – xxx, 68
Toombs – xxx, 116
Tubman – xxx, 34, 142
Tucker – xxx, 195
Turney – xxx, 198
Tuttle – xxx, 162
Tyree – xxx, 15, 77, 89, 90, 95–96, 104, 111, 185, 196, 201

Upson – xxx, 144, 162

Vienna Bakery (Philadelphia) – xxx, 124
Virginia Cook Book – 53, 91, 111

Wallace – xxx, 96, 163
Walsh – xxx, 86–87
Washington – xxx, 142
White House Cake and Pastry Department – 118

White – xxx, 124, 195
Whitlock – xxx, 199
Whitlock House (Marietta) – 51
Whitney – xxx, 33
Williams – xxx, 150
Winn – xxx, 44, 54, 59
Wisconsin Dairyman's Association – 27
Woodrow – xxx, 60

Wrenn – xxxi, 172
Wright – xxx, 21, 22, 259
Wyatt – xxxi

Yorston – xxx, 94
Youman's Dictionary – xxx, 55, 174
Young – xxx, 206–207

ONLY 50 CENTS A YEAR!

The Phœnix Agriculturist,

UNIQUE IN THE HISTORY OF JOURNALISM!

The only Farmer's Magazine in the world printed and published literally in the field itself, by farmers and for farmers. Twenty-six pages of interesting reading monthly, and the neatest printed magazine in the State.

THE OFFICIAL ORGAN

of the COBB COUNTY AGRICULTURAL ASSOCIATION, comprising twelve District Clubs. Circulation rapidly increasing. Goes into nearly every household in Cobb county, and into nearly every county in the State. A splendid medium by which

ADVERTISERS

may reach our people direct. A most interesting feature of the current year will be the publication of the Reports of 225 representative Farmers, from all portions of the State, upon their respective systems and methods of farming. Send for the PHŒNIX AGRICULTURIST and make the acquaintance of "UNCLE MALACHI."

Printed and published out in the woods of Cobb county, thereby putting our county, in this respect, ahead of any other locality in the United States—David Landreth, the Seedsman, says so.

R. B. GOODMAN AND H. N. STARNES,

Publishers and Proprietors,

P. O., MARIETTA, GEORGIA.
ONLY 50 CENTS A YEAR!

Sample copies sent FREE on application.

www.ingramcontent.com/pod-product-compliance
Lightning Source LLC
Chambersburg PA
CBHW031519010425
24436CB00002B/30